Hands-On Microsoft Lists

Create custom data models and improve the way data is organized using Lists in Microsoft 365

João Ferreira

Rene Modery

BIRMINGHAM—MUMBAI

Hands-On Microsoft Lists

Associate Group Product Manager: Pavan Ramchandani

Publishing Product Manager: Aaron Tanna

Senior Editor: Keagan Carneiro

Content Development Editor: Divya Vijayan

Technical Editor: Saurabh Kadave

Copy Editor: Safis Editing

Project Coordinator: Manthan Patel

Proofreader: Safis Editing

Indexer: Tejal Daruwale Soni

Production Designer: Nilesh Mohite

First published: June 2021
Production reference: 1110621

Published by Packt Publishing Ltd.
Livery Place
35 Livery Street
Birmingham
B3 2PB, UK.

ISBN 978-1-80107-504-6

www.packt.com

To my family, especially my parents, Maria Oliveira and Carlos Ferreira, for their constant support, and my grandparents, for the valuable lessons I learned from them over the years.

– João Ferreira

To my families in Singapore and Germany, for supporting me throughout the years. To my children, Alyssa and Frédéric, for their love and inspiration and for helping me grow every day.

– Rene Modery

Contributors

About the authors

João Carlos Oliveira Ferreira is a Microsoft MVP, in the Office Development and Windows Insider categories. With a degree in computer science, João has been working with Microsoft Technologies for the last 10 years, mainly focused on creating collaboration and productivity solutions that drive the adoption of Microsoft Modern Workplace. A true tech enthusiast, book author, and author of four blogs, he writes weekly about SharePoint, Microsoft Teams, and Microsoft Lists.

Last year I had the pleasure of publishing my first book with Packt and never thought that it would be possible to get my second title published just 14 months after the first one.

None of this would have been possible without the support of my family, my girlfriend, Francisca Peixoto, and my friends, who gave me confidence and helped me to keep up the writing pace.

Thanks to Rene Modery, who made the two-handed writing process a breeze; thanks to everyone at Packt who taught me so much about the book-writing process and offered valuable suggestions that ultimately will make you a Microsoft Teams hero.

Lastly, I want to thank my friend, David Ramalho, for assuming the technical reviewer role for this book and for providing valuable insights that helped to improve this book.

Rene Modery is a Microsoft Office Apps and Services MVP, working as an APAC Digital Workplace Project Manager in Singapore. For more than 15 years, Rene has lived and worked in Europe and the Asia Pacific in various regional and global roles. The main focus of his work nowadays lies in Microsoft 365 and the Digital Workplace, especially in providing guidance and change management for regional projects and initiatives. He is a regular speaker at user groups and conferences and generally likes to share his knowledge and experiences with others.

This is the first book I have had the pleasure of publishing with Packt, and I would like to thank everyone on the Packt team who helped with their guidance and support during the writing.

Thanks also go to my co-author, João, who was a great help and guide during the writing process, and who regularly supported me in getting chapters completed.

Lastly, I want to thank my wife, Wenna, and my family for their support. None of this would have been possible without having some dedicated time for writing, often at the expense of spending time together. Thank you for letting me contribute my knowledge and experience to this book.

About the reviewer

David Ramalho is a Microsoft MVP in Apps and Services, a SharePoint developer, a content creator, and the owner of the SharePoint-tricks blog. He has worked with Microsoft technologies for 4+ years with a primary focus on SharePoint and Microsoft Teams. That has allowed him to earn experience that has led to him sharing blog posts that help users to improve their Microsoft 365 experience. He also holds a few Microsoft certifications, including Teams Administrator Associate.

Table of Contents

3
Microsoft Lists Core Features

4
Collaborating on Microsoft Lists

5
Creating Microsoft Lists Views

6

Customizing Microsoft Lists

7

Customizing Microsoft Lists Views

8

Customizing Microsoft Lists Forms

9
Integrating Microsoft Lists with the Power Platform

10
Microsoft Lists for Admins and Advanced Users

11
Extending Microsoft Lists Using SPFx

Other Books You May Enjoy

Index

Preface

Microsoft Lists is a new application added to the Microsoft 365 ecosystem to help users track, share, and organize their work.

Released as an evolution of SharePoint lists, Microsoft Lists is a lightweight database that you can use to build and customize data according to your business requirements without the need to worry about the rules of the more complex relational databases.

If you've never used SharePoint lists before, this book will teach you everything about them, covering the new and old features that made SharePoint one of the most trusted collaboration platforms in the world.

Who this book is for

Professionals who work with Microsoft 365 tools such as SharePoint and Microsoft Teams and want to improve how data is structured, managed, and consumed inside an organization will benefit from this book. For administrators with permission to manage access to Microsoft Lists, this book will give them all the basic concepts, suggestions, and best practices they need to ensure good governance. Basic knowledge of SharePoint and Excel is assumed.

What this book covers

Chapter 1, *Getting Started with Microsoft Lists,* provides an introduction to Microsoft Lists. It explains the historical background (SharePoint lists) and gives a short overview of the possibilities and functionalities. The chapter sets the stage for the subsequent chapters and ensures that you have a basic understanding of Microsoft Lists before moving on to more detailed topics.

Chapter 2, *Creating Your First List,* guides you through the creation of your first lists. It starts by explaining the different entry points for creating a new list. We then proceed to describe the list creation process, showing how to create new blank lists and how to leverage existing list templates. At the end of the chapter, you will know how to create lists.

Chapter 3, Microsoft Lists Core Features, covers all the default features of Microsoft Lists. We will provide a detailed explanation of all the out-of-the-box features, such as personal lists, shared/team lists, and list templates. This chapter will also explain where the Microsoft Lists data is stored.

Chapter 4, Collaborating on Microsoft Lists, teaches you how to collaborate with other people on your lists. You will learn how to invite others, see who has access to your list, and how to add comments to list items.

Chapter 5, Creating Microsoft Lists Views, takes your basic knowledge about how to create lists and moves forward into the more advanced features of filtering and formatting list data.

Chapter 6, Customizing Microsoft Lists, is where you will learn how to customize how your data looks in a list, by formatting several data types using JSON and by following the provided examples.

Chapter 7, Customizing Microsoft Lists Views, shows you how to customize list views to make the information stored in a list stand out, using JSON and the provided examples.

Chapter 8, Customizing Microsoft Lists Forms, covers the default list forms and explains how to modify them using the options in the Microsoft ecosystem to meet your business needs.

Chapter 9, Integrating Microsoft Lists with the Power Platform, is about how to automate business processes without writing code, making use of the Power Platform. You will be able to create actions based on data that is added, modified, or deleted from Microsoft Lists. Additionally, you will learn how to visualize your data with Power BI.

Chapter 10, Microsoft Lists for Admins and Advanced Users, will give you the tools you need to disable/enable Microsoft Lists features if you are an administrator in your organization or an advanced user.

Chapter 11, Extending Microsoft Lists Using SPFx, is where you will learn how to extend the default features of Microsoft Lists using SharePoint. With the use of list view command set extensions, you will be able to bring your business logic to Microsoft Lists and complement the OOB features.

To get the most out of this book

The Microsoft 365 platform, which Microsoft Lists is a part of, is constantly changing and growing. Microsoft does not add new features and functionalities on a predefined schedule, such as every 6 months, but rather provides these improvements in a very fast-paced manner. Therefore, when you look at Microsoft Lists today, it may look and behave slightly differently compared to yesterday, as new changes may have been published.

For this book, this means that the content presented here is correct at the time of writing, but we expect things to change. To give you an example, the Microsoft Lists menu through which you can access Power Automate flows was changed during the writing of *Chapter 9, Integrating Microsoft Lists within with the Power Platform*. While it is a relatively small change, where the corresponding menu items are now located within the **Integrate** section instead of **Automate**, this also meant that we had to update several text and image references.

If your version of Microsoft Lists looks and behaves slightly differently from what is described in this book, it is most likely due to the constantly evolving nature of Microsoft Lists. If you are interested in seeing recently published changes, as well as what Microsoft is currently working on, please visit `https://roadmap.office.com` to see the public roadmap for all of Microsoft 365. You can search for `microsoft lists` to see only those roadmap items that are related to Microsoft Lists.

Software/hardware covered in the book	OS requirements
Microsoft Lists	Windows, macOS, Linux, or iOS

If you are using the digital version of this book, we advise you to type the code yourself or access the code via the GitHub repository (link available in the next section). Doing so will help you avoid any potential errors related to the copying and pasting of code.

Download the example code files

You can download the example code files for this book from GitHub at `https://github.com/PacktPublishing/Hands-On-Microsoft-Lists`. In case there's an update to the code, it will be updated on the existing GitHub repository.

We also have other code bundles from our rich catalog of books and videos available at `https://github.com/PacktPublishing/`. Check them out!

Download the color images

We also provide a PDF file that has color images of the screenshots/diagrams used in this book. You can download it here: `https://static.packt-cdn.com/downloads/9781801075046_ColorImages.pdf`.

Conventions used

There are a number of text conventions used throughout this book.

`Code in text`: Indicates code words in text, database table names, folder names, filenames, file extensions, pathnames, dummy URLs, user input, and Twitter handles. Here is an example: "If you want to disable a specific template, you can provide the template's ID as part of the `DisableModernListTemplateIds` parameter while executing `Set-SPOTenant`."

A block of code is set as follows:

```
"txtContent": "@currentField.title"
"txtContent": "[$Address].Address.City"
```

When we wish to draw your attention to a particular part of a code block, the relevant lines or items are set in bold:

```
"txtContent": "@currentField"
"txtContent": "[$Author]"
```

Any command-line input or output is written as follows:

```
Get-SPOTenant | select DisablePersonalListCreation
```

Bold: Indicates a new term, an important word, or words that you see onscreen. For example, words in menus or dialog boxes appear in the text like this. Here is an example: "Select **SPFx Columns** from the site columns dropdown."

> Tips or important notes
> Appear like this.

Get in touch

Feedback from our readers is always welcome.

General feedback: If you have questions about any aspect of this book, mention the book title in the subject of your message and email us at customercare@packtpub.com.

Errata: Although we have taken every care to ensure the accuracy of our content, mistakes do happen. If you have found a mistake in this book, we would be grateful if you would report this to us. Please visit www.packtpub.com/support/errata, selecting your book, clicking on the Errata Submission Form link, and entering the details.

Piracy: If you come across any illegal copies of our works in any form on the Internet, we would be grateful if you would provide us with the location address or website name. Please contact us at copyright@packt.com with a link to the material.

If you are interested in becoming an author: If there is a topic that you have expertise in and you are interested in either writing or contributing to a book, please visit authors.packtpub.com.

Reviews

Please leave a review. Once you have read and used this book, why not leave a review on the site that you purchased it from? Potential readers can then see and use your unbiased opinion to make purchase decisions, we at Packt can understand what you think about our products, and our authors can see your feedback on their book. Thank you!

For more information about Packt, please visit packt.com.

1
Getting Started with Microsoft Lists

Microsoft Lists is a new application that's been added to the Microsoft 365 ecosystem to help users track, share, and organize their work.

If you are one of the 200 million users already using SharePoint, the transition and adoption of Microsoft Lists will be a breeze for you. This is because this new application makes accessing the lists you know and love easier than ever before.

If you've never used SharePoint Lists before, don't worry – this book will teach you everything about it. We will do this by covering both the old and new features of Lists that made SharePoint one of the most trusted collaboration platforms in the world.

In this chapter, we will start with the basics by covering the following topics:

- What is Microsoft Lists?
- How can I access Microsoft Lists?
- Getting familiar with Microsoft Lists' user interface
- What does a list look like?

What is Microsoft Lists?

If you are familiar with SharePoint, the concept of lists won't be new to you. In reality, Microsoft Lists is an evolution of the original SharePoint Lists, which became a separate application for aggregating all the new lists that are created with Microsoft Lists, as well as all the preexisting lists that were created with SharePoint.

Microsoft Lists was designed to help you track and organize your work, thus giving you a holistic view of all the lists you have on the sites you have shared with your teams, as well as your own personal lists.

If you are not familiar with the concept of lists yet and are starting from scratch, think of Microsoft Lists as a lightweight database that you can build and customize according to your business requirements, without the need to worry about the rules of more complex relational databases.

Lightweight databases aren't just used to store and share data – they are much more powerful than that. For example, you can use them to build custom workflows on top of data automating business processes for you and your teams.

We can also use them to format information by using custom views, formatting, and filters – all the information you need is literally one click away.

How can I access Microsoft Lists?

To get started with Microsoft Lists, first, you need to know how to access the application.

Lists is available for a variety of platforms, and you can use it through any of the following:

- A web browser
- A Microsoft Teams application
- A mobile application

Each version has its own layout, but they all follow the same design language. This makes using Microsoft Lists across all platforms very natural and intuitive.

Microsoft Lists on the web

Microsoft Lists is available as a web app and can be accessed directly from a browser from the Microsoft 365 context. Currently, there are no direct links to access the application, so to access Lists, you must do the following:

1. From your Microsoft 365 environment, click on the app launcher icon located at the top-left corner. You can do this in any application. Clicking on this icon will open a list containing all the Microsoft 365 applications you have access to.

2. Locate the **Lists** icon and click on it:

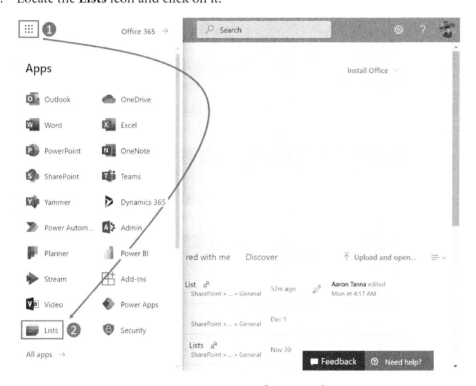

Figure 1.1 – Accessing Microsoft Lists – web version

After a few seconds, the app will open and leave you on the Microsoft Lists landing page.

If you want to share the new awesome application you've just discovered with your colleagues, make sure you instruct them to open Lists by following the instructions described here. The link to the application is unique for each user. You must combine the respective URL with the user's personal email, like so: `https://contoso-my.sharepoint.com/personal/joaoferreira_contoso_com/_layouts/15/Lists.aspx`.

You can save this link in your browser's bookmarks for quick access, but keep in mind that if you share it with any other users from your organization, all they will see is a 404 error page.

Microsoft Lists on Microsoft Teams

Microsoft Lists is available as a Microsoft Teams app that can be used in the context of your teams as a tab. This version of Microsoft Lists was designed with collaboration in mind and despite being a bit different, you can still use the same list features you can find in the web version.

To use Microsoft Lists in the context of Microsoft Teams, do the following:

1. Open Microsoft Teams and select the team channel where you want to add a list.

2. Once in the channel, click the + icon to add a new tab.

3. If the Lists app is not visible immediately, use the search bar to locate it. Once you can see the **Lists** icon, click on it to add the application:

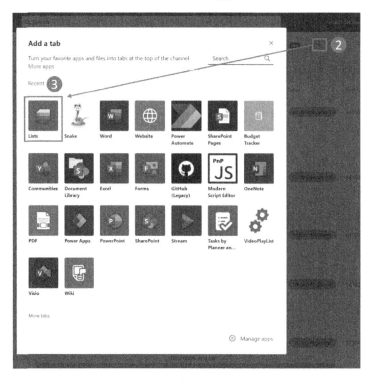

Figure 1.2 – Accessing Microsoft Lists – Microsoft Teams version

4. On the pop-up that appears, click on the **Save** button.

The main difference you will find between Microsoft Lists on the web and Microsoft Lists on Microsoft Teams is that the app will not work as a central repository for all your lists; instead, it acts as a container for individual lists.

Microsoft Lists on mobile

As an application that aims to help you track and organize your work in modern workplace environments, Microsoft Lists is also available on mobile devices so that you can access your data on the go.

If you have a smart phone or tablet with iOS on it and want to have Microsoft Lists just a tap away, do the following:

1. Open the application store on your mobile phone.
2. Search for Microsoft Lists and install it.
3. Once the application has been installed, open it and provide your Microsoft 365 credentials.
4. Once you've successfully authenticated, you will see the same information you can see in the web version but adjusted to a smaller screen size.

Note: At the time of writing this book, Microsoft Lists for Android is not available yet. However, it is planned to be released by the end of 2021.

Lists on SharePoint

As we mentioned at the beginning of this chapter, Microsoft Lists is an evolution of SharePoint Lists, which means that lists can also be accessed directly from SharePoint.

Compared to the Microsoft Lists application, SharePoint only lets you view the lists that exist in the context of the SharePoint site, making the experience a bit more limited.

To access your lists from SharePoint, you must do the following:

1. On your SharePoint site, click on the **cog** icon in the top-right corner.
2. From the menu, click on **Site Contents**. **Site Contents** is also available from the quick launch menu on your SharePoint site.

3.   After a few seconds, you will land on the **Site Contents** page of your SharePoint site. Here, you will find document libraries and lists in the same location:

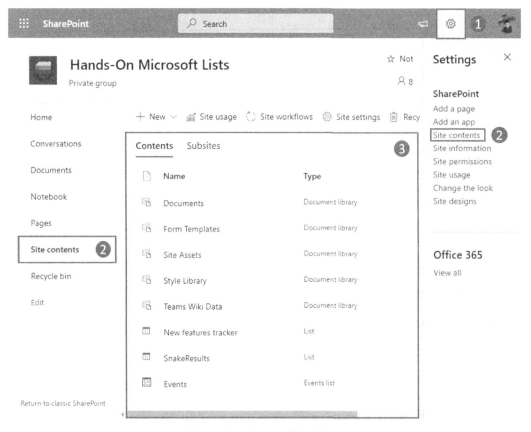

Figure 1.3 – Lists on SharePoint

Now that you know how to access Microsoft Lists, let's look at the application in more detail.

Getting familiar with Microsoft Lists' user interface

In this section, you will become familiar with the layout of Lists on the four platforms where it is available.

After completing this section, you will have the foundations to move on and start learning how to create and manage your own lists.

Microsoft Lists on the web

The following screenshot represents the web version of Microsoft Lists. Its main components have been identified with numbers:

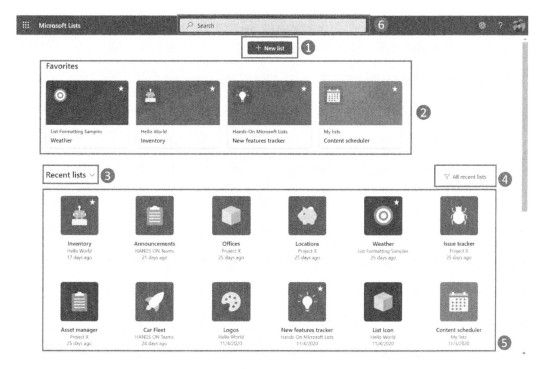

Figure 1.4 – Microsoft Lists main screen – web version

Let's look at these components in more detail:

1. **New Lists**: This button allows you to create new lists on the platform. **New Lists** has several options, all of which will be explained in detail in *Chapter 2, Creating Your First List*.

2. **Favorites**: The **Favorites** section allows you to mark the lists you use the most and pin them to the top of the page. Besides being displayed at the top of the page, favorites lists are displayed differently from regular lists. While regular lists are represented as a square with an icon and a background color, favorite lists are represented in a rectangular card.

To add or remove a list from your favorites, all you have to do is click on the star in the top-right corner of the list tile, as highlighted in the following screenshot:

Figure 1.5 – Adding/Removing lists from favorites

3. **View Selection**: As we will see in *Chapter 2, Creating Your First List,* you can create team and personal lists; this view selection allows you to select between them.

a) **Recent Lists**: This option displays the most recent lists in the system and aggregates personal and team lists in the same view.

b) **My Lists**: This option only displays your personal lists.

4. **Filters**: The filter option allows you to refine the view selection even further. Here, you will find the following options:

a) Recent lists filter:

All Recent lists: This option displays all your lists organized in chronological order.

Recent lists I created: This option displays all the lists **created by you**, organized in chronological order.

b) My Lists:

Name A-Z: This option displays your personal lists, organized alphabetically from A to Z.

Name Z-A: This option displays your personal lists, organized alphabetically from Z to A.

Newest: This option displays your personal lists, organized chronologically from the newest to the oldest.

Oldest: This option displays your personal lists, organized chronologically from the oldest to the newest.

5. **List grid**: This section displays all your lists according to the selections you made via the **View** selection and the **Filters** section.

6. **List search**: Located at the top of the page, this option allows you to easily discover any lists in your Microsoft 365 ecosystem. You can search by the name of the list. This works globally in all the locations that you have access to:

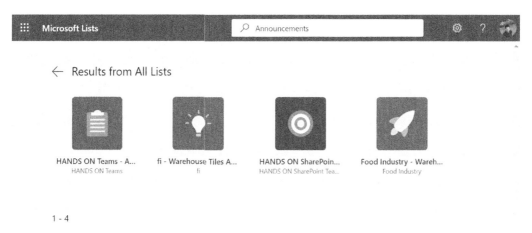

Figure 1.6 – Microsoft Lists search results

Microsoft Lists limits

The Favorites and Recent lists both have a maximum limit in terms of the items they can display. You can favorite up to 30 lists, while the Recent list will just display the first 100.

As you have already seen, the Microsoft Lists landing page is easy and intuitive to use. However, there are certain aspects that we haven't covered yet. You should become familiar with them before you start using the application.

The following screenshot shows a list on the Microsoft Lists landing page, with all the main components highlighted. For reference, we are using a screenshot representing a Favorite and a Regular list:

Figure 1.7 – List representation with highlighted components

Let's look at these components in more detail:

1. **List name**: This is the title of the list defined by the user.

2. **List location**: This is where the list is stored. Personal lists that are only available to you are displayed with the **My Lists** label, while team lists are displayed via the name of the SharePoint site where they are located.

3. **Favorite**: This button allows you to add or remove a list from the **Favorite** section. When a list is not one of your favorites, you can only see the start icon's outline and only appears when you hover over the list card. Favorite lists display the star in a solid color, and it is always visible.

4. **Open actions**:... only appears when you hover over the list cards. Once you click on them, it opens the list actions menu, which allows you to **Customize** and **Share** the list. In the case of recent lists, it also allows you to **remove it from the recent list gallery**. This option also allows you to delete personal lists. The following screenshot shows all the options that are available in the action menu:

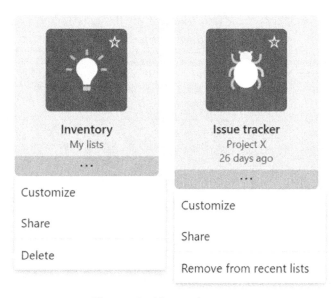

Figure 1.8 – More actions menu

5. **List Icon**: The icon, along with its background color, are used to define the list for better identification, as we will see in *Chapter 2*, *Creating Your First List*, there are 12 icons and 12 different colors that can be combined when a new list is created, or its properties are modified.

6. **Last modified date**: This value is only available in the lists that are not in your favorites and displays the date when the list was last modified.

Microsoft Lists on Microsoft Teams

The Microsoft Lists experience for Microsoft Teams was adapted to collaboration work, and the application looks and behaves a bit different than the web version. In this section, we will teach you how to use it and what the application looks like when you add it to one of your teams.

The following screenshot shows the first screen you will see once you add the application to one of your teams. The main components have been identified with numbers here:

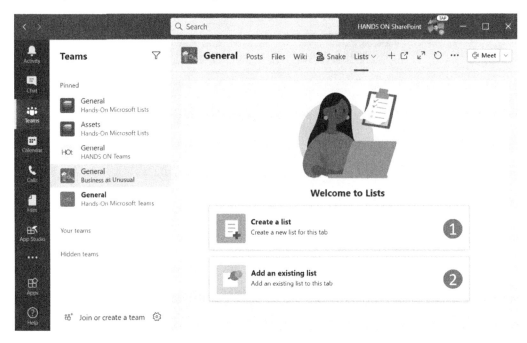

Figure 1.9 – Microsoft Lists main screen – Microsoft Teams version

Let's look at these components in more detail:

1. **Create a list**: This option opens a new page where you can create a new list on Microsoft Teams. This list will be stored in the context of the team where the app was added. There are several options available here, all of which will be explained in detail in *Chapter 2, Creating Your First List*.

2. **Add an existing list**: This option allows you to add an existing list to the tab.

The visual representation of lists in the Teams version is a bit different than in the web version. The following screenshot shows the screen that is displayed once you choose to add an existing list. Its main components have been identified here:

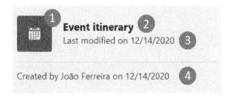

Figure 1.10 – List representation with highlighted components – Microsoft Teams version

Let's look at these components in more detail:

1. **List icon**: The icon, along with its background color, are used to define the list so that it can be identified with ease.

2. **List name**: This is the title of the list defined by the user.

3. **Last modified date**: This value displays the date when the list was last modified.

4. **Creation details**: This value shows who created the lists in the site and when.

Microsoft Lists on mobile

Now that you know what Microsoft Lists looks like on your web browser and Microsoft Teams, it is time to see what it looks like on your mobile device. The concept of Lists for mobile devices is the same as for the web; the interface will provide the same options but adjusted to smaller screens.

The following screenshot shows the main components of Microsoft Lists on iOS mobiles:

Figure 1.11 – Microsoft Lists main screen – mobile version

Let's look at these components in more detail:

1. **Favorites**: The **Favorites** section allows you to quickly access the lists you use the most and pin them to the top of the home screen of the mobile application. Besides being displayed at the top of the page, favorite lists are different in shape, similar to what we saw in the web version.

2. **Recent Lists**: This option displays the most recent lists in the system and aggregates them in the same way as personal and team lists. On mobile, these lists are ordered by the date they were modified.

3. **Home**: The **Home** button is always present at the bottom of the application and allows you to navigate back to the home screen from any location inside the app.

4. **New**: The **New** button allows you to create new lists in the platform. You have several options here, all of which will be explained in detail in *Chapter 2, Creating Your First List*.

5. **My Lists**: The **My Lists** button allows you to open all your personal lists. On mobile, this button and the **Home** button have the same functionality we saw in the view selection of the web version. Unlike the recent list, **My Lists** allow you to sort lists alphabetically, as shown in the following screenshot:

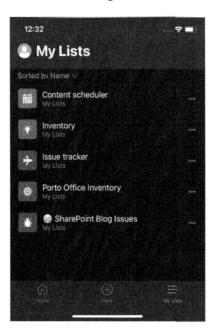

Figure 1.12 – My Lists on mobile

6. **Search**: This option allows you to easily discover any lists you have in the Microsoft 365 ecosystem. You can search by the name of the list and all locations that you have access to are searched.

7. **Profile**: With the mobile version of Microsoft Lists, you can add multiple accounts to the same application. This allows you switch between and access data stored in multiple organizations with ease. The following screenshot shows the profile menu in detail:

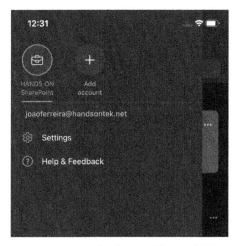

Figure 1.13 – Account selection on Microsoft Lists mobile

As we saw with the web version, the mobile application of Microsoft Lists also provides more options that you should become familiar with.

In the following screenshot, you can see a list, with all the main components highlighted:

Figure 1.14 – List representation with highlighted components

Let's look at these components in more detail:

1. **List name**: This is the title of the list defined by the user.

2. **List location**: This is where your lists are stored. Personal lists that are only available to you are marked with the **My Lists** label, while team lists are displayed with the name of the SharePoint site where they are located.

3. **Last modified date**: This value is only available in the lists that are not in your favorites and displays the date when the list was last modified.

4. **List icon**: The icon, along with its background color, are used to define the list so that it can be identified with ease.

5. **Open actions**: These three dots open the actions menu for each of the lists. From there, you can **Add/Remove to favorites**, **Rename**, **Share**, and **Delete** your lists:

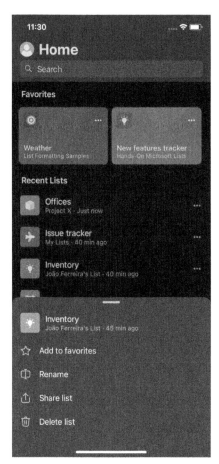

Figure 1.15 – Microsoft Lists actions menu

Since lists are also available in SharePoint, it is important to know what they look like so that you can identify them in the context of this application.

Lists on SharePoint

SharePoint had a huge update in 2016 that Microsoft has called modern experience; since the classic experience is still around and you can still enable it in your tenant, you must meet the lists layout in SharePoint for both experiences.

Starting with modern SharePoint, the following screenshot shows how a list is represented:

Figure 1.16 – Modern SharePoint – List representation

Let's look at these components in more detail:

1. **List icon**: Compared to Microsoft Lists, lists in SharePoint are all displayed with the same icon and their background colors aren't displayed, even if they were defined in the Microsoft Lists application.

2. **Name**: List name defined by the user.

3. **Actions**: The **Actions** menu, which consists of the following components:

   a) **Delete**: This option is self-explanatory and allows you to delete the list from the SharePoint site. A list deleted in SharePoint will also disappear from Microsoft Lists.

   b) **Settings**: This is where you can manage your lists, add/delete more columns, and create new views. All these concepts will be explained in the subsequent chapters of this book.

   c) **Details**: This option will show you the type of app that a list represents on SharePoint. You can also create a new list from here.

4. **Type**: This field is used to identify the type of element in the SharePoint site's contents. All the lists will display the relevant work **List**.

5. **Items**: This field is the number of items you have inside of your list.

6. **Modified**: This field shows the date when the last item was added to/modified in the list.

If you are using Microsoft Lists for the very first time, then it is very unlikely that you will see the classic layout of SharePoint, but in case you have never seen it, this is how a list is represented:

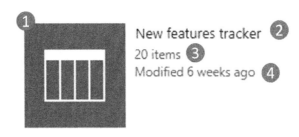

Figure 1.17 – Classic SharePoint – List representation

Let's look at these components in more detail:

1. **Icon**: This is the icon that represents lists in classic SharePoint and is the same for all lists. Despite having a background color defined, it is not related to the background color that you've defined and will be visible in Microsoft Lists. This color is inherited from SharePoint's branding.

2. **List name**: List name defined by the user.

3. **Items**: This is the number of items you have inside your list.

4. **Last Modified**: This field shows the date when the last item was added to/modified in the list.

> **Quick Tip**
>
> SharePoint Lists can easily be opened in the Microsoft Lists application, without the need for you to open Microsoft Lists and look for the desired list. With the list open in SharePoint, all you have to do is add a query string to the end of the URL, as shown here: `https://handsonsp.sharepoint.com/Lists/New_Features/AllItems.aspx?`**`env=WebViewList`**.
>
> By adding this parameter to the URL, the list will immediately open inside Microsoft Lists.

Now that you know how to open Microsoft Lists on all the platforms where it is available, it is time to have a look at a real list's layout.

What does a list look like?

The following screenshot shows what a list looks like. The main components of the application and the list itself are highlighted here:

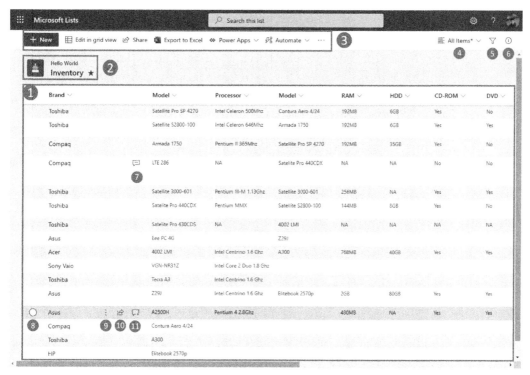

Figure 1.18 – List layout with data and the main components highlighted

Let's look at these components in more detail:

1. **List view**: This is where you will see the data stored in your lists. The view shown here is the default one you will see in a list. It can take on different formats and can be customized, as we will see in *Chapter 5, Creating Microsoft Lists Views, Chapter 6, Customizing Microsoft Lists, and Chapter 7, Customizing Microsoft Lists Views.*

2. **List identification**: This shows you the list's icon and color, the list's name, the list's location, and if the list is one of your favorites.

3. **Command bar**: The command bar is where you will find the options to perform actions on your list, such as creating a new item, editing the list, or exporting the list to Excel. This is one of the places that you can extend with extra functionality to bring your own commands to your lists. You will learn more about how to extend the command bar in *Chapter 11, Extending Microsoft Lists Using SPFx.*

4. **View selection**: This option allows you to change the data you visualize in the application. Microsoft Lists comes with a couple default views, but you can create and customize your own. You will learn more about the creation and customization process for views in *Chapter 5, Creating Microsoft Lists Views*, and *Chapter 6, Customizing Microsoft Lists:*

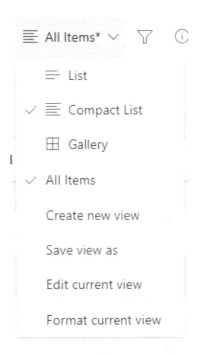

Figure 1.19 – Microsoft Lists view selection

5. **Filters**: Filters allow you to refine the information that is visible in the view. The filter panel is generated automatically based on your list schema and the view's content. The following screenshot shows the filters that were generated for the list shown in this section:

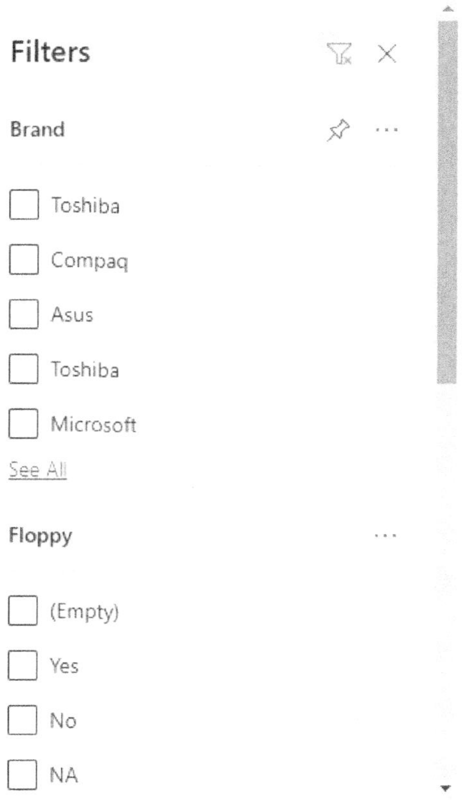

Figure 1.20 – Microsoft Lists filter pane

6. **List information**: This pane shows who has access to the list and a resume of the latest activities that have occurred, such as comments that were made about the list items.

7. **Item comment**: This icon tells the user that the item has a comment attached to it. Once you click on this icon, a new pane will appear, showing the item's details and the comments associated with it. More information about list item comments can be found in *Chapter 3, Microsoft Lists Core Features*:

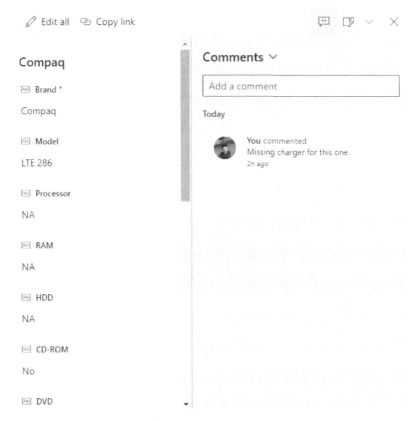

Figure 1.21 – Microsoft Lists item with a comment

8. **Item selector**: This option allows you to select one or multiple items. When a user selects an item, the options in the command bar change to allow actions such as editing an item or deleting all the selected items.

9. **Item actions**: This option displays a menu that shows all the options related to the list item. Here, you can do things such as delete the item, share the item, or copy the direct link to the item.

10. **Share item**: This option allows you to share an individual item with other users. To share an item, you will need to provide the emails of the relevant users and define the level of permissions those users will have in the list. Invited users receive an email with a link to open the item:

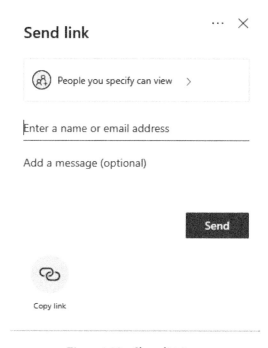

Figure 1.22 – Share list item

11. **Add a comment**: This button allows you to add unstructured data to the list item that does not follow any of the rules that have been defined by the list schema. Once you click to add a comment, a new pane will open that displays the item and a comment box, similar to the **Item comment** icon.

Summary

In this chapter, you learned what Microsoft Lists is and how to access it from Microsoft 365, as well as from a web browser, Microsoft Teams, and the Microsoft Lists mobile application.

You also became familiar with the basic components of Microsoft Lists. These let you manage your lists effectively and are the foundation of the subsequent chapters.

In the next chapter, you will learn more about these basic concepts and create your first Microsoft list.

2
Creating Your First List

In the previous chapter, we explained the history of Microsoft Lists and reviewed the core functionalities that are available. In this chapter, we will look at the different ways we can create our own lists. We can do this manually by starting with a default, empty list, and adding additional columns as needed. Alternatively, we can reuse existing list structures and create new lists based on Excel spreadsheets or other lists. Finally, we will review how to maintain data in lists.

This chapter will cover the following topics:

- Personal lists and team lists
- Creating a blank list
- Adding and maintaining columns on a list
- Creating a list from Excel
- Creating a list from an existing list
- Maintaining list data

Personal lists and team lists

Before we look at how to create lists, first, we need to establish the different scopes that they can be set up in. When you create a list, you need to decide whether the list should be made available to a small scope of people or just yourself, or whether there is an existing group of people that should be allowed to access and possibly contribute to it.

For the first case, you would have to set up the list so that it's stored in the My Lists space, which creates it within your personal OneDrive account in Microsoft 365. Initially, only you will be able to access the list and its contents until you share it with others.

However, often, you already have an existing group of people that collaborate on a SharePoint site or within a team, and you want to create a new list that all those people have access to. In such cases, you would have to create your list within that existing space and make it available immediately to everyone with existing access. Both these cases will be considered in this chapter, and further information around how to share a list with more people will be provided in *Chapter 4, Collaborating on Microsoft Lists.*

An important thing to note is that you will only be able to create lists in your own OneDrive account, as well as in SharePoint sites where you were given the rights to do so. This is the case when you are added as a member or owner of a SharePoint site through a Microsoft 365 Group, for example, which also happens when you get added to a team in Microsoft Teams. For sites that you have no access to, or sites that you were only given view rights to, you will not be able to create a list.

Creating a blank list

When it comes to creating a new, blank list, there are different starting points. You can create a new list from the home page of a modern SharePoint site, from the Lists app in Teams, or from the Lists app in the Microsoft 365 app launcher. In the following subsections, each of these options will be explained. However, as there are many similarities between the three different options, including common functionalities, steps, and options, they will only be explained once; any differences will be highlighted.

Creating a new list from the Microsoft Lists app

As the Lists app in the Microsoft 365 app launcher provides the most flexibility, we will look at what benefits we get from creating a list there. Once you've navigated to the Lists app, you will see a **New list** button at the top of the page. Clicking on it provides you with the **Create a list** dialog, which provides various options you can choose from:

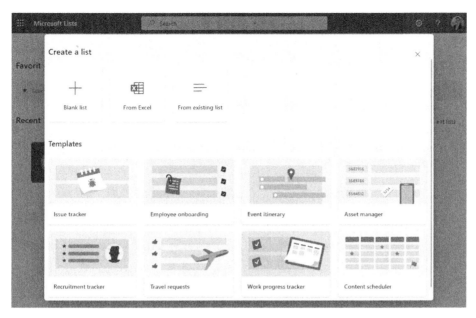

Figure 2.1 – Creating a new list

There are three options for creating a new list, and the list templates we explained in the previous chapter are at the bottom of the dialog. To create a new list not based on one of the templates, you can start from the following entry points. You can either start with a blank canvas or, depending on any already existing data structures you may have, use an existing spreadsheet containing data or another list as a base:

- **Blank list**: This option allows you to create a new, empty list without any specific structure or data in it. It is used as the standard starting point in most cases. While this option provides you with the simplest initial setup, it also gives you the greatest flexibility in terms of how to set up your list.

- **From Excel**: If you already have a structure set up in an Excel spreadsheet, likely containing some existing data, then this is the best option for creating a new list while using it. You would choose this option, for example, when you are already tracking information in a spreadsheet and want to convert it into a list to make use of additional functionality. This option will be covered in detail in the *Creating a list from Excel* section of this chapter.

- **From existing list**: Finally, if you already have an existing list that you want to duplicate, this option allows you to do so. For example, if there is an asset tracking list in use that another department is also interested in, you could use this option to create a new copy. We will explain this in the *Creating a list from an existing list* section.

Once you've selected **Blank list**, the dialog will present you with a range of options so that you can configure your list:

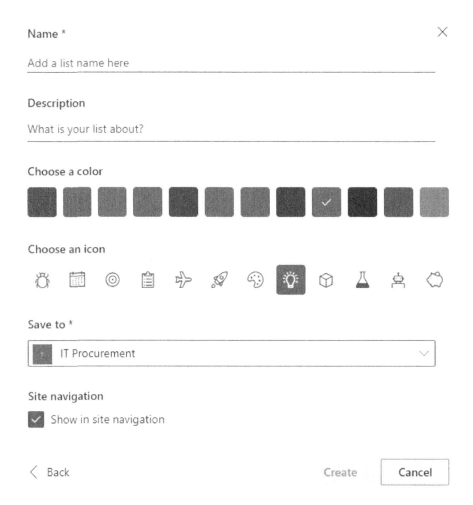

Figure 2.2 – Setting up a new blank list

Except for the last option, **Save to**, all the other options can be changed again after their initial setup:

- **Name** defines the display name of your list. It is recommended that you choose a unique and descriptive name right at the beginning, as the list name is the first thing that people usually see before they see a description or data. Thus, the more specific you are here, the easier it is for people to understand the purpose of the list.

- **Description** allows you to provide further information about the purpose of your list. As an example, if you have an "Asset Tracking List" to manage your physical IT assets, an appropriate description could be "This list is used to manage the life cycle and allocation of all physical IT assets, including notebooks, speakers, and others."

- **Choose a color** is one of two options that helps you define a logo for your list. You can choose from 12 different colors to use as the background color for the logo.

- **Choose an icon** is the second option for defining your logo. As with the colors, there are 12 different choices available to you, including a calendar icon, an airplane icon, and a tracking chart icon. The icon you select here will also use your selection from **Choose a color** as the background color to provide you with a preview of the final logo.

- **Save to** is an option where you will need to make a very conscious choice:

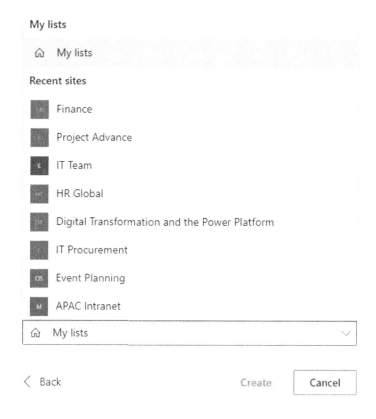

Figure 2.3 – Save to options

Here, you decide where your list will be created, a choice that cannot be changed as easily without additional migration or copy and paste effort compared to the other options. You can choose to save to **My lists**, which will create a personal list in your OneDrive account that you can share later with others. Alternatively, you can select from a range of **Recent sites**, which includes regular SharePoint sites as well as sites connected to Microsoft Teams. Selecting one of those will create the list in this site, and any existing access rights to the site will also apply to your new list.

- **Site navigation** is an option that only appears if you have selected a SharePoint or Teams site under **Recent sites** in the **Save to** field. It allows you to define whether your list should be displayed in the left-hand navigation of the site where you want to create the list, and thus be easily accessible to site visitors.

> **Note**
>
> In this chapter, we will use the following scenario for our list:
>
> Your company does not use any software system that allows you to track and manage your annual leave. You want to use Microsoft Lists to keep note of any leave requests that you made, their status, and when the leave is scheduled for. You are planning to call this list Leave Tracker, and you will not share it with anyone else initially, so you will create it within My Lists.

Once you click **Create**, the list will be created in your selected location, and your browser will navigate to it:

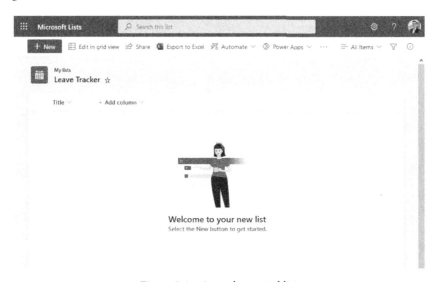

Figure 2.4 – A newly created list

As you can see, it only contains the default column called **Title**, which is available in every list, and no data has been added yet. Adding additional columns to your list will be covered in the *Adding columns to a list* subsection.

As we mentioned previously, you can change some of your list settings again once you've created the list. When you are viewing the contents of a list, clicking on the name of the list in the top-left corner will make a small dialog appear with familiar options:

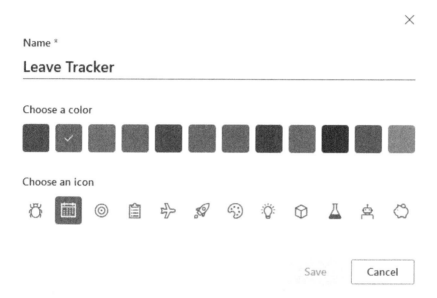

Figure 2.5 – Changing your list's name and icon

This allows you to change the name and the logo of your list later if needed.

Creating a new list in a SharePoint site

If you want to create a new list in a SharePoint site directly, you can do so by navigating to your site's home page or **Site contents** page and selecting **List** from the **New** dropdown. The dialog that appears will show the same **Create a list** options and templates as in the Microsoft 365 app launcher. However, selecting **Blank list** will show you a slightly different next step:

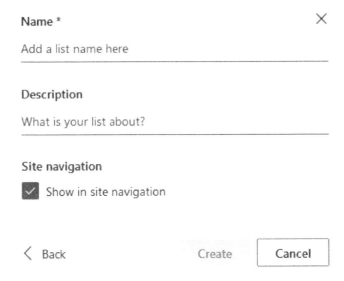

Figure 2.6 – Setting up a new blank list in a site

As you can see, you can still configure the **Name** and **Description** areas and whether the list should be displayed in **Site navigation**. However, you can't update the logo of your list.

Once you have entered all the required information and clicked **Create**, the list will be created within the site and you will be redirected to it.

Creating a new list in Microsoft Teams

The third option for creating a new list is available in Microsoft Teams. Usually, there are already people collaborating within Microsoft Teams and leveraging the flexibility of creating and using dedicated teams and channels to focus on specific work. The Lists app can be added to a team and is then available in all the channels within this team. You can create a new list for and within a selected channel, and anyone who has access to the channel can then work on data within that list.

Within a channel in a team, you can add a new tab at the top, and then select **Lists** from the options provided:

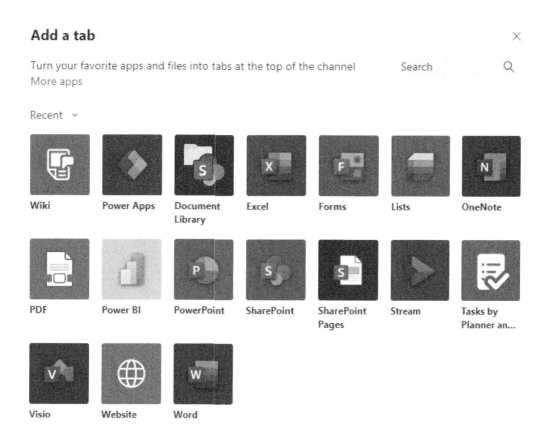

Figure 2.7 – Add a tab window in Microsoft Teams

Once the tab has been added, you have the option to either create a new list or add an existing list to be displayed within this tab. If you choose to add an existing list, it should be noted that the list does not have to reside in the current team and its dedicated SharePoint site; instead, it can be a list that has been created in another SharePoint site:

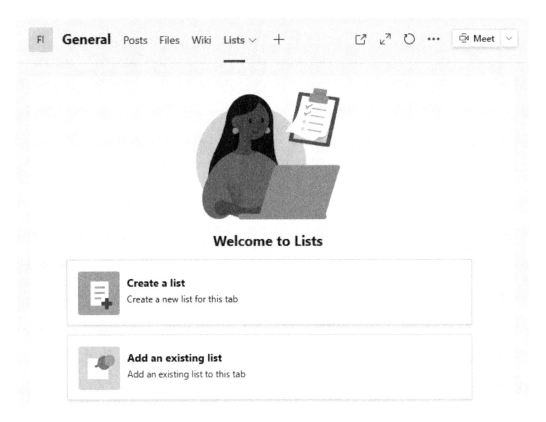

Figure 2.8 – Create a list and Add an existing list options

Once you click **Create a list**, a familiar view will be shown in the tab, providing you once again with the options to create a blank list, create one based on an Excel spreadsheet or a duplicate of an existing list, or select from predefined templates:

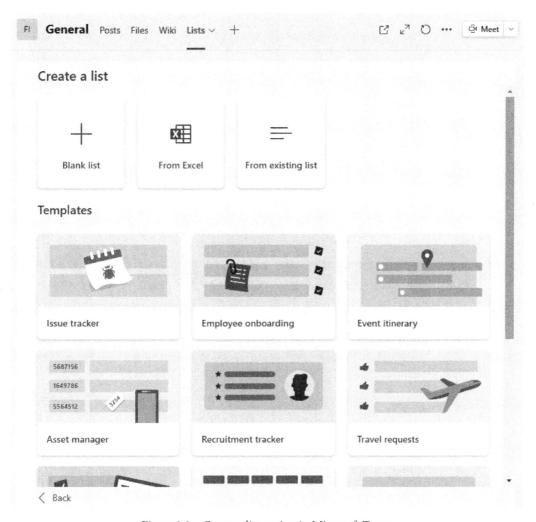

Figure 2.9 – Create a list option in Microsoft Teams

When you choose to create a blank list from here, you can define the name, description, and logo of your new list:

Figure 2.10 – Configuring your new list in Microsoft Teams

Once the list has been created, members of your team can work with it directly within Microsoft Teams by accessing it from the Channel's tab.

In this section, you learned how to create a new blank list from the Microsoft 365 app launcher, a SharePoint site, and from within Microsoft Teams. Next, you will learn how to configure your list according to your needs by adding an appropriate structure for your data.

Adding and maintaining columns on a list

Columns are used to provide structure for lists and store individual pieces of data. Now that you have created your first list, you will want to add some additional columns to your Leave Tracker so that you can track information properly.

There are various column types that can be used, all of which will be shown in more detail in *Chapter 3, Microsoft Lists Core Features*. In this chapter, we will use a subset of them to explain their purpose and usage. To continue with the Leave Tracker list, we are going to add the following columns with the corresponding column types:

- **Start Date**: A **Date and Time** column that will be used to track the beginning of when you take leave

- **End Date**: A **Date and Time** column that will be used to track the last day of when you take leave

- **Days**: A **Number** column where we manually provide the number of days in the leave period

- **Leave Type**: A **Choice** column to track whether it is **Annual Leave**, **Medical Leave**, or **Others**

- **Status**: A **Choice** column to track whether it is **Planned**, **Approved**, **Cancelled**, or **Taken**

Adding columns to a list

To add a new column, open your list. At the top of your list is a header bar showing various columns that are available. How you can control the visibility of these columns, and how you can manage different views to provide various viewpoints of your data, will be covered in *Chapter 5, Creating Microsoft Lists Views*.

Selecting **Add column** provides you with a list of the available column types that can be used for your new column:

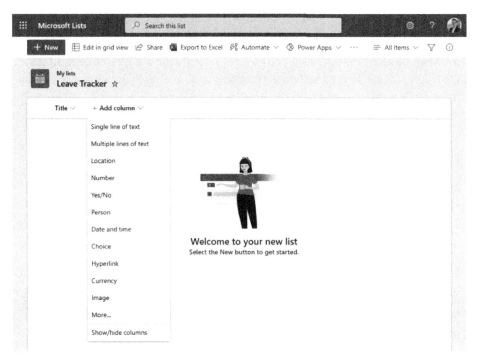

Figure 2.11 – Adding a new column to your list

Once you've selected any of these types, a new pane will open on the right-hand side of your browser, giving you even more fields that you can fill in and provide information about the column that you want to create.

The first three fields are always shown by default:

- **Name** asks you for the name you want to use for your new column.

- **Description** allows you to provide further information about the purpose of your column.

- **Type** lets you decide on the column type you want to use. The type you chose initially is selected here, but you can still switch to any of the other types during the creation process. Please note that once you have made a selection and created a column, it is not always possible to switch the type. While some types allow you to change to another type after column creation, such as from **Single line of text** to **Multiple lines of text**, other types, such as **Person** or **Group**, are not as flexible and are locked after creation. Due to this, you should be clear about the type of data you want to store in your column from the beginning and make a conscious choice.

When you choose a **Type**, the bottom section of the pane gets updated dynamically with additional configuration options. We will look at all the column types and their respective options in *Chapter 3, Microsoft Lists Core Features*. For example, for the **Date and Time** column, you can decide whether it should be a date-only field, whether the time should be included as well, and whether the column data should be displayed in a friendly format. Friendly format means that instead of having the date shown in your regular locale, such as 3/2/2021, a more appealing format will be used and might say "4 days from now" or "March 2," as an example. In addition, you can define a **Default** value to be used for any new items, and you can set the column to be optional or mandatory:

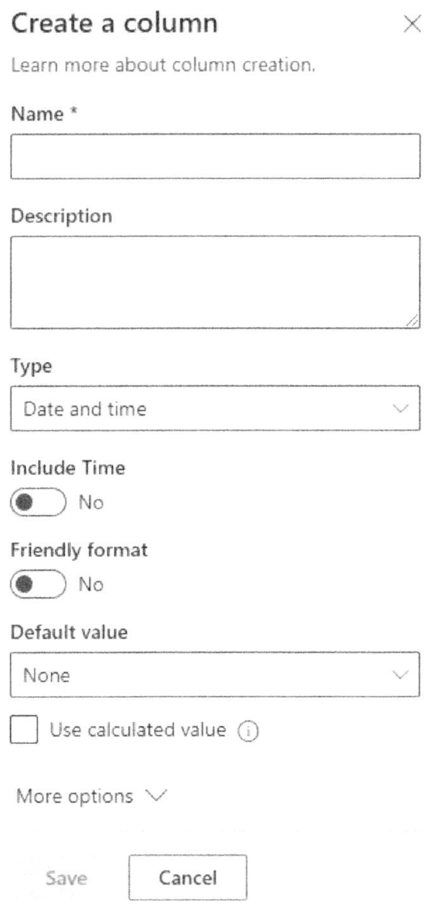

Figure 2.12 – Creating a Date and Time column

As we mentioned previously, different types offer you different configuration options. The **Choice** column type, for example, allows you to define different available and valid choices, and even a supporting color for each that will be used as the background color to highlight the value. That way, you not only let people who view your data see the different values, but make it more appealing to them and help them differentiate between these values easily. If you use a **Choice** column to keep track of projects, you can easily create a **Red, Amber, Green** (**RAG**) status column to let project managers select the corresponding status value, such as *on track*, while also providing a visual clue about the value itself:

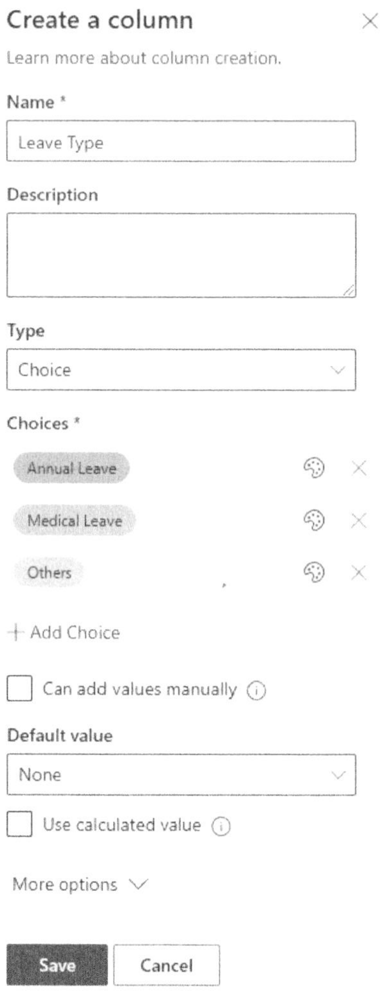

Figure 2.13 – Creating a Choice column

Once you have added multiple columns and added some data, this is what your Leave Tracker should look like:

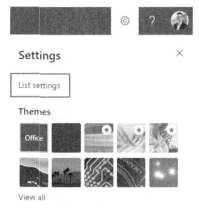

Figure 2.14 – List with multiple columns and data

Now that we have seen how to add columns, let's look at how we can edit and delete them.

Editing and deleting columns from a list

Often, you will find yourself in a situation where you need to modify your column's settings. This could be changing your **Single line of text** column to a **Multiple lines of text** column, switching the **Friendly format** option of your **Date and Time** column on/off, adding an additional option to a **Choice** column, and so on. In other cases, you will want to delete a column completely, such as when it does not capture any relevant information and you do not require it or any previously captured data anymore.

To make any such changes, you need to access your list's settings. This can be done by clicking on the **gear** icon in the top-right corner of Office 365 and selecting **List settings** while you have your list open. While the menu that appears when you click on the **Gear** icon is context-dependent, which means that, in a SharePoint site, you will see different additional options compared to what you do in the Microsoft Lists app, the **List settings** option will appear in both cases:

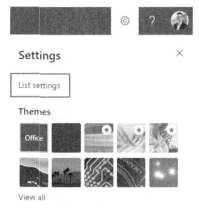

Figure 2.15 – Accessing List settings

On the **List settings** page, you will find a dedicated section for the columns of the selected list. All the columns are listed with their respective types, and it is specified if a column is mandatory:

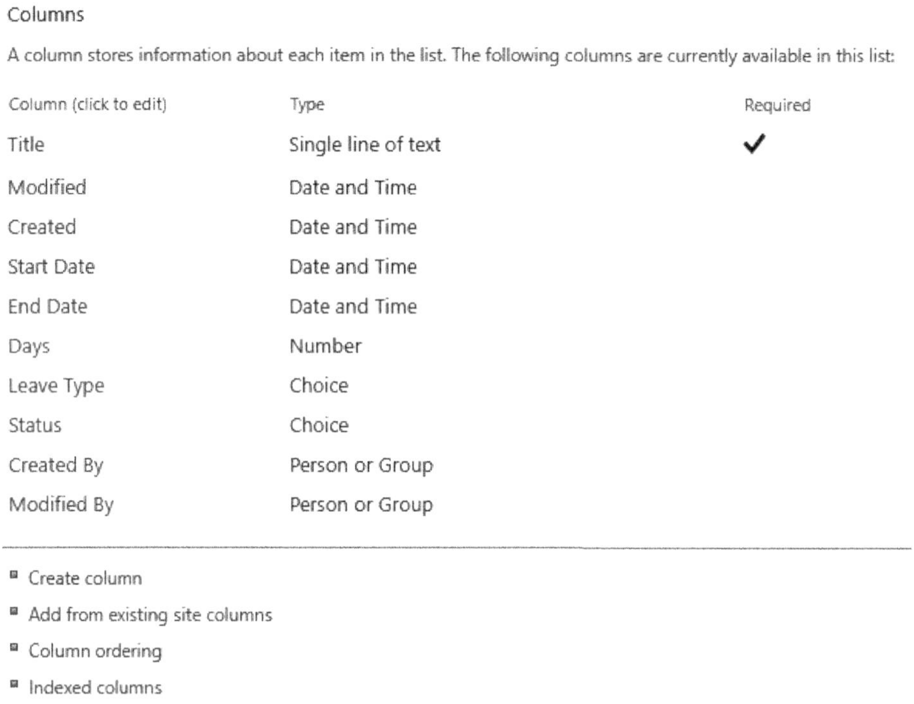

Columns

A column stores information about each item in the list. The following columns are currently available in this list:

Column (click to edit)	Type	Required
Title	Single line of text	✔
Modified	Date and Time	
Created	Date and Time	
Start Date	Date and Time	
End Date	Date and Time	
Days	Number	
Leave Type	Choice	
Status	Choice	
Created By	Person or Group	
Modified By	Person or Group	

- Create column
- Add from existing site columns
- Column ordering
- Indexed columns

Figure 2.16 – Columns section of the List settings page

Clicking on a column's title will bring you to the column's settings page. This page shows all the available type-specific properties and provides you with information about any potential type changes. As we mentioned previously, not all types can be switched to another type once a column has been created, and such an option may not be available:

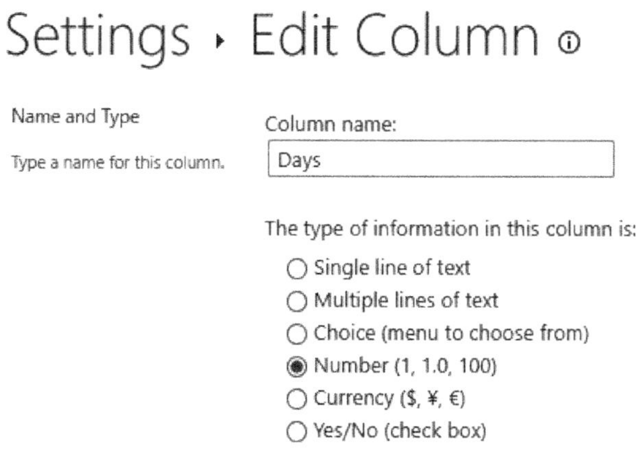

Settings ‣ Edit Column ⓘ

Name and Type	Column name:
Type a name for this column.	Days

The type of information in this column is:

○ Single line of text
○ Multiple lines of text
○ Choice (menu to choose from)
◉ Number (1, 1.0, 100)
○ Currency ($, ¥, €)
○ Yes/No (check box)

Figure 2.17 – Changing your column's type

In the **Additional Column Settings** section, you can update the column's available options, similar to when you created the column initially. For the **Days** column, which uses the **Number** type, you can specify **Number of decimal places** as **0** so that only whole numbers are accepted, and even provide a minimum and maximum allowed value:

Additional Column Settings	Description:
Specify detailed options for the type of information you selected.	

Require that this column contains information:

○ Yes   ◉ No

Enforce unique values:

○ Yes   ◉ No

You can specify a minimum and maximum allowed value:

Min: [   ]   Max: [   ]

Number of decimal places:

[0   ▾]

Default value:

◉ Number ○ Calculated Value

[   ]

☐ Show as percentage (for example, 50%)

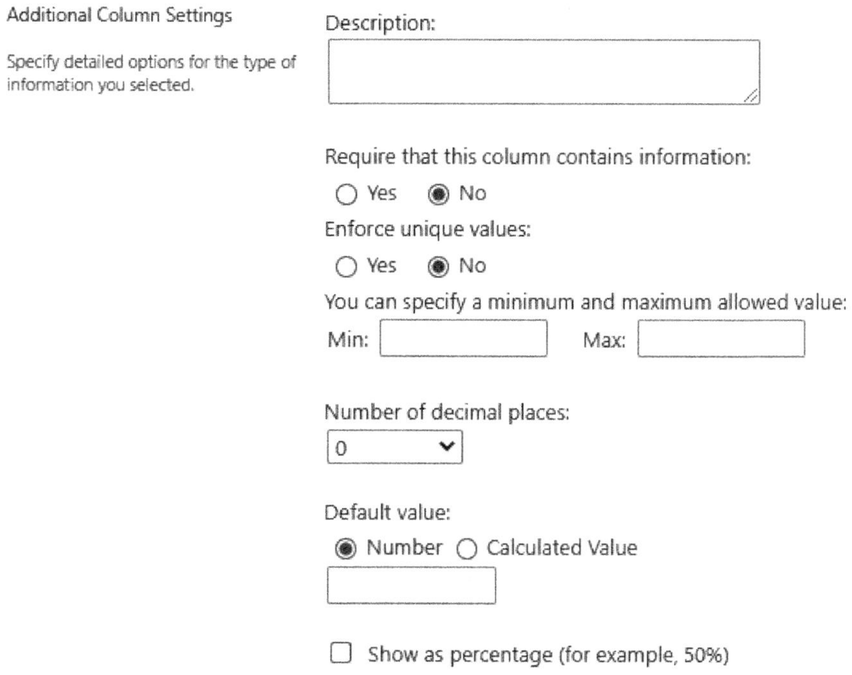

Figure 2.18 – Additional Column Settings window

At the bottom of the page, you will find three buttons to complete your desired action. You can click **Cancel** to discard any changes, click **OK** to save all the updates that you've made, or click **Delete** to remove your column from the list permanently.

> **Deleting a Column**
>
> When you delete a column from a list, all the information that was entered previously will be removed as well. If you want to retain the data but do not want the column to appear anymore in your list's public views, you can simply hide the column from any such locations.
>
> Deleting a column and the corresponding data is a process that cannot be reversed. Once you've deleted it, the column and the data cannot be restored anymore.

In this section, you learned how to set up your list with a structure for your data, and you also know how to add, edit, and delete columns. This way, you can create and maintain lists according to your requirements easily. However, there are also other, more efficient ways to create lists from an existing structure, all of which will be covered in the next two sections.

Creating a list from Excel

Often, you won't want to create a new list when starting from a blank canvas, as you may have already defined the data structure and potentially even have existing data. A lot of corporate and personal information resides in Excel spreadsheets. In some cases, you may want to take this information from an existing spreadsheet and put it into a list, in order to make use of additional functionalities such as formatting columns or creating a workflow to respond to changes.

If we have a spreadsheet where we keep track of our annual leave, we will likely have the structure of our information already defined, and will also have some data already available in this spreadsheet:

	A	B	C	D	E	F	G
1							
2							
3		Title	Start Date	End Date	Days	Leave Type	Status
4		Family Visit	11/1/2021	12/1/2021	2	Annual Leave	Approved
5		Chinese New Year	16/2/2021	19/2/2021	4	Annual Leave	Planned
6		School Holidays	15/3/2021	16/3/2021	2	Others	Approved

Figure 2.19 – Existing spreadsheet with a data table

As we saw previously, Microsoft Lists can be created from such existing Excel spreadsheets. Generally, it is highly recommended to review and clean up the data inside your spreadsheet before you perform any imports. Any data that exists in the table you want to import from your spreadsheet will be added to your list as new items. But if you do not want to import everything, performing a cleanup in Excel beforehand is easier than doing the cleanup afterward in your list.

When you start the process of creating a new list, you can select **From Excel** as a starting point. The dialog that appears allows you to either upload a local file or select an existing file from the current site's **Documents** library:

Figure 2.20 – Creating a new list from an Excel spreadsheet

Once you have selected your spreadsheet, the import process will start by examining the file for any existing tables. If no tables are available in your file, you will be informed about how to format your data accordingly to make use of the import functionality:

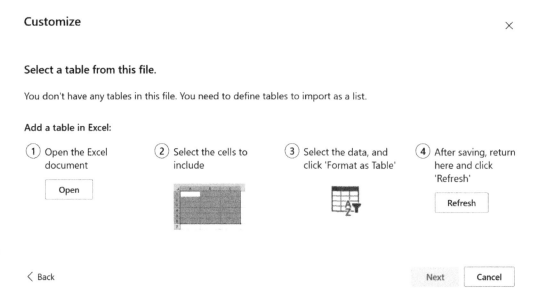

Figure 2.21 – Information dialog informing you of how to format your spreadsheet

If tables are found in your document, the import process will ask you to select the table to be used. If there are multiple tables in your spreadsheet, you need to define which single table should be used. You can also review the identified column from the selected table and define which column type to use, respectively. Depending on the format of the data in your spreadsheet, different options are available.

For example, a column that has been formatted as a date or as a number in Excel can be set up as text, number, choice, date, or currency in your list:

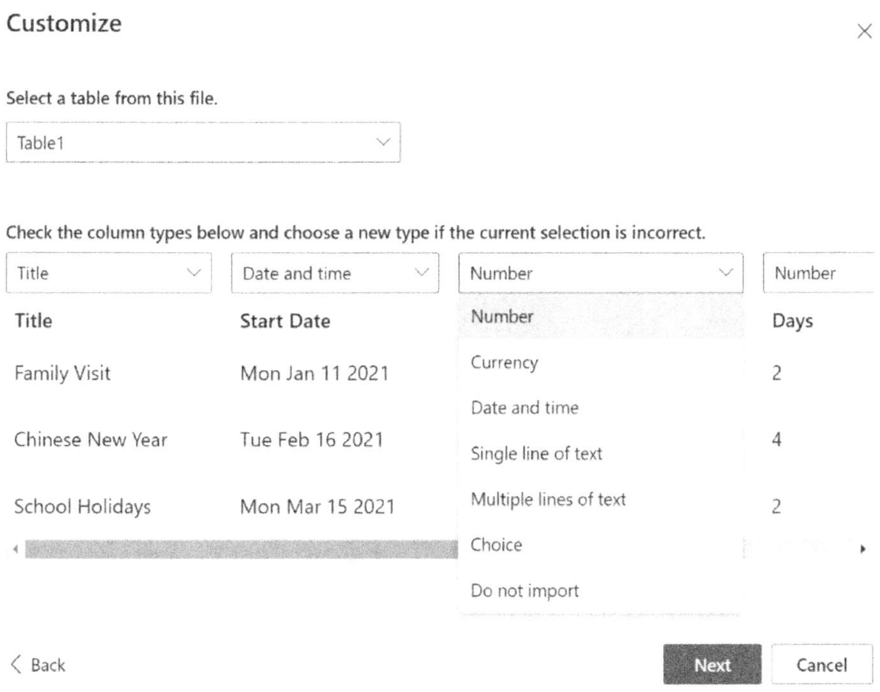

Figure 2.22 – Import dialog showing the column type options for columns with number values

If the column is formatted as text only, the provided options are restricted to text and choice only:

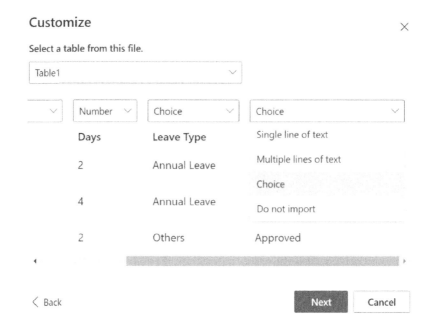

Figure 2.23 – Import dialog showing the column options for columns with text values

If desired, you can also choose to exclude columns from your table by selecting **Do not import** as the column type. It should also be noted that not all column types can be imported. Complex types, such as **Person** or **Group**, can't be imported easily, so they can't be selected. When you import a spreadsheet, you should consider this limitation and plan for it accordingly. Further configuration and manual data imports might be required.

Once you've confirmed the column configuration, you can define a name and description for your list and complete the process. The list will then be set up with the selected columns, and any available data from the spreadsheet will be imported into it:

Figure 2.24 – A list created from an Excel spreadsheet

Instead of creating a blank list and adding columns manually, you now know how to leverage the **From Excel** creation functionality to easily and quickly set up a new list based on an existing spreadsheet. As a lot of corporate data is often stored in Excel spreadsheets first, this method is extremely useful for converting such spreadsheets into a list in a convenient manner.

With that, we have seen how to create our own lists by starting from scratch and adding relevant columns as needed, and we have also looked at how to create a list based on an existing Excel spreadsheet. The next step is to learn how to duplicate a list that already exists.

Creating a list from an existing list

In many cases, you have an existing list for a specific purpose, but you may also have some interest in it from different groups. For example, the Leave Tracker list, which we are using in this chapter, is something that other colleagues or even teams could be interested in. Instead of setting it up the same way repeatedly, it is more efficient to create a copy for new audiences whenever it's needed.

In the **New list** creation dialog, once you've select the **From existing list** option, you need to decide which list you want to duplicate. You can do this by selecting the team or site where the list has been created, followed by selecting the specific list:

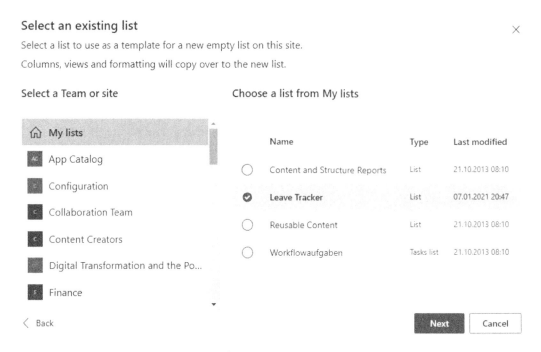

Figure 2.25 – Selecting an existing list to duplicate

Afterward, the familiar options dialog where you can define the list's name and other properties, among which is the destination location, such as a different site or My list, will appear again. Once you click **Create**, a copy of your list will be created in the selected destination, including all the previously created columns.

This method is useful when an existing list has been deemed valuable and should be used in other locations as well. Instead of setting up the same list structure again or using a third-party tool to create a copy, this out-of-the-box functionality provides you with a convenient way to create duplicates of a list.

Maintaining list data

Regardless of whether you've created an empty list or imported a list with data from Excel, the next step is usually to add some information to your list, followed by updating any existing information.

Adding items to a list

To create a new entry in a list, click on the **New** button. A new form will appear, where you will be able to provide relevant information based on the columns that you've added to the list:

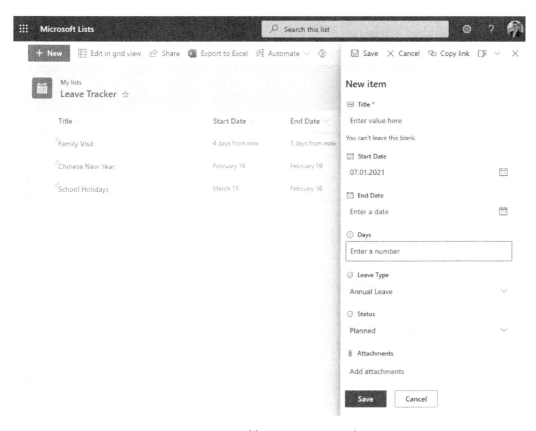

Figure 2.26 – Adding a new item to a list

Depending on the column type, the individual controls are rendered differently. For example, for simple text fields, a normal text area will be shown, where you can enter required information. Where possible, more user-friendly controls are used. For date fields, date pickers are shown, allowing users to either enter the date manually or select it from the date picker control. Clicking **Save** will create the new entry, whereas clicking **Cancel** will close the dialog without storing anything that was entered.

Another way to add information is to use **Edit in grid view** mode, as you will see in the next chapter. While this mode is mainly used to edit existing entries, you can also use the **Add new item** row at the bottom of your list to create a new entry and add relevant data directly into the cells shown:

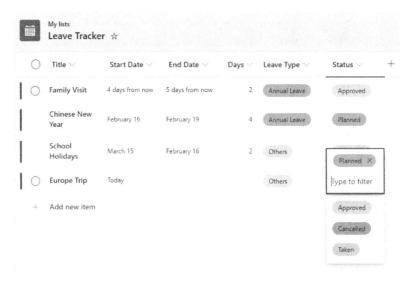

Figure 2.27 – Adding a new entry in grid view mode

One benefit of doing so is that items are rendered directly on screen. As an example, for a **Choice** column with entries that are different colors, you will be able to see these background colors when you're entering your data, something that is not available in the regular **New entry** form.

Editing items in a list

To edit an item, you can click on the item's **Title** value, which opens a preview pane. Here, you can edit the column values individually, or you can click on **Edit all** at the top to open the full edit form. The edit form can also be accessed by clicking on the ellipsis of the item and choosing **Edit**:

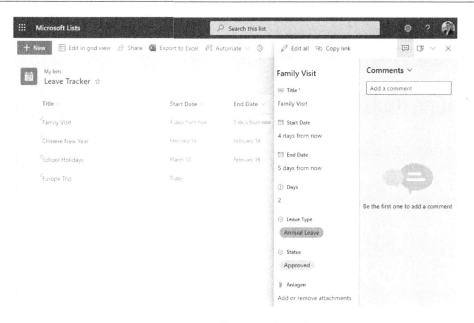

Figure 2.28 – Editing an existing item

It is also possible to edit items individually or in bulk in **Edit in grid view** mode. One of the benefits of doing so is that you can easily update a column for multiple items with the same value. You can select multiple cells within the same column by selecting the first item to be selected, pressing the *Shift* button, and finally selecting the final item to be selected. All the cells for the items between these two will be highlighted, and you can paste a value into all of them in one go. Alternatively, if you want to copy the value from the first cell into the cells below, you can select the first cell by clicking on the small square in the bottom-right corner of it and dragging it down across all the cells to be filled with the selected cell's value:

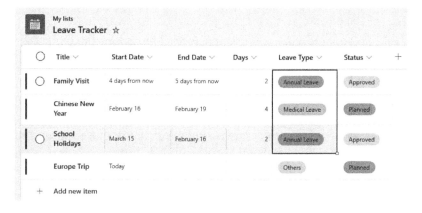

Figure 2.29 – Editing the items in a list in bulk

Any changes that you've made to items and cells will be saved immediately in the grid view, as well as in the preview pane. Only in the full edit form are you required to click on **Save** to save your changes.

Deleting items from a list

The last action we want to cover is deleting items from a list. When an item is no longer required, you can right-click on it and select **Delete** either from the menu that appears or from the options menu on top of the list. If there are multiple items you wish to delete, you can also select all of them first by clicking on the checkbox in front of each relevant item, and then selecting **Delete**:

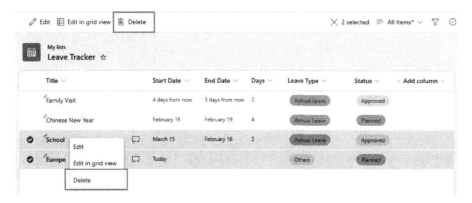

Figure 2.30 – Selecting and deleting multiple items

Items that you delete will be moved to your site's recycle bin, where they will remain for the duration of the retention period that has been set up. The default duration for this is set to 93 days, during which you are still able to restore deleted items when needed.

A list without any data in it does not provide any value. In this section, we have shown how to maintain entries in your list by adding new items, editing them, and also deleting them when they are no longer required. This equips you with the knowledge to utilize your lists efficiently and to start using them within your organization.

Summary

In this chapter, we went through the various available processes for creating a new list and explained the differences between them. We also added additional columns to our list and looked at how to manage and maintain list data.

In the next chapter, we will review the available out-of-the-box Microsoft Lists features that can help you set up, manage, and use your lists effectively.

3
Microsoft Lists Core Features

Now that we know how to access Microsoft Lists and how to create new lists, it is time to look at its core features and how you can use them when building your own lists.

To get the best out of Microsoft Lists, you will need to understand all the core features described in this chapter, which will help you decide later which is the appropriate feature to use for the different scenarios you will face.

In this chapter, you will gain an overview of the following main topics:

- Modern and classic list features
- What are the out-of-the-box Microsoft Lists features?
- Where is Microsoft Lists data stored?

Modern and classic list features

As mentioned in *Chapter 1, Getting Started with Microsoft Lists*, SharePoint had a major update in 2016 when Microsoft introduced the modern experience in SharePoint. Despite having been released in 2016, the modern experience rollout is not yet complete and there are areas of the product that still only exist in the classic version, even though Microsoft Lists has been introduced as a modern application.

> **Note**
>
> Microsoft Lists features that are available in the modern and classic versions are shown and explained in the modern layout within this book. The classic experience will gradually disappear, and we believe that you will take more advantage of the system if you use it exclusively in the modern experience. All the features that are only available in the classic experience and are still relevant will be highlighted within the text.

The easiest way to access the classic options of a list is by opening the list settings page. To do that, you need to perform the following steps:

1. In Microsoft Lists, with your list open, click on the **Settings** icon in the top-right corner of the page.

2. From the menu, select **List settings**:

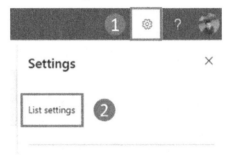

Figure 3.1 – Microsoft Lists settings

3. You will notice that the list settings page will open inside SharePoint. From there, you will be able to access multiple list options, such as the list columns, list views, and advanced settings, among others. Any option marked in this book as classic only can be accessed from this classic experience screen:

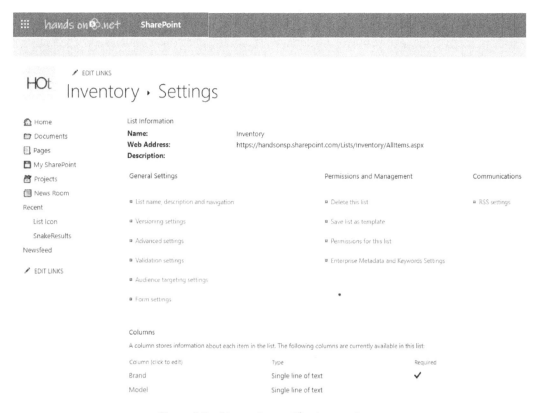

Figure 3.2 – List settings – Classic experience

As Microsoft continues to evolve SharePoint and Microsoft Lists, it's expected that all the features will become available in the modern interface. However, until such time, do keep in mind how to access the classic settings page, as explained previously in this section. Next, we will take a look at the different features available that Microsoft Lists offers.

What are the out-of-the-box Microsoft Lists features?

The Microsoft Lists application comes with several out-of-the-box features that will help you to build your own lists to manage your work and to collaborate with your co-workers.

To better help you understand each one of these features, we will describe them throughout the chapter with real-world scenarios whenever this is justified.

Column types

Column types are the main foundation of Lists, as you saw in *Chapter 2, Creating Your First List*. Each column has a data type associated with it that is responsible for the way data is displayed and stored in lists.

Microsoft Lists has a very complete set of column types that will allow you to easily define text, images, and locations, among other things. In the following list, you can find a definition for all the column types you will find when creating a new column:

- **Single line of text**: This is the most basic column type you will find in Lists. You must use it whenever you want to store small amounts of text, such as a product name, a book title, or a department name. With a single line of text, you are limited to a maximum of 255 characters. If you need to store a larger amount of text, you must use multiple lines of text.

    The single line of text comes with a few options that you can use to ensure that the information in this cell meets your business requirements, including the following:

    a) **Default value**: If you want this field to be prepopulated with information when a user creates a new list item, use this option to define it.

    b) **Maximum number of characters**: Despite having a maximum limit of 255 characters, you can sort the size of your column by defining your own maximum size for the single line of text column, using a number between 1 and 255.

    c) **Enforce unique values**: By default, this option is set to **No**. However, if your column is unique and you do not want the user to introduce multiple entries in different rows with the same value, this option gives you that possibility. For example, you are creating a list to store all the departments of your company and want to make sure that the list only displays one entry for each department. To achieve your goal, you can create a list column to store the department name and turn **Enforce unique values** to **Yes**.

    d) **Calculated**: This option allows you to transform the single line of text into a calculated column. You can learn more about this column type in this section in the *Calculated (classic only)* column.

e) **Column validation**: Column validation allows you to define custom rules for a data format when a user is creating new list items. This field allows you to define the formula that must be true to get the item saved and the error message that the user will see if the formula returns false. For example, you are creating a list to store information pertaining to all the vehicles in your company. One of the things you want to save is the license plate number, which always has eight characters and you want to ensure that this value has exactly eight characters before the item is saved. From the column validation setting, you will be able to define a formula that will make sure your requirement is validated when a user presses the **Save** button:

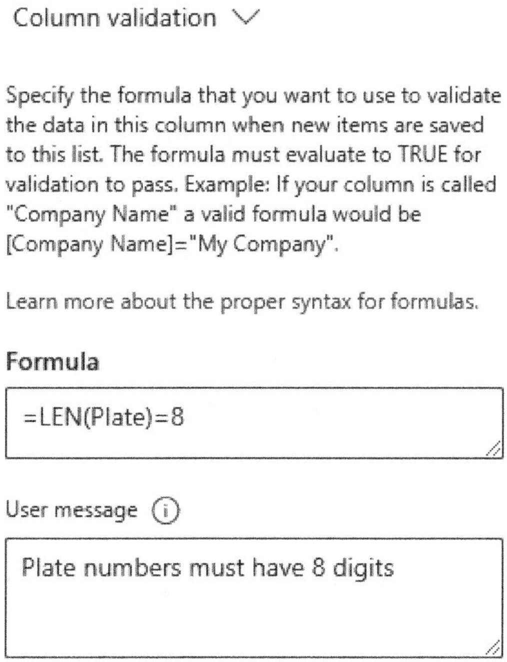

Column validation ∨

Specify the formula that you want to use to validate the data in this column when new items are saved to this list. The formula must evaluate to TRUE for validation to pass. Example: If your column is called "Company Name" a valid formula would be [Company Name]="My Company".

Learn more about the proper syntax for formulas.

Formula

=LEN(Plate)=8

User message ⓘ

Plate numbers must have 8 digits

Figure 3.3 – Column formula validation

- **Multiple lines of text**: This type of column must be used when you want to store text that surpasses the limits of the single line of text. A multiple lines of text column can have up to a maximum of 63,999 characters and comes with a few options that allow you to set it up to meet your business requirements, including the following:

a) **Default value**: If you want this field to be prepopulated with information when a user creates a new list item, use this option to define it.

b) **Rich text**: This option allows you to add rich text elements to the column. You will be able to format your text with basic formatting styles such as bold, italic, hyperlinks, or tables. By default, this option is set to **No**.

c) **Append Changes**: This option will only work if your list has versioning enabled. You can learn more about versioning in *Chapter 4, Collaborating on Microsoft Lists*. With this option enabled, other users will be able to append text to this column without deleting the pre-existing values. By default, this option is set to **No**.

d) **Calculated**: This option allows you to transform the multiple lines of text into a calculated column. You can learn more about this column type in this section in the *Calculated (classic only)* column.

- **Choice**: This type of column is used when you want people to choose from a predefined list of values defined by the creator of the list. Each choice can be customized with a color, which will assist in identification when you are viewing the list data:

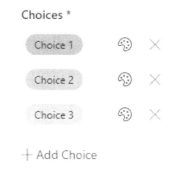

Figure 3.4 – Choices with customizations

A choice field also has other options that allow you to customize it further, including the following:

a) **Can add values manually**: This option allows people to type in new values for this column.

b) **Display choices**: This option allows you to define how the choices are presented to the user in the new item form. There are two options available: **Drop-Down Menu** and **Radio Buttons**.

c) **Allow multiple selections**: This option allows a user to select more than one option from the choices available.

d) **Enforce unique values**: By default, this option is set to **No**, but if your column is unique and you do not want the user to introduce multiple entries with the same text, this option gives you that possibility.

- **Location**: This column is integrated with the Bing Maps service and your organization directory. It allows you to easily search for a location and store it in the list, giving you the option to immediately complete the following fields based on the location selection:

a) Street Address

b) City

c) State

d) Country or Region

e) Postal Code

f) Coordinates

g) Name:

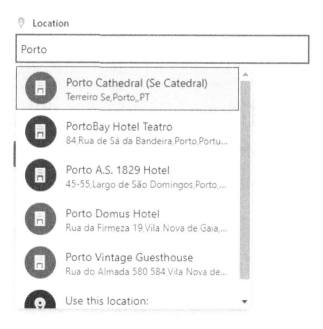

Figure 3.5 – Location selection in a list form

- **Number**: This column is meant to be used with the numeric values you need to store in a list, except currency values. A number in a list can be defined with several options, including the following:

a) **Number of decimal places**: The description of the option is self-explanatory, and you can define the decimal places between 0 and 5.

b) **Show as a percentage**: This option allows you to display a value as a percentage.

c) **Default value**: If you want this field to be prepopulated with information when a user creates a new list item, use this option to define it.

d) **Minimum allowed value**: Use this option to define the minimum value a user can introduce in the field.

e) **Maximum allowed value**: Use this option to define the maximum value a user can introduce in the field.

f) **Enforce unique values**: By default, this option is set to **No**, but if your column is unique and you do not want the user to introduce multiple entries with the same text, this option gives you that possibility.

g) **Calculated**: This option allows you to transform the number into a calculated column. You can learn more about this column type in this section in the *Calculated (classic only)* column.

- **Yes/No**: This field is used to store the logical values – True (Yes) and False (No). This type of column is one of the simplest you will find in lists and only has one option:

a) **Default value**: The default value is set to **Yes**.

- **Person or Group**: This column allows you to select users or groups that exist in your tenant. When creating a column of this type, you will find several configuration options:

a) **Allow selection of groups**: This option allows you to select not just a person but also an Office 365 group.

b) **Allow multiple selections**: This option allows you to select multiple users or groups.

c) **Enforce unique values**: By default, this option is set to **No**, but if your column is unique and you do not want the user to introduce multiple entries, this option gives you that possibility:

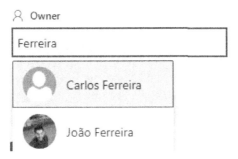

Figure 3.6 – Person or group selection in a list form

- **Date and Time**: With this column type, you can store date values in several different formats that you can customize with these field type options:

  a) **Include time**: This option gives you the possibility to define your date with or without the time. By default, this option is set to **No**.

  b) **Friendly format**: This option allows you to define how you see the date. Here, you can see examples of standard and friendly formats:

  i) **Standard**: 12/16/2020, 12:00 AM

  ii) **Friendly**: Yesterday at 12:00 AM

  c) **Calculated**: This option allows you to transform a date into a calculated column. You can learn more about this column type in the section in this *Calculated (classic only)* column.

- **Hyperlink**: This column allows you to store a URL in your list and make it clickable when a user accesses the data in the list. A hyperlink is always defined by two fields, one to store the URL and another one to store the alternative text, which is the value that appears as visible in the list:

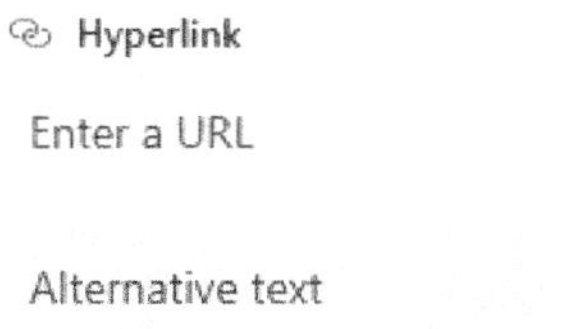

    ⚭ **Hyperlink**

    Enter a URL

    Alternative text

Figure 3.7 – Hyperlink in a list form

- **Currency**: This is the column you must use when dealing with currency values. It includes options to format the currency in the country format. In the currency column type, you will find the following options:

  Number of decimal places: The description of the option is self-explanatory, and you can define the decimal places between 0 and 5.

  Currency format: This option allows you to select the symbol and how the number will be formatted. It has 131 options available, which allows you to select any type of currency available in the world.

  Default value: If you want this field to be prepopulated with information when a user creates a new list item, use this option to define it.

- **Minimum allowed value**: Use this option to define the minimum value a user can introduce in the field.

Maximum allowed value: Use this option to define the maximum value a user can introduce in the field.

Enforce unique values: By default, this option is set to **No**, but if your column is unique and you do not want the user to introduce multiple entries with the same text, this option gives you that possibility.

Calculated: This option allows you to transform the currency into a calculated column. You can learn more about this column type in this section in the *Calculated (classic only)* column.

- **Image**: This type of column allows you to display images in your list. The image is saved in the context of the SharePoint site, as we will see in the following section of this chapter, *Where is Microsoft Lists data stored?*

- **Lookup** (classic only): This type of column allows you to enforce a relationship between different sources of data in your site. For example, you have a list where you store the information of all your suppliers and you are now building a list to keep track of your stock. Each item in the stock list should display the name of the supplier and you can only select suppliers previously added to the suppliers list:

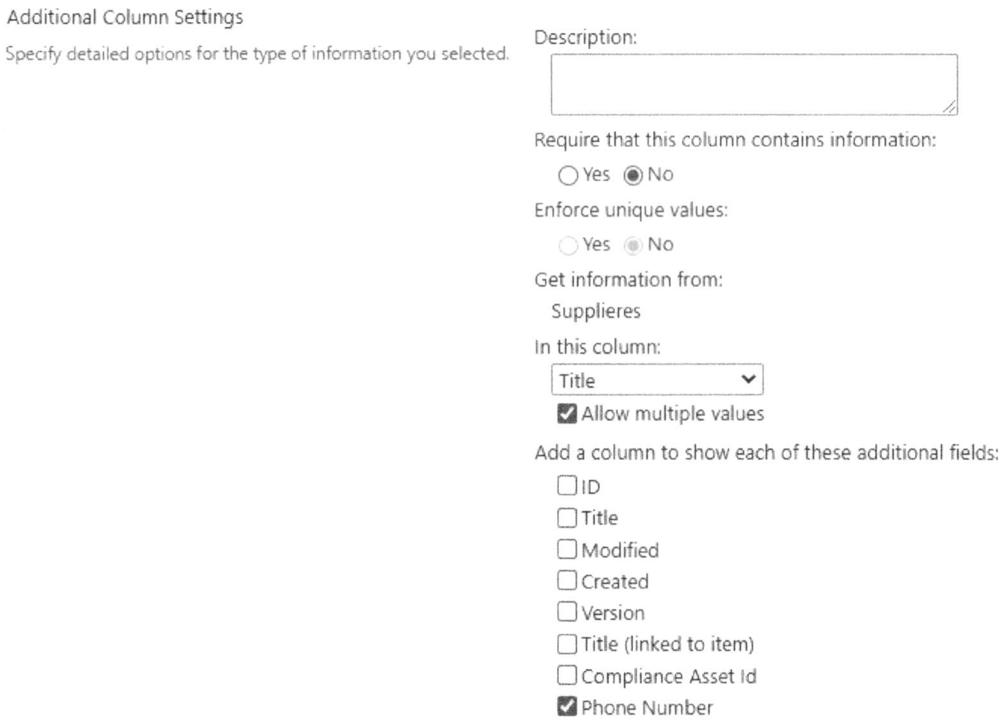

Additional Column Settings

Specify detailed options for the type of information you selected.

Description:

Require that this column contains information:

○ Yes ● No

Enforce unique values:

○ Yes ● No

Get information from:

Supplieres

In this column:

Title

☑ Allow multiple values

Add a column to show each of these additional fields:

☐ ID
☐ Title
☐ Modified
☐ Created
☐ Version
☐ Title (linked to item)
☐ Compliance Asset Id
☑ Phone Number

Figure 3.8 – Lookup column configuration

A lookup column will be displayed as a dropdown in list form and will always be updated with the values you have in the source list.

- **Calculated** (classic only): This is one of the more powerful column types you will find in lists. With it, you will be able to calculate a value based on any other column you have in the lists. For example, you are creating a list to store all your products with their prices. You only have the price of the product without VAT, but you also want to store the prices with VAT in the list and have it calculated automatically.

The result of a calculated column can be created with different types of data:

Single Line of text

Number

Currency

Date and Time

Yes/No:

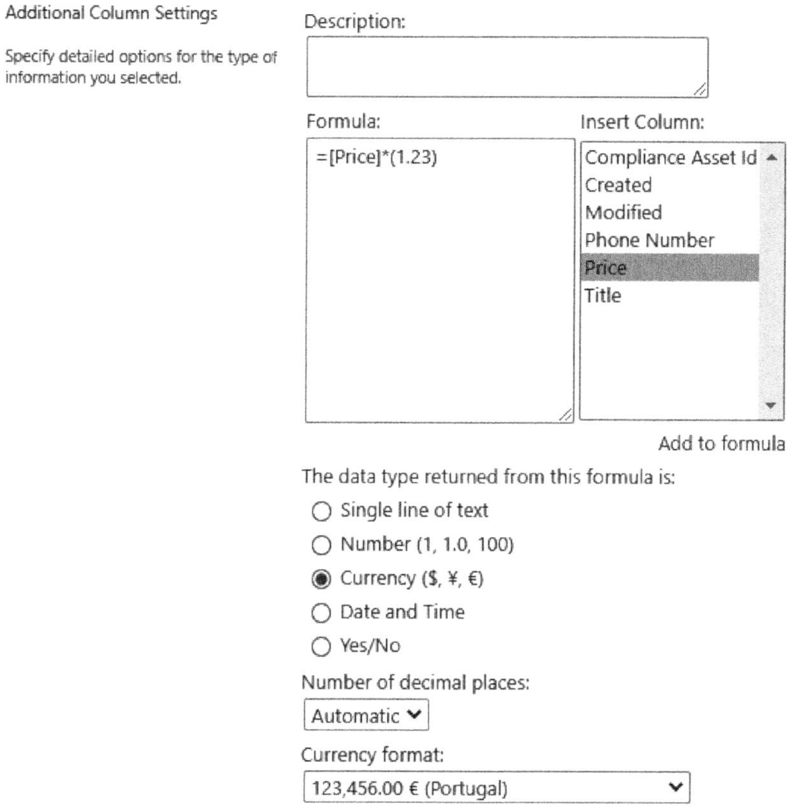

Figure 3.9 – Calculated column configuration

A calculated column will not be present in the new item form and you will only see it in the Lists view.

> **Note**
>
> Microsoft Lists supports dozens of formulas in the calculated fields and throughout the book, you will see some examples of them. For future reference, we recommend that you have a look at the following Microsoft link: `https://support.microsoft.com/en-us/office/ examples-of-common-formulas-in-lists-d81f5f21- 2b4e-45ce-b170-bf7ebf6988b3`.

- **Managed metadata** (classic only): If your company has information organized and categorized with metadata, you can use this type of column to promote the consistency in your lists aligned with the definitions of the company. Creating a managed metadata column requires the previous configuration of metadata in SharePoint if you are not familiar with it. We recommend that you have a look at `https://docs.microsoft.com/en-us/sharepoint/managed- metadata` for a topic written by Microsoft.

In the following screenshot, you can see what the interface for selecting the terms defined previously looks like in Lists:

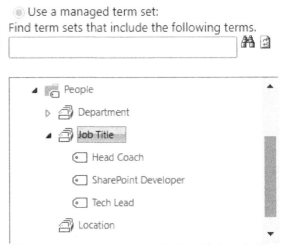

Figure 3.10 – Term Set Settings column configuration

Lists views

Lists views allows you to see a particular selection of items or to see the items sorted in a particular order or format, as you will learn in detail in *Chapter 5, Creating Microsoft Lists Views*. Lists views allows you to filter the information through the selection of the columns you want to see and the use of conditions, among a few other settings.

In this section, you will learn what are the default views you will find when you create a new list and what view formats are available:

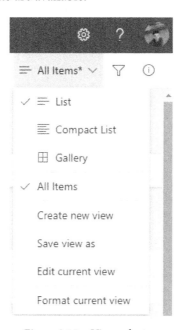

Figure 3.11 – View selector

When you first create a list, the only view you will get is **All Items**. This is the default view in all lists. It displays all the columns created by a user ordered by their creation ID, which means that a new item will always be displayed at the end of the list.

Despite being ordered by the item ID, from the view, you will be able to sort the list by any of the existing columns. All you have to do is click on the arrow next to the column name to get access to the sorting options. Your default view can also be filtered from the UI using the filtering pane that you can open next to the view selector:

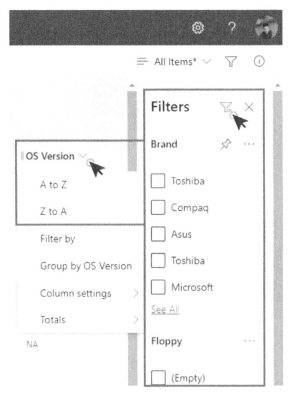

Figure 3.12 – Viewing the sort and filter options

Along with the **All Items** view, you will get three default formatting options that can be applied to any view to change the way information is presented in the list – **List**, **Compact List**, and **Gallery**.

List and **Compact List** have a similar layout, with the compact list displaying a smaller height for each item. The layout is provided by default with an alternating row style, with the odd rows displayed with the gray background, while the white rows are displayed with a white background:

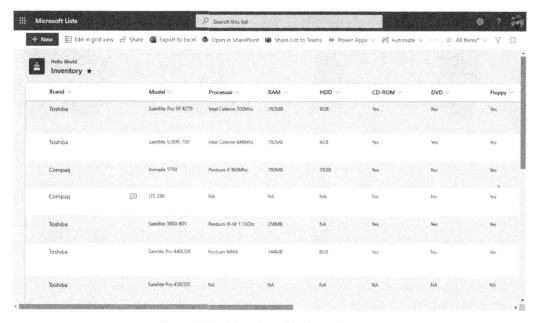

Figure 3.13 – Lists view with alternating rows

The **Gallery** view creates a card layout where the image columns are displayed in a prominent position. This default layout focuses importance on the media elements and may hide some of the columns that are only displayed when a user clicks in the Lists detail.

The **Gallery** view displays the first five columns of the list and highlights the first image or person column defined in the list schema.

The following screenshot illustrates the same list displayed to illustrate the List and Compact list layouts, but with the gallery layout applied:

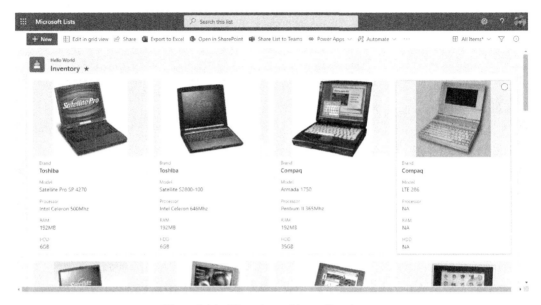

Figure 3.14 – Lists view with a gallery layout

List forms

List forms are the components that allow you to introduce data into your lists. Forms are generated and updated automatically when you add, modify, or delete a new column from a list. In a default form, each input is created based on the column type. Despite being generated automatically, list forms can also be customized and custom-made, as you will see in *Chapter 8, Customizing Microsoft Lists Forms*:

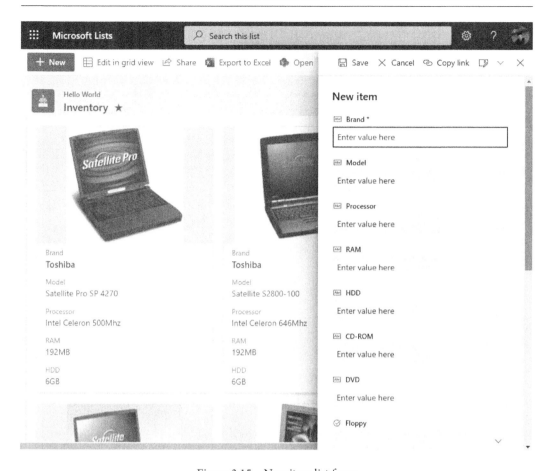

Figure 3.15 – New item list form

List item comments

Lists are lightweight databases and the data stored on them follows the rules that are defined in the list definition. Despite storing structured data, Microsoft Lists also allows you to add unstructured data to each item in the format of a comment.

Comments inherit the permissions defined in SharePoint and Microsoft Lists, which means only users with editing permissions will be able to create/delete comments, while users with read-only permissions will only be able to read the comments.

The option to create a new comment and to view existent comments will appear next to the item details in a vertical pane, as shown in the following screenshot:

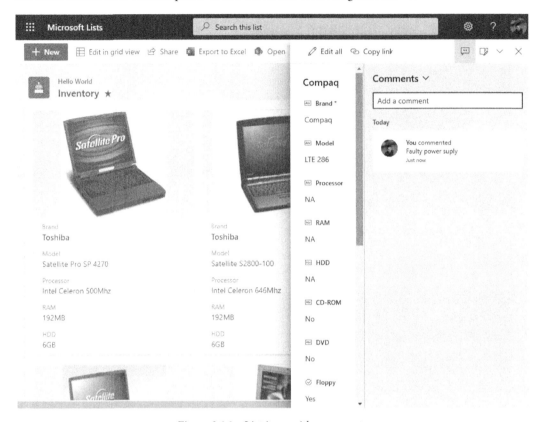

Figure 3.16 – List item with comments

List item attachments

Each list allows you to attach one or multiple files to the list. Despite being handy in certain scenarios, you should not consider this feature to use your list as a main repository for files.

If you are looking for a solution for files, you should look into SharePoint document libraries that are, in definition, very similar to lists.

The option to attach files to a list appears in the new item form and can be disabled in the list settings of each list individually.

List rules

List rules allow you to implement workflows on top of the data in your lists, and you have four different conditions that you can use to notify someone regarding data modifications:

- A column changes
- A column value changes
- A new item is created
- An item is deleted:

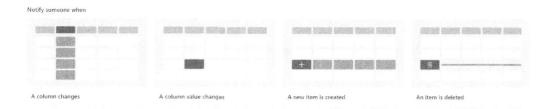

Figure 3.17 – Microsoft Lists rules

List rules can easily be customized, and the interface is not technical at all. With the use of natural language, you will be able to easily create your notification system. Microsoft Lists rules are explained in detail in *Chapter 4, Collaborating on Microsoft Lists*:

Figure 3.18 – Rule creation language

List sharing

Microsoft Lists has built-in sharing features that allow you to easily share lists and list items with other members of your organization or external members if your organizations have external collaboration enabled.

The sharing feature for a list is in the command bar and gives you the possibility to do the following:

- Enter the email addresses of users to send list access.

- Define the permissions the users will have in the list.

- Add an optional message.

- The option to notify users by email that a new list has been shared:

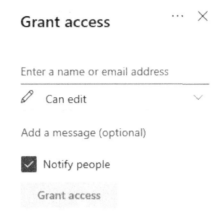

Figure 3.19 – Sharing a list option

The permissions you select when sharing the list will give the user different levels of actions in terms of the list data. Keep the following table in mind when sharing a list with someone:

Actions	Can View	Can Edit	Full Control
View items in the list	✔	✔	✔
Edit items in the list		✔	✔
Add new items to the list		✔	✔
Share the list with others			✔
Modify the list schema			✔

The sharing feature of a list item is available in two different places. You can access it from the command bar if the list item is selected, or you can use the share button located in the item when you hover over it. The sharing list items features include the following options:

- Enter the email addresses of users to send list access.
- Add an optional message.
- Select the permissions for people with access to the link.
- Set an expiration date for the link.
- Set a password to access the list item:

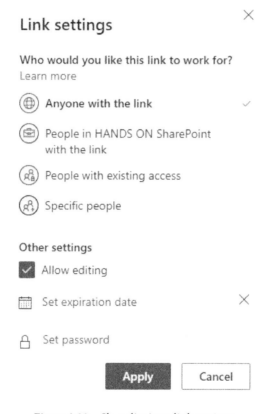

Figure 3.20 – Share list item link settings

List templates

Microsoft Lists comes with 12 out-of-the-box templates that cover the most typical scenarios of several vertical sectors and will help you to get started with the creation of a new list:

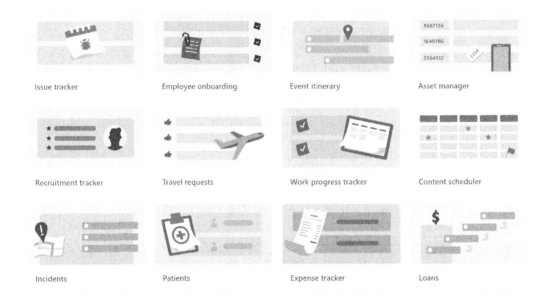

Figure 3.21 – Microsoft Lists templates

- **Issue tracker**: Track issues and bring them to closure in this list.

- **Employee onboarding**: Manage your new employee's onboarding process from day 1. Share resources and contacts, and get your new hire up to speed quickly.

- **Event itinerary**: Organize all your important event details in one place so that everything runs smoothly.

- **Asset manager**: Keep track of all the devices in your organization, and when they are checked in and returned.

- **Recruitment tracker**: Manage the recruitment pipeline in your organization or team with this simple tracker that helps you keep your finger on the pulse in terms of feedback for all candidates.

- **Travel requests**: Manage all your travel requests and keep an eye on budgets.
- **Work progress tracker**: Track priorities and progress as you work toward delivering products and services.
- **Content scheduler**: Plan, schedule, and manage your content with this template. Filter down to just the items that are due soon or get notifications when authors check in their drafts.
- **Incidents**: Track and manage incidents and events and keep the team up to date regarding their status and severity.
- **Patients**: Record the needs and status of patients so that care teams can monitor and coordinate care.
- **Expense tracker**: Record all your expenses anytime, anywhere.
- **Loans**: Provide a place for your loan origination team to track loans and work together to move them through the approval process.

When using Microsoft Lists, you will notice that not all 12 templates are available in all Microsoft Lists clients. In the following table, you can see that each template is available in each client. Once the list is created from a template, it will be accessible from all the Lists clients:

	Web	Teams	iOS
Issue tracker	✔	✔	✔
Employee onboarding	✔	✔	✔
Event itinerary	✔	✔	✔
Asset manager	✔	✔	✔
Recruitment tracker	✔	✔	✔
Travel requests	✔	✔	✔
Work progress tracker	✔	✔	✔
Content scheduler	✔	✔	✘
Incidents	✘	✔	✘
Patients	✘	✔	✘
Loans	✘	✔	✘
Expense tracker	✘	✘	✔

Each template is provided just with the list schema without any content in it. However, all of them have a preview available and through it, you will see what the content will look like with all the formatting that is included:

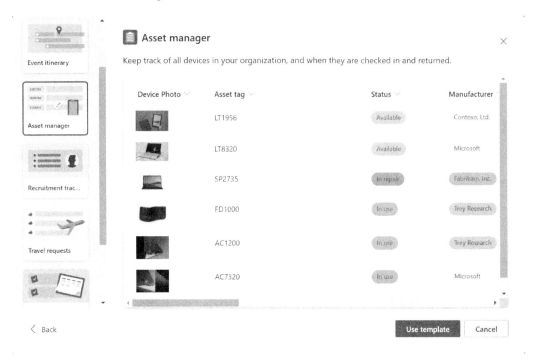

Figure 3.22 – Lists template preview

Despite being pre-made, templates can be modified and adjusted to your business needs. This feature is still limited to Microsoft only and you will not be able to save one of your lists as a custom template.

Edit mode

The data you enter in Microsoft Lists is not static and, over time, you will be able to modify it. The Lists application comes prepared with three different modes to edit your content that will help you to do things faster and to be more productive.

The first mode is **Edit in grid view** and the option to enable it can be found in the command bar. Once you click on this button, your list will enter into edit mode and all the cells will be editable. If you are familiar with Excel, the experience you will find here is very similar to the spreadsheet application:

Figure 3.23 – Microsoft Lists in quick edit mode

This mode is appropriate for scenarios where you need to change data in multiple columns. One important feature it has built in is the possibility to **Undo** and **Redo** your modifications in case you have made any mistakes. These options are available in the command bar while in edit mode and can also be used with the keyboard shortcuts, *Ctrl+ Z* and *Ctrl + Y* on Windows, and *Command + Z* and *Command + Y* on macOS.

Microsoft Lists also allows you to edit a single item at a time; however, the interface will be different, and the modification of the elements will be made in a similar form to the one that is used to add data to the list.

To edit a single item, all you have to do is select the item and click on the **Edit** button in the command bar. A new left pane will open with the item form in edit mode:

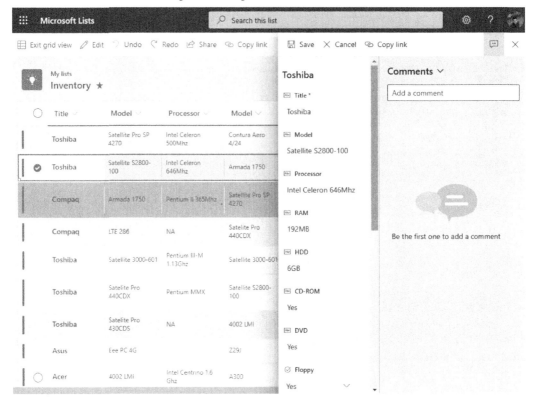

Figure 3.24 – Edit list item

The third available method that allows you to modify data in your list is the bulk editing of list items. To do this, you have to select all the items that you want to edit to have the same values in the edited columns.

Once you have the items selected, click on the **Edit** button in the command bar. Instead of getting access to the form pre-filled with the existing data, you will see it empty. All the columns that you change on it will then be saved with the same value to all the items:

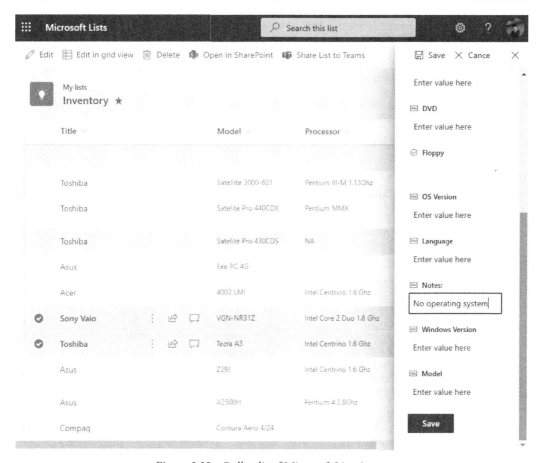

Figure 3.25 – Bulk edit of Microsoft Lists items

Now that we are familiar with the various features of Microsoft Lists, next we will find out how to determine where exactly are the data displayed on lists stored.

Where is Microsoft Lists data stored?

Despite being fully integrated, you will find data that is displayed in the lists being stored in different locations. Lists are stored in SharePoint, as we mentioned several times before, but depending on the type of list you select, they will end up in different locations:

- **Site/Team Lists**: These lists are stored in the context of the SharePoint site where they are created, and the permissions for the list are inherited by default from the SharePoint site.

- **My Lists**: My lists or personal lists are created on the user's site and are only accessible to the user who owns it.

List comments and attachments are the unstructured data inside lists as they do not follow any rule defined by the list schema. Despite their nature, the content of comments and attachments is stored in the list schema inside the SharePoint storage platform and is only directly accessible from the list context.

Image is the only column type that stores the data outside of the list schema. A picture uploaded to a list is stored in the same SharePoint site where the list exists, but in the Site Assets library in a folder with the unique list identifier:

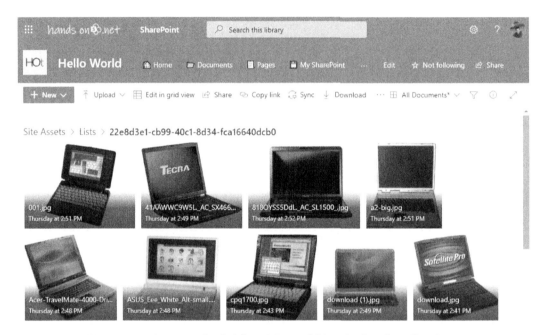

Figure 3.26 – Images uploaded from Microsoft Lists displayed on SharePoint

> **Quick tip**
>
> To find the correct folder in the library where the images are stored, you need to first find the unique identifier (GUID) for the list. To discover the GUID of your list, you must go to the List Settings page. Once on the page, the GUID will be visible in the URL; for example, `https://handsonsp.sharepoint.com/_layouts/15/listedit.aspx?List=76b55d3c-ad46-42c4-9899-8e52fb12cbf8`.

Summary

This chapter provided an introduction to the main features included in Microsoft Lists and gave you an overview of how they work and what they look like. In the upcoming chapters, you will learn how to make use of these features to create and manage lists.

In the next chapter, you will learn how to build a collaboration system using Microsoft Lists.

4

Collaborating on Microsoft Lists

Now that you have created your first list and understood its core features, it is time to look at how you can get more value out of it by making it available for others in your organization and working on the list data together. In this chapter, you will learn how to invite others to your list and see who has access to it. We will also review how to collaborate on list items more effectively by adding comments.

This chapter will cover the following topics:

- Managing access to your list
- Collaborating with others through comments
- Managing notifications through alerts and rules
- Tracking multiple changes through list versioning

Managing access to your list

If you have created a list on a SharePoint site, anyone who has access to the site will, by default, also have access to this list. When you add somebody new to the site, that person will also be able to work with the list. And correspondingly, when somebody's permissions on the site are removed, this person also loses access to the list.

However, there are often cases where you may want to share the list with a few more people, but not necessarily grant them access to the site itself. For example, you could have an *IT Budget* site where your various IT managers and other relevant staff have been granted access. Within the site, you also have a *Planned IT Projects* list, where you want to keep track of potential future projects and their estimated cost. There are people who are expected to provide details for such IT projects and add entries to this list, but they should not be allowed to see anything else within the site.

This is where sharing a list or even an individual list item is helpful. You can control in detail who has access to your list without having to manage the permissions of the site itself, allowing you to create small collaboration spaces on your site where more people can contribute. It is the same with your personal lists in your OneDrive as well – only you have access to your OneDrive, but you can share the lists you create within with others as well.

Sharing a list

Sharing a list with somebody else is a relatively straightforward process. Open the list that you want to share and at the top of the list, click on the **Share** button:

Figure 4.1 – Sharing a list through the Share button

In the dialog that opens, you have a few options to grant access to the list:

Figure 4.2 – Grant access to a list

1. Enter the name or email address of the person that you want to invite. Note that, if your organization allows it, you could even invite somebody from outside your company. Furthermore, after you have selected a person, you can add more people in the same field.

2. Define the permissions for the people you want to invite:

   - **Full control** allows them to fully configure, edit, and share this list. This is useful if you want them to be allowed to invite others as well.

   - **Can edit** grants them the right to edit or add items. However, unlike **Full control**, they are not able to share the list.

   - **Can view** only allows the selected people to view the list and the data, but not to make any changes.

3. Optionally, you can add an invitation message that will be shared with the people you are inviting via the notification email.

4. Lastly, you can choose whether you want to **Notify people** – that is, send a notification email with your message and the link to the list. This is selected by default. If you choose to disable this, the message from the previous step will be hidden in the dialog.

Clicking **Grant access** will set up the corresponding permissions on the list and, if selected, inform the invited people:

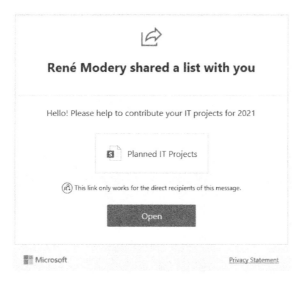

Figure 4.3 – Notification email with a custom message that was sent to an invited person

Please note that if you grant someone access to your list this way, if the list inherited permissions before as is the default, this inheritance will be broken. As mentioned before, new lists on SharePoint sites inherit their permissions from the site itself, so that anyone who can access the site can also access the list. When the inheritance is broken, changes to the site's permissions will likely no longer be reflected. New members of groups, which have access to a site and a list, will still be able to access the list itself as long as the group has rights. However, any newly added people or groups to the site's permissions will not be added to the list.

To give an example, have a look at the following permissions setup:

Object	Permissions
IT Budget site	IT Managers Group – Contribute CIO – Full Control Finance Team Members – Contribute Selected IT Staff – Read
Planned IT Projects	Permissions are inherited, and thus equal to the IT Budget site

If you now share the *Planned IT Projects* list with the CFO and grant them **Read Access**, the new permissions look as follows:

Object	Permissions
IT Budget site	IT Managers Group – Contribute CIO – Full Control Finance Team Members – Contribute Selected IT Staff – Read
Planned IT Projects	IT Managers Group – Contribute CIO – Full Control Finance Team Members – Contribute Selected IT Staff – Read CFO – Read

The risk now is that if you share the *IT Budget* site with an additional group, for example, granting the compliance team read access, these permissions will no longer be reflected on the *Planned IT Projects* group:

Object	Permissions
IT Budget site	IT Managers Group – Contribute
	CIO – Full Control
	Finance Team Members – Contribute
	Selected IT Staff – Read
	Compliance Team - Read
Planned IT Projects	IT Managers Group – Contribute
	CIO – Full Control
	Finance Team Members – Contribute
	Selected IT Staff – Read
	CFO - Read

Therefore, before you readily share your list this way, make sure that your permissions are working the way you expect them to.

Sharing permissions

In order to be allowed to share a list in SharePoint, the *Manage permissions* right is needed. By default, this is granted to site owners only, for example, through the *Full Control* permissions. If a site member or site visitor tries to share a list, an approval request will be sent to the site owners.

Thus, even if you are not a site owner and are not allowed to manage a site and its permissions, you can still request to share lists.

Sharing a list item

Now that we have seen how to share a list with others, you may also think of scenarios where you do not want to share a whole list, but only individual list items with others. For the *Planned IT Projects* list, you could have multiple entries where you need some business stakeholders to provide further information, but you do not want to grant them access to the site and the list. In such a case, you can share a list item itself.

Select the list item you want to share and click on the **Share** button at the top of the list. Unlike when you share a list generally, the dialog that will appear is no longer called **Grant access** but **Send link**:

Figure 4.4 – Share a list item by sending a link

As in the **Grant access** dialog, you can again specify the people you want to share the list item with, as well as an optional notification message. However, instead of defining the permission level as you did previously for a list, here you have different options to define what can be done with the list item via the link you are creating. Click on the dropdown at the top to change the type of the link by accessing **Link settings**:

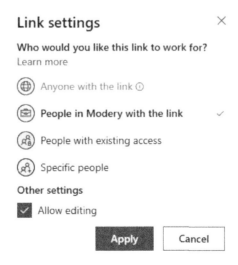

Figure 4.5 – Changing the link settings

The options that are available are the following:

- **Anyone with the link** allows, as the name says, anyone who has this particular link to access the item. This includes both people within your organization as well as anyone outside of it. While this is useful if you want to make an item available to a larger audience, it should also be noted that this means that if the link is shared publicly with others, you have no control over who accesses your list item. The link could be shared with people who you didn't intend to grant access in the first place. For this reason, this option is disabled in the majority of organizations.

- **People in [Your Organization] with the link** is similar to the first option as it allows easy sharing of an item without defining the exact people who should have access. However, only people that are within your Office 365 tenant's organization can access it; externals will not be able to.

- **People with existing access** simply generates a new link to the list item without granting new people access. This type of link is useful when you want to share a link to a specific list item with someone you know already has access, for example, if you want to ask a colleague to review a particular project in your list, and they are already listed as one of the members of your SharePoint site, you can create a link of this type to notify them about their task.

- Lastly, **Specific people** gives you the opportunity to specify directly which people you want to share the link with. You would select this option when you do not want to add a larger audience to the list of people who can access your list item, but only the specified people, which can include internal and external people.

At the bottom of the **Link settings** dialog, you can also define whether the people who will be granted access should be allowed to edit the list item, or whether they should only be allowed to view it.

> **Sharing settings grayed out**
>
> Depending on your organization's sharing settings, some of the available options may be grayed out. In such a case, discuss with your Office 365 administrator whether the corresponding setting can be enabled, or if it is disabled, for example, due to legal or compliance concerns.

After you have defined the link settings and your recipients of the link, you then have three options:

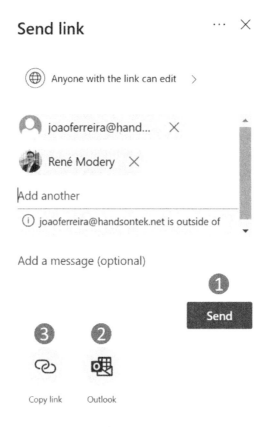

Figure 4.6 – Different options to send a list

1. Clicking **Send** sends an automated email with a default branding to all the people you specified.

2. If you want to customize the email, you can click on the **Outlook** icon. A new link will be created, and Outlook Online will open with a new email.

   The body of this email will contain the link, and the people you specified in the dialog will be added as recipients of this email. This gives you greater flexibility in terms of what you want to share in the notification email:

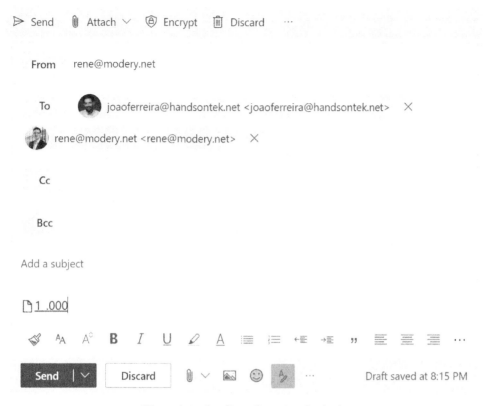

Figure 4.7 – Sending a list using Outlook

3. The last option, **Copy link**, is the simplest, but yet also the most flexible option. It creates a link and copies it onto the clipboard, from where you can paste it to where you need it – an email, a Teams message, a Word document, and so on.

Once a link has been created, access through this link is only possible as long as the link exists. After the link has been removed, the permissions granted through it will be revoked as well.

Reviewing and modifying access

After content has been shared, you will also want to review access to your list or list item, and potentially remove permissions if they are no longer required. In this section, we will focus on how you can do so for the sharing options discussed previously. Reviewing permissions for a SharePoint site, and thus any inherited permissions for any lists that are created within this site, will not be covered.

To review and modify access to a list, select the **Information** icon in the top right corner of it, and select **Manage access**:

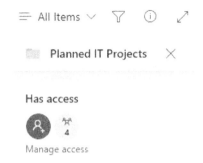

Figure 4.8 – Accessing the list information pane and managing access

You will then be able to see whom the list has been shared with, including any permissions that have been set up previously. Under the **Direct access** section, you will see a list of all users and groups that have been given direct access. A pencil icon indicates edit rights, whereas a crossed-out pencil shows view rights. Furthermore, you can also change permissions here by selecting the dropdown next to the user or group and choosing either **Can view**, **Can edit**, or **Stop sharing**. Please note that any such change stops the list's permission inheritance:

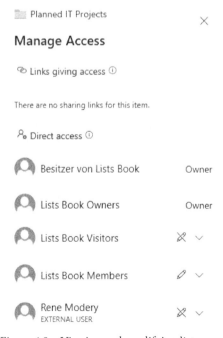

Figure 4.9 – Viewing and modifying list access

For list items, you can access the same dialog by selecting the item you want to review, and clicking on the same **Information** icon, whose scope has now changed from the whole list to the selected item only:

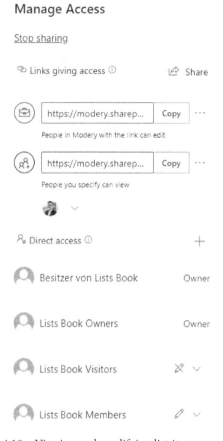

Figure 4.10 – Viewing and modifying list item permissions

You will notice that the **Direct access** section looks nearly the same as for the list, with the only difference being a **Plus** icon that allows you to open the **Grant access** dialog for the list item itself.

List item permission warning

Please note that it is generally recommended not to grant direct access to individual list items, as doing so would break the inheritance from the list. Any changes to the list's permissions would no longer be applied to such a list item. The same applies to updating the permissions. Any changes here also break the permission inheritance.

More importantly, under the **Links giving access** section, you will find all sharing links that were created. Here, you can copy the existing link again in case you lost it, add more people to a specific link or remove them from it, change the rights on the link, or remove the link completely:

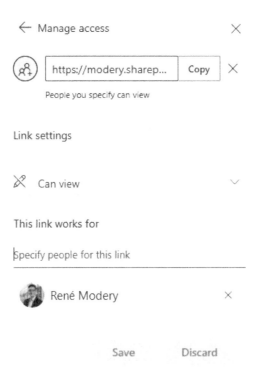

Figure 4.11 – Updating a sharing link's settings

This section showed you how you can share your lists and list items with others, and how you can manage existing permissions. As mentioned before, updating permissions can have unexpected consequences if not planned and executed properly, so careful planning of how you want to share content and with whom is strongly recommended.

Collaborating with others through comments

We saw in *Chapter 3, Microsoft Lists Core Features*, that you can add comments to list items. This functionality is especially useful when you have multiple people working on a list item and they want to share notes with each other. For our IT projects list example, this could mean that a business stakeholder could add a comment stating that they are currently still reviewing the requirements and that the cost is expected to be provided later this week. Or some details about delayed cost estimates could be shared so that while there is some missing information in the list data, reviewers can easily see why. The goal of the **Comments** functionality is not to provide an area for lengthy discussions, detailed reports, or similar, but a location where short, relevant pieces of information can be added:

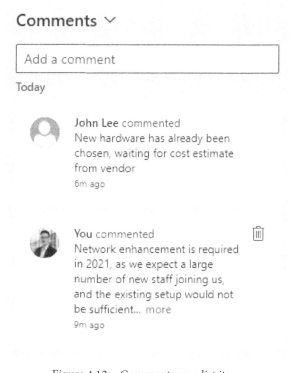

Figure 4.12 – Comments on a list item

Anybody who can edit a list item can also add comments to it, as well as deleting the comments of others that have been added. Once a comment has been added, it cannot be modified. To access the **Comments** area, select the item to be commented on. A preview pane of the item will open to the right side of the browser, showing the item's details as well as the additional **Comments** pane:

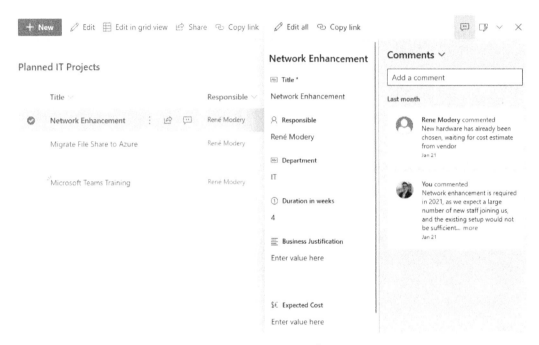

Figure 4.13 – Viewing an item and its comments

Here, you can add a new comment by typing it into the textbox at the top and submitting it, as well as reviewing previous comments added by yourself or others.

Once comments have been added to a list item, an indicator icon is shown near the title of the list item. Clicking on the icon will open the **Comments** pane again:

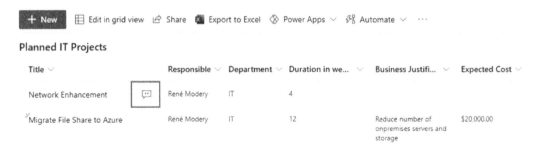

Figure 4.14 – List item with comments

One of the drawbacks of comments is that they don't get indexed for searching. This means that any comment added cannot be discovered through Office 365 searching, and are thus not as visible as other list content. Furthermore, it is not possible to format comments, such as highlighting text in bold or italics or adding bullet points. If any of these are required, it may be better to leverage a custom column of **Multiple lines of text** to cater to such needs, even though the content of these columns is not as structured as comments.

Now that we have seen how you can easily collaborate with others on lists and list items by inviting them and sharing comments with them, the next step is to learn how to get updated about any changes made to list items.

Managing notifications through alerts and rules

When multiple people work on the same set of data, you will often want to be notified about changes that are made by others. Or, as an owner of a list, you want to make sure that specific people receive updates about those changes. This is where the built-in alerts and rules come in handy. The **Alert Me** functionality allows you to specify under which conditions which people should receive an email notification, whereas rules provide some more detailed conditions, such as changes to specific column values only.

Using the Alert me functionality

Alerts on lists and list items can be set up by anyone with access to them. Additionally, as a list owner, you can also set them up for others. To create a new alert, navigate to your list and select **Alert me** from the navigation:

Figure 4.15 – Setting up an alert on a list

The dialog that appears has been used in previous versions of SharePoint and should be familiar if you used those:

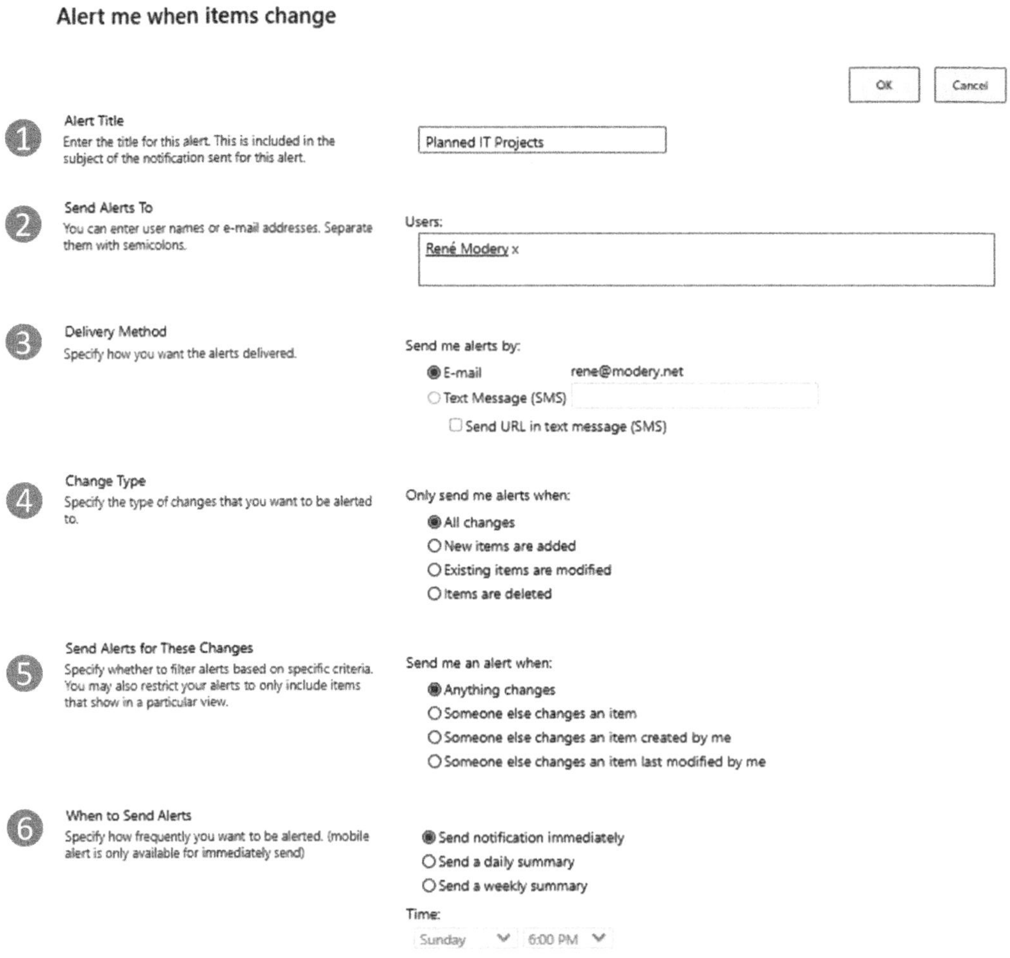

Alert me when items change

OK   Cancel

1 Alert Title
Enter the title for this alert. This is included in the subject of the notification sent for this alert.

Planned IT Projects

2 Send Alerts To
You can enter user names or e-mail addresses. Separate them with semicolons.

Users:

René Modery ×

3 Delivery Method
Specify how you want the alerts delivered.

Send me alerts by:

● E-mail   rene@modery.net
○ Text Message (SMS)
☐ Send URL in text message (SMS)

4 Change Type
Specify the type of changes that you want to be alerted to.

Only send me alerts when:

● All changes
○ New items are added
○ Existing items are modified
○ Items are deleted

5 Send Alerts for These Changes
Specify whether to filter alerts based on specific criteria. You may also restrict your alerts to only include items that show in a particular view.

Send me an alert when:

● Anything changes
○ Someone else changes an item
○ Someone else changes an item created by me
○ Someone else changes an item last modified by me

6 When to Send Alerts
Specify how frequently you want to be alerted. (mobile alert is only available for immediately send)

● Send notification immediately
○ Send a daily summary
○ Send a weekly summary

Time:

Sunday   ∨   6:00 PM   ∨

Figure 4.16 – Configuring a new alert

It provides you with a range of options to customize the alert to your needs:

1. **Alert Title** is the title you want to give your alert. This will be used in the notification emails.

2. **Send Alerts To** allows you the possibility to define who should be notified by this alert. Note that this field only shows up when you are an owner, the only case when you are allowed to set up alerts for others. If you are, for example, just a visitor to a list, you can set up an alert for yourself only.

3. While **Delivery Method** provides you with two options, **E-mail** and **Text Message**, only **E-mail** works in SharePoint Online. Thus, there is nothing here that needs to be configured.

4. **Change Type** defines under which condition the notification should be sent:

- **All changes** is the default and triggers when a new item gets added to the list, or when an existing item gets updated or deleted.

- **New items are added** only triggers when a new item gets created. For example, you may want to notify specific project management Office team members when a new project gets added to the *Planned IT Projects* list.

- To receive a notification about changes to existing items, select **Existing items are modified**.

- Lastly, if you want to know when something gets removed, you can select **Items are deleted**.

5. **Send Alerts for These Changes** allows you to define some additional conditions to be evaluated when your previously selected **Change Type** triggers:

- **Anything changes** is the default and simply means that you will be notified about all updates. This also means that you would receive notifications about changes done by yourself.

- **Someone else changes an item** helps with the just mentioned scenario and stops you from getting notified about your own changes. It is recommended to use this option if you do not intend to use notifications about your own changes in any way.

- **Someone else changes an item created by me** takes things one step further and will only notify you about changes made to items that you created. For the *Planned IT Projects* list, you could use this setting to get notified about changes to your own projects.

- **Someone else changes an item last modified by me** restricts the scope only to those items for which you were the last person to make an update. Once someone makes a change, and you are thus no longer the last person to update the item, you will no longer be notified again for this item until you update it.

6. Finally, **When to Send Alerts** lets you define the frequency at which you want to be notified:

- **Send notification immediately** sends, as the name says, an immediate email. However, if there are frequent changes, this could result in a large number of emails cluttering up your inbox.

- **Send a daily summary** helps to reduce the number of notification emails, and simply sends a daily summary of all the changes that occurred in the past 24 hours. This option also allows you to define at what time the summary email should be sent.

- **Send a weekly summary** works similarly and sends a summary email once a week. Besides the time, you can also define the day on which the email should be sent.

Once the alert has been set up, email notifications will be sent when the conditions you configured are met. The notification email contains relevant information about the change, for example, the list name, who made the change, and what change was made:

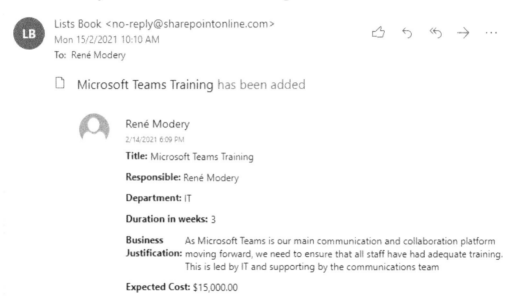

Figure 4.17 – Email notification of a new item

If you do not want to set up an alert on all items on a list, you can also reduce the scope to a single list item only. Instead of selecting **Alert me** on the list's navigation, you can open an item's menu and choose **Alert me** there. A similar dialog will appear, with the major difference being that you are not offered the option to select **Change Type**. All other options remain the same:

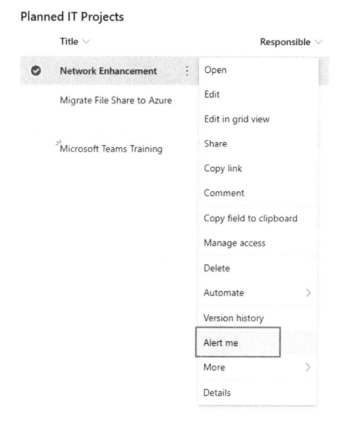

Figure 4.18 – Setting up an alert on a list item

Alerts have been available in SharePoint since SharePoint 2003, and have proven themselves very useful over the years. When many people are accessing a list regularly and making modifications to list items, they offer an easy-to-set-up and convenient way to stay up to date on those changes. However, the default notification email uses a very simple design only and provides no customization capabilities. If you require an email notification with your company's branding or other additional information as part of the notification, using Power Automate to create a flow is a possibility. Enhancing Microsoft Lists with Power Automate will be covered in *Chapter 9, Integrating Microsoft Lists with the Power Platform.*

Using rules to get informed about changes

Similar to *Alert me,* rules allow you to set up notifications about changes for yourself or others. However, there are some differences to alerts, such as not being able to specify daily or weekly summaries. Instead, you have the possibility to get notified if values in a specified column change, and not just when any value for an item changes.

To create a new rule, access the **Automate** menu item in your list. You can select either **Create a rule**, or **Manage rules**:

Figure 4.19 – Managing rules on a list

When you create a new rule, a new dialog will appear that will provide you with four different entry points:

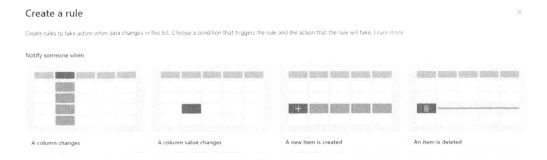

Figure 4.20 – Entry points

You can choose to notify yourself or someone else when the following occurs:

1. **A column changes**, which triggers whenever a value for a specified column gets updated. You can either define the specific person to notify, or you can make use of dynamic values from inside your list as provided through the **Person** field type. As an example, for our *Planned IT Projects* list, we can notify the new person selected as **Responsible** when this particular column gets updated, as shown in *Figure 4.20*.

2. **A column value changes**, which goes one step further. Here, you do not just specify the column, but also specify a comparison condition. You can either get a notification when the column value is equal to a provided value or not equal to it. This could be used to set up notifications when the *Department* column is set to HR, and we thus want to inform the HR manager about it.

3. **A new item is created** or **An item is deleted**. In these two cases, we only specify whom to inform; no further configuration is possible:

When **Responsible** changes

send email to Enter a name or email address .

Suggestions from this list

Responsible

Created By

Modified By

Other suggestions

Me

Figure 4.21 – Notify the new person selected when the Responsible column gets updated

Once created, the rule will be active immediately, and emails will be sent accordingly when a trigger condition is met:

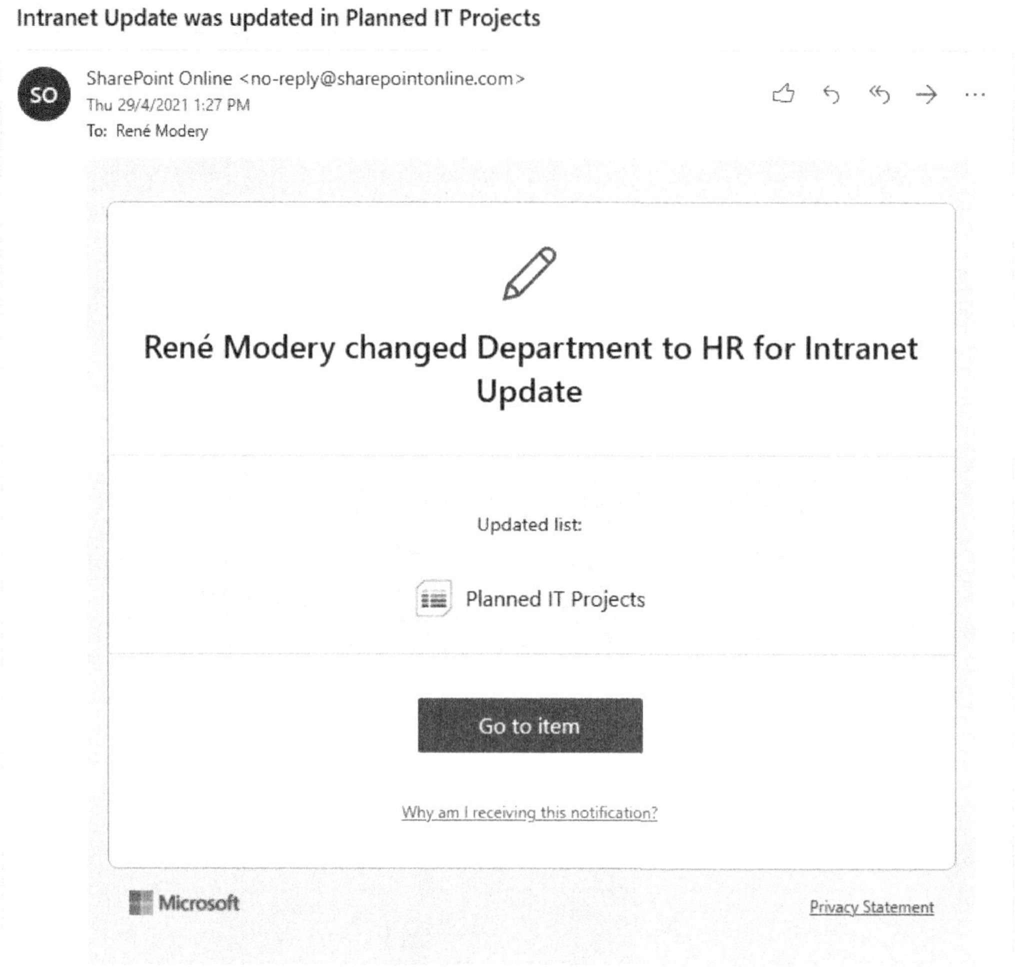

Intranet Update was updated in Planned IT Projects

SO   SharePoint Online <no-reply@sharepointonline.com>
Thu 29/4/2021 1:27 PM
To: René Modery

👍 ↩ ↞ → ⋯

René Modery changed Department to HR for Intranet Update

Updated list:

▦ Planned IT Projects

Go to item

Why am I receiving this notification?

Microsoft   Privacy Statement

Figure 4.22 – Notification about a column value change

To see the rules that have been set up on a list, open the **Automate** menu item and select **Manage rules**. On the overview screen, you can find the rules that you have created and can either modify them, delete them, or simply turn them off while keeping them:

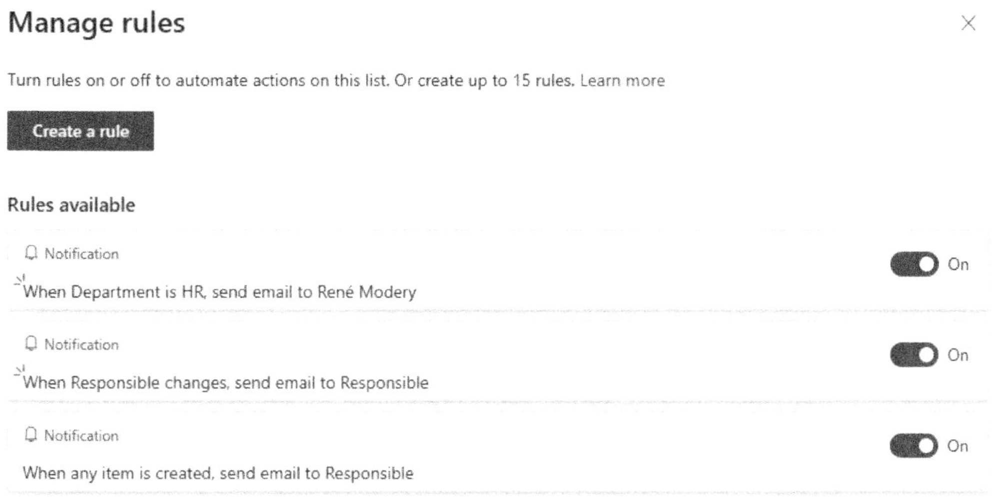

Manage rules   ✕

Turn rules on or off to automate actions on this list. Or create up to 15 rules. Learn more

[Create a rule]

Rules available

🔔 Notification   ⬤ On
⌃ When Department is HR, send email to René Modery

🔔 Notification   ⬤ On
⌃ When Responsible changes, send email to Responsible

🔔 Notification   ⬤ On
When any item is created, send email to Responsible

Figure 4.23 – Managing rules set up on a list

As we have shown, while rules do not provide the same functionality as alerts, they do provide some valuable additional functionality when you want to get notified about changes to specific columns only. Both alerts and rules are quite useful and can be used together on the same list, helping you to stay informed.

Now that you have learned how to stay up to date on any changes, you will also want to learn how to manage tracking these changes directly within lists. For this purpose, we will review the out-of-the-box versioning functionality next.

Tracking item changes through list versioning

With multiple people editing the same dataset comes the risk of unwanted changes. Somebody updates an item and sets a value to something that is not correct, not wanted, and so on. Additionally, it becomes more important to see which people collaborated on and contributed to an item, and which changes they made. This is what versioning can be used for. Versioning tracks all changes made to list items and includes information about the person who modified the item and at which time. It also allows you to restore a previous version, and view and delete older versions:

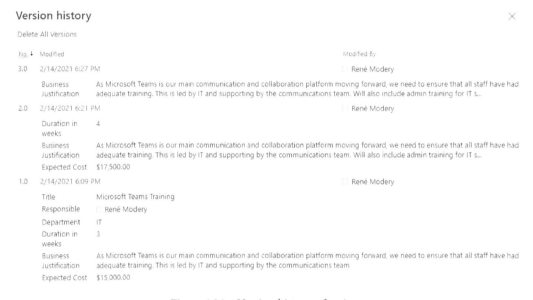

Figure 4.24 – Version history of an item

Currently, versioning on new Microsoft lists is set to keep 50 versions but was disabled when Microsoft Lists was first introduced. While Microsoft may change this default number sometime in the future if there is a need to increase or decrease it generally, you have full control over the versioning settings once a list has been created. To review a list's versioning settings, do the following:

1. Open the list's **Settings** page, and select **Versioning settings**:

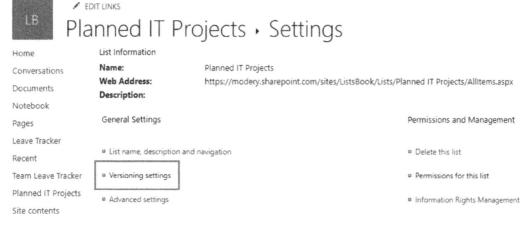

Figure 4.25 – List versioning settings

2. On the **Versioning Settings** page, there are a few configuration options to define how your versions should be managed:

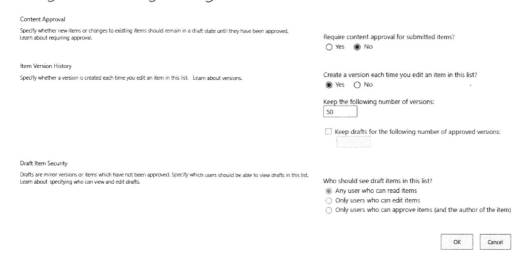

Figure 4.26 – Versioning Settings page

- **Content Approval** provides you with the possibility to keep new and modified items in a draft state until they are approved, which is when they are published and visible to everyone. This setting is by default turned off and is not required in most scenarios, and it will not be covered in detail in this book.

- **Item Version History** gives you the option to define how many versions you want to keep for the items in your list. While you can turn the setting here off, so that only the latest, current version is kept, it is highly recommended to use this functionality and set the number of versions to keep it to something suitable. In most scenarios, the default number of 50 versions should be sufficient. If you have a scenario with a lot of editing of list items within a short timeframe, you can increase this number to something higher depending on your needs. Valid values are between 1 and 50,000, though you should evaluate carefully whether you require a high number. The final configuration option, **Keep drafts for the following number of approved versions**, is only available if you have **Content Approval** enabled.

- The last setting, **Draft Item Security**, is also only configurable if you have **Content Approval** enabled. It allows you to define who should be allowed to view draft items – anyone who can read items, anyone who can edit items, or anyone who can approve items.

Once versioning is enabled on a list, any modifications to list items, whether they are done manually by someone in the browser or even automatically through a PowerShell script or another tool, get recorded. To see an item's **Version history**, open the item's ellipsis menu, and select the corresponding menu item:

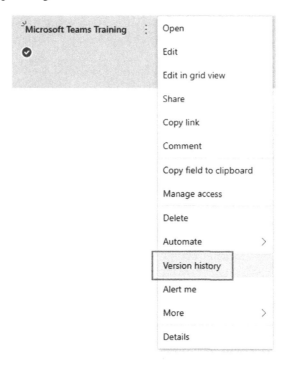

Figure 4.27 – Accessing an item's version history

As shown previously, the version history will show the previous versions and highlight which changes were made in which version by whom and when. You can easily track these changes and review them.

If you need to restore an older version, you can do so from the **Version history** dialog. Any changes that were made after the version you want to restore will still be tracked in the version history but will be overwritten by the previous version's values. For example, if we restore version 2 in *Figure 4.27 – Accessing an item's version history*, this will mean that the change to the **Business Justification** field made in version 3 will be overwritten again with the value of version 2, but version 3 itself will still be kept. Restoring a previous version does not remove any versions created after this version, but simply creates a new copy of the older version as the latest version.

Each version has a menu that allows you to **View** the full item with all of its columns and not just the changes from that version, to **Restore** the version, and also to **Delete** the version:

Version history

Delete All Versions

No. ↓	Modified	Modified By
3.0	2/14/2021 6:27 PM	☐ René Modery
	Business Justification	As Microsoft Teams is our main communication and collaboration platform moving forward, we need to ensure that all staff have had adequate training. This is led by IT and supporting by the communications team. Will also include admin training for IT s...
2.0		☐ René Modery

View

Restore

Delete

icrosoft Teams is our main communication and collaboration platform moving forward, we need to ensure that all staff have had uate training. This is led by IT and supporting by the communications team. Will also include admin training for IT s...

500.00

Figure 4.28 – Opening a version's menu

When you delete a version, the entry will be removed from the version history and moved into the site's recycle bin, from where you could restore it again if required. When you restore a version, a duplicate of this version will be created as the latest version:

Version history

Delete All Versions

No. ↓	Modified		Modified By
5.0	2/14/2021 7:01 PM		☐ René Modery
	Duration in weeks	3	
	Business Justification	As Microsoft Teams is our main communication and collaboration platform moving forward, we need to ensure that all staff have had adequate training. This is led by IT and supporting by the communications team	
	Expected Cost	$15,000.00	
3.0	2/14/2021 6:27 PM		☐ René Modery
	Business Justification	As Microsoft Teams is our main communication and collaboration platform moving forward, we need to ensure that all staff have had adequate training. This is led by IT and supporting by the communications team. Will also include admin training for IT s...	
2.0	2/14/2021 6:21 PM		☐ René Modery
	Duration in weeks	4	
	Business Justification	As Microsoft Teams is our main communication and collaboration platform moving forward, we need to ensure that all staff have had adequate training. This is led by IT and supporting by the communications team. Will also include admin training for IT s...	
	Expected Cost	$17,500.00	
1.0	2/14/2021 6:09 PM		☐ René Modery
	Title	Microsoft Teams Training	
	Responsible	☐ René Modery	
	Department	IT	

Figure 4.29 – Version history after restore and delete operations

Figure 4.29 shows a scenario where the previous version 1.0 was restored and is now seen as version 5.0. Additionally, it can be seen that version 4.0 was deleted at some point.

Versioning is a valuable and helpful feature that supports collaboration on Microsoft Lists. It allows you to track changes easily, revert them if required, and generally make sure that the data in your lists does not get lost or modified in unexpected and unrecoverable ways. Being familiar with this functionality will help you to work on lists with greater security and accountability.

Summary

This chapter showed you how you can work with other people, both inside and outside your organization, on lists and list data. You have learned how you can invite others to view or maintain list data, and you have seen how you can leverage comments to provide further context on list items. Lastly, you saw how you can leverage versioning in lists to easily track changes and restore older data if required.

In the next chapter, we will look at how you can customize Microsoft Lists views to your and your colleagues' needs, in order to increase the usefulness and flexibility of them even further.

5
Creating Microsoft Lists Views

After you have created a list and defined its structure by providing additional columns, you will also want to provide different ways to view and consume this data. Different people who access your list will likely have different needs: members of the finance department may be more interested in the project costs in your *Planned IT Projects* list, whereas the infrastructure team is more interested in seeing how long certain IT infrastructure projects have been planned for.

For this purpose, you can leverage list views to cater to different needs, and use advanced features such as grouping, sorting, and filtering to narrow down your list data and save extracts as custom views.

This chapter will cover the following topics:

- What are Microsoft Lists views?
- Default Microsoft Lists views
- Managing custom Microsoft Lists views

What are Microsoft Lists views?

As shown in *Chapter 2, Creating Your First List*, you can extend your list with additional columns. However, you do not always want to show all these columns at the same time and in the same order, and sometimes you may also want to provide prefiltered data. This is where list views come in.

Views allow you to define which columns to display and how to sort, group, and filter the underlying data. This way, instead of showing all data on one large screen, you can provide multiple views to show relevant extracts of your data to the people accessing your list, with the goal of making it easier to see and process. For example, if you think of the *Planned IT Projects* list from the previous chapter, you can have a main view to show all IT projects with important columns. Additionally, you can also add a view to only show projects that have an expected cost of greater than $25,000, so that high-cost projects can be seen much more quickly. Or, if you have a **Status** column to keep track of the status of your projects, you can create a view that groups your items by this column to easily show which projects are currently planned, which ones are ongoing, and which ones are completed.

Additionally, you can also use view formatting to make the data consumption more appealing, for example, by providing visual indicators, conditional formatting, and other formatting. Formatting will be covered in *Chapter 6, Customizing Microsoft Lists.*

Default Microsoft Lists views

Whenever you create a list, a default view called **All Items** will be set up with it. As the name implies, it does not apply any filters and shows all items sorted by their creation date, with the oldest items on top. This view is shown by default when you navigate to the list, but once you have created other views, one of them can be set as the default.

With Microsoft Lists, you can now also switch between different view modes for the currently selected view. A view mode allows you to see the data from the current view in different ways:

- **List** is the default mode and shows the list data in the known tabular format.
- **Compact List** reduces the whitespace that is used for showing the data and allows you to see more list items on your screen compared to **List**.
- **Gallery** shows your list data on so-called cards, which are configurable and display a row of information.

To select a different view mode, open the **View options** menu in the top-right corner of your list by clicking on the view name:

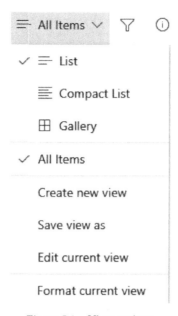

Figure 5.1 – View options

If you want to select another view mode as the default for your current view, you can do so by switching to it and selecting **Save view as** from the **View options** menu:

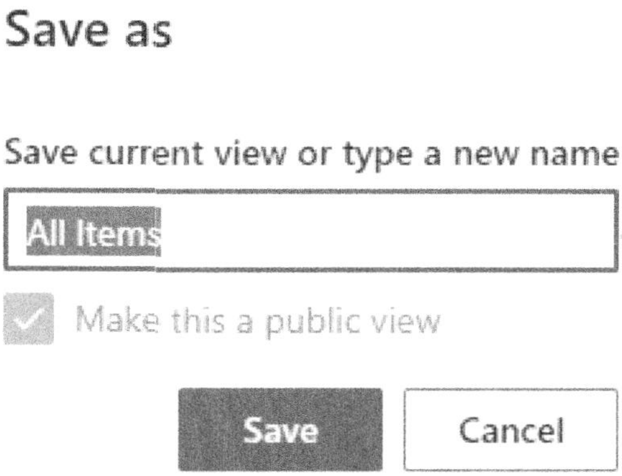

Figure 5.2 – Save as dialog

The dialog that appears allows you to either save your changes to the current view or create a new view with your changes under a new name:

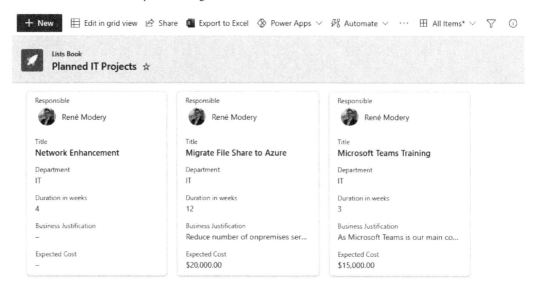

Figure 5.3 – Gallery mode of a view

The potential of leveraging list views should be clearer now, and as the next step, we will look at how you can create and maintain views in your list.

Managing custom Microsoft Lists views

To provide more possibilities for people to make the best use of your list, you can create additional views. However, once created, you may also want to modify them based on feedback you receive or delete them when you realize that they are no longer required.

Creating a view

To create a new view, open the **View options** menu in a list and select **Create new view**:

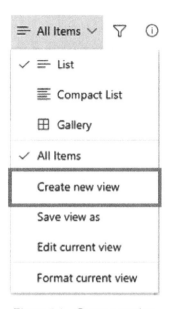

Figure 5.4 – Create new view

In the dialog that appears, you have three configuration options:

1. In the **View name** option, you define the name of the view. It is recommended to use a short but descriptive name here, to make it easy for people accessing your list to understand the purpose of this view.

2. Under **Show as**, you can configure a view mode. Besides the known **List** and **Gallery**, you can also select **Calendar** here. This third mode is useful when you want to highlight dates from your list item in a calendar view, and allows you to select a column from your list to be used as the **Start** date, and another column to be used as the **End** date.

3. Lastly, **Visibility** allows you to define whether your view is public, which means that it is visible to everyone who has access to your list, or whether it is personal and only shown to you. For example, you can create a personal view to see data that is important to you only and not to others:

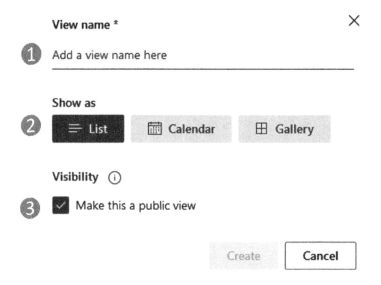

Figure 5.5 – Options to create a new view

Once you click **Create**, your new view will be set up. The newly created view with **Show as List** looks like the following screenshot:

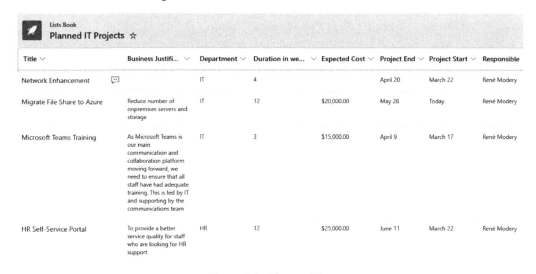

Figure 5.6 – Show as List

The following screenshot shows the newly created view with **Show as Calendar**:

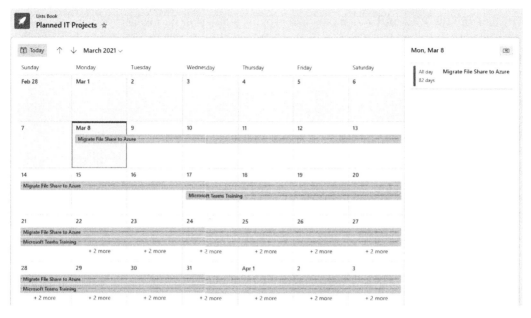

Figure 5.7 – Show as Calendar

And this is the newly created view with **Show as Gallery**:

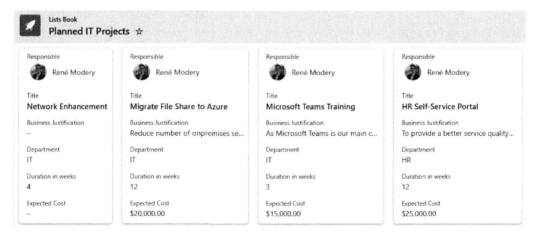

Figure 5.8 – Show as Gallery

If you want to create a copy of an existing view or make small changes to one, you can do so without creating a new view as just described. Instead, simply select the **Save view as** option from the **View options** menu, but provide a different name. This will create a copy of the view that you had open when you performed this action with the same grouping, sorting, and filtering options applied. As the next step, you will want to make changes to your new view, such as changing which columns are displayed and in which order, or changing the other options just mentioned.

Editing and deleting a view

There are various options for you to update a view. First, you can modify the order of the currently visible columns by dragging a column header and dropping it where you want it to appear. This way, you can easily arrange the order of your columns, and show more important information toward the left:

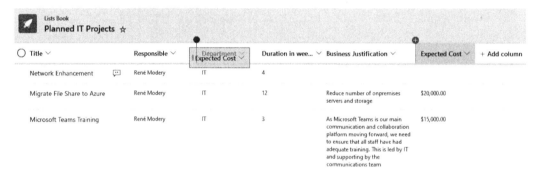

Figure 5.9 – Rearranging columns in a list view

Furthermore, you can also change the width of the columns. For example, a column that only shows a single number should not need to take up too much space, whereas a column with a few lines of text naturally requires more space. To change the column width, simply move your cursor to the right side of the column you want to resize, and drag the column divider that appears accordingly to define the new column width:

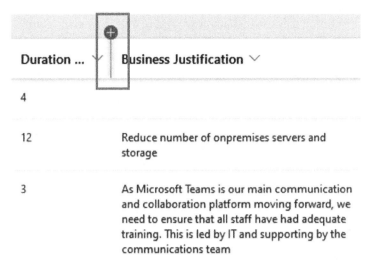

Figure 5.10 – Changing the width of a column in a view

You can also add additional, previously created columns to a view, or remove currently shown columns from the view without deleting them from the list. To show an existing column, or to hide it, move the cursor in the list header to the position where you want to place it and click on the plus icon that appears. At the bottom of the menu, select **Show/ hide columns**:

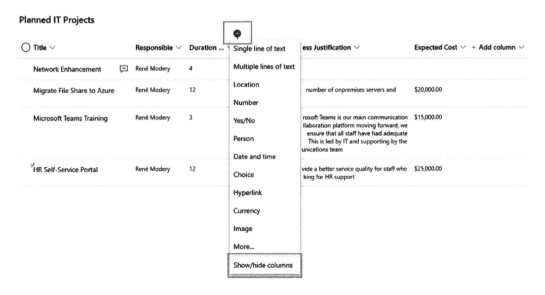

Figure 5.11 – Show or hide a column in a view

A new pane opens to the right side that allows you to edit the current view's columns. All columns of your list are shown, and a checkbox indicates whether a column is shown in the current view or not. Additionally, when you hover over a column's name, up and down arrows appear, allowing you to rearrange the order of your columns:

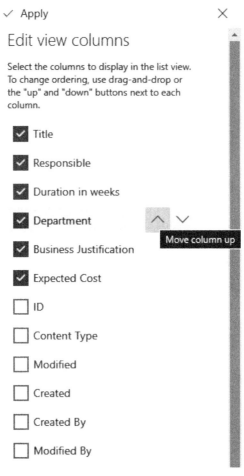

Figure 5.12 – Edit view columns

Once you click **Apply**, your current column selection and order are applied to your view.

Next, you can also change how the list data in your view is sorted. To do so, click on a column header to see the available options. Depending on the column type, there will be different options displayed. Some column types, such as *Single Line of Text* columns, do not support sorting. Other columns allow you to sort in ascending or descending order and will provide you with corresponding options such as **Smaller to larger** and **Larger to smaller** for numbers, or **A to Z** and **Z to A** for text:

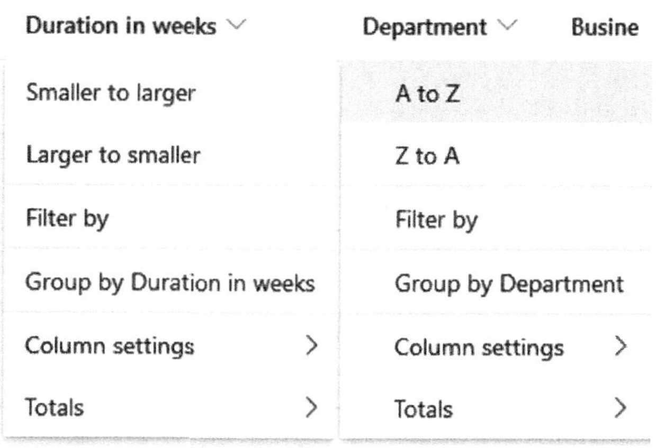

Duration in weeks ∨		Department ∨	Busine
Smaller to larger		A to Z	
Larger to smaller		Z to A	
Filter by		Filter by	
Group by Duration in weeks		Group by Department	
Column settings	>	Column settings	>
Totals	>	Totals	>

Figure 5.13 – Changing the sort order of a column

Sorting and grouping by multiple columns

You can only sort or group by a single column when you're inside a view of a list. If you want to sort or group by multiple columns, such as sorting by column A first and then by column B, you will need to define the sorting and/ or grouping in the advanced view editor explained later in this chapter.

As can be seen in *Figure 5.14*, you can also group columns, so that all items with the same value in the grouped column are shown together, with the group displaying the grouped column's value and the number of items in it. This also works with sorting, so that when a grouped column is sorted, the individual groups are shown in ascending or descending order. An example of this is shown in *Figure 5.14*, where the **Department** column is grouped and sorted from **A to Z**:

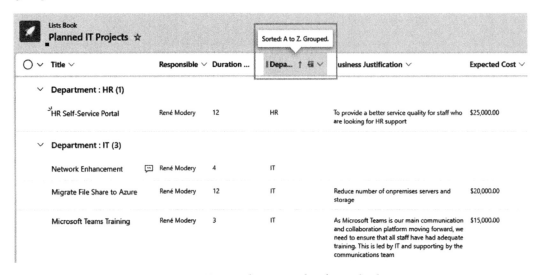

Figure 5.14 – View with a grouped and sorted column

The column's **Options** menu also allows you to apply a filter to most column types, which can be accessed through the **Filter by** menu item. Once selected, a filter pane will open to the right side and recommend appropriate filter values. For example, for the **Duration in weeks** column and the list items shown in *Figure 5.15*, the available options are **3**, **4**, and **12**:

Figure 5.15 – Filter pane with recommended filter values

The filter pane allows you to select one or more values and apply the filter, or clear all filter values set. Once a filter has been applied, the list items shown are the ones that match the filter criteria.

Another configuration option for a view is to provide column totals for some column types. You can get the most value out of this out of the number columns, as it allows you to easily display different calculations, such as the sum of the values, the maximum or minimum value, and more. To add this to a column, select the **Totals** option in the chosen column's drop-down menu, and select one of the provided options:

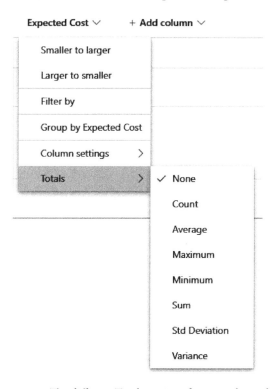

Figure 5.16 – The different Totals options for a number column

Once added, the selected calculated **Totals** will be shown at the bottom of the corresponding column. Only items that are shown in the current view are considered for the calculation. If you have a filter applied, only items that match the filter are used, and if you have a grouping applied, **Totals** will be shown for each group individually as well as for the list in total:

Planned IT Projects

Title ∨	Responsible ∨	Duration ... ∨	Department ∨	Business Justification ∨	Expected Cost ∨
Network Enhancement	💬 René Modery	4	IT		
Migrate File Share to Azure	René Modery	12	IT	Reduce number of onpremises servers and storage	$20,000.00
Microsoft Teams Training	René Modery	3	IT	As Microsoft Teams is our main communication and collaboration platform moving forward, we need to ensure that all staff have had adequate training. This is led by IT and supporting by the communications team	$15,000.00
HR Self-Service Portal	René Modery	12	HR	To provide a better service quality for staff who are looking for HR support	$25,000.00
		Average **7.75**			Sum **$60,000.00**

Figure 5.17 – Displaying an Average and a Sum for two number columns

The benefit of using **Totals** is that it can provide you with some additional insights into your data. For our projects example, we can calculate the average duration of a project, and see the total expected cost of all projects.

The modern interface of Microsoft Lists allows you to easily and quickly update your views and immediately see your changes. However, sometimes you may need to perform certain actions that are currently not yet possible here, such as sorting by multiple columns in a specified order. Or you may want to see all currently applied configuration options in a single view. This is where the classic view editor for SharePoint lists can be used. The fastest way to access it for a currently selected view is to select **Edit current view** from the **View options** menu:

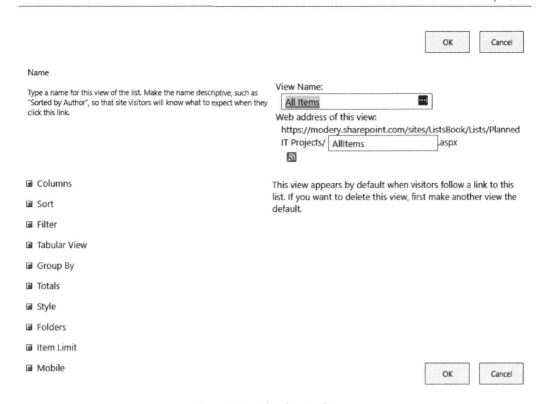

Figure 5.18 – The classic edit view

This edit view page has been in use in SharePoint for a long time already and should be quite familiar to anyone who has worked with older versions of SharePoint. It allows you on a single page to define which columns to show in which order, how to sort, filter, and group them, and which totals to display. There are also some additional configuration options available here for legacy purposes, such as **Style** or **Mobile**, however, it is not recommended to use them any longer, as they are no longer applicable to modern views such as the ones used in Microsoft Lists.

Nevertheless, this page can be quite useful if you want to review all the settings that have been applied to a view easily and quickly.

Summary

In this chapter, we have explained what list views are and how they work. You have seen how you can create your own views and customize them according to your needs, including how to group, sort, and filter data in them. In the following chapter, we will look at how you can take one step further and make your columns and views more useful by providing more appealing visuals through column and view formatting.

6

Customizing Microsoft Lists

Microsoft Lists allows you to tailor lists to your own needs, as well as your business needs, with the use of custom formatting.

With the formatting options available, you will be able to easily bring your corporate brand to the list, or easily identify a critical bug by the red color that is applied to the column or item.

In this chapter, you will learn how to take your lists to the next level by covering the following main topics:

- Understanding Microsoft Lists formatting
- Column formatting

Technical requirements

You can find the code files present in this chapter on GitHub at `https://github.com/PacktPublishing/Hands-On-Microsoft-Lists/tree/main/Chapter06`.

Understanding Microsoft Lists formatting

The formatting options available in Microsoft Lists allow you to improve the way columns and views are displayed.

These formatting options are available to anyone who has permissions to manage the list and create views. Once the formatting has been applied, it becomes visible to all users.

We have decided to group the formatting options into three different categories, starting with the simple customizations available to any power user, all the way up to the more complex scenarios only available to developers.

WYSIWYG formatting

What You See Is What You Get (WYSIWYG) is a term used to describe functionalities that provide an immediate preview of the customization that is being made to the user.

This formatting option is the simplest one available and can be found in the column settings of some column types. Using the user interface, you can define conditions and customizations that will then be applied to columns or views.

An example of a WYSIWYG formatting option that you will find in Microsoft Lists is the **Choice** column definition, which allows you to define colors for each of the options:

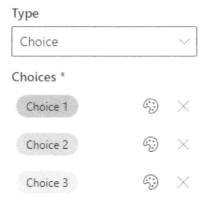

Figure 6.1 – Choice column formatting

If the customization options provided in the interface are not enough, you can use JSON to customize it even further, as explained in the following section.

JSON formatting

JSON is an acronym for **JavaScript Object Notation** and it is a lightweight format used to define data models in the web. JSON structures can easily be understood as they are self-describing, and this method was chosen by Microsoft to define the advanced formatting for columns and views.

The following code represents what a JSON object for defining a car looks like:

```
{
    Brand: "BMW",
    Model: "i8",
    Color: "White and Blue",
    Year: "2018",
    Plate Number: "98-8I-NN"
}
```

As you can see, you can easily read all the attributes of the car by looking at the property names and their respective values.

SharePoint Framework formatting

SharePoint Framework, also known as **SPFx**, is the framework that's used to extend SharePoint. Using SPFx extensions, you can customize columns and create new commands that will allow you to perform actions on your list from the command bar.

This extension method requires previous knowledge of development and is explained in detail in *Chapter 11, Extending Microsoft Lists Using SPFx*.

Now that we have a good idea of the options available to format lists, we will explore in detail the manner in which we can format columns

Column formatting

Column formatting allows you to manipulate how data is displayed to the users, without you needing to change the values that have been stored for the formatted column in the list.

Formatting a column requires the user to have basic knowledge of HTML and JSON as Microsoft combined both to create the formatting languages available in Microsoft Lists. If you are not familiar with the web programming language, you can use the basic formatting options available in the Microsoft Lists interface.

Any user with permissions to create or manage views will be able to format columns in a list.

Supported column types

Formatting is possible in most of the columns, but you will find some column types where this option is not available.

The following table shows each column type and the supported formatting options. Columns that support WYSIWYG allow you to create basic formatting without the need to write code:

Column Type	WYSIWYG	JSON
Calculated	✔	✔
Choice	✔	✔
Currency	✔	✔
Date and Time	✔	✔
Hyperlink	✔	✔
Location	✘	✔
Lookup	✔	✔
Managed Metadata	✘	✘
Multi-line of Text	✘	✔ *
Number	✔	✔
Person or Group	✔	✔
Image	✘	✔
Single line of Text	✔	✔
Yes/No	✔	✔

* Column formatting is only available for columns that don't contain rich text.

How to format a list column

Before we start exploring the more technical areas of column formatting, you must know how to format a column.

To gain access to the customization interface, do the following:

1. Open your list.
2. Next to the column's name, click the down arrow to open the column context menu.
3. Expand the **Column settings** section.
4. Click on **Format this column**:

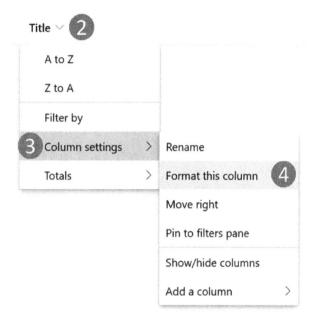

Figure 6.2 – Open format column interface

5. If the column supports WYSIWYG formatting options, you will see them listed with a link at the bottom to open **Advanced mode**. If the column only supports JSON formatting, you will see the text editor. Both options are exemplified in the following image:

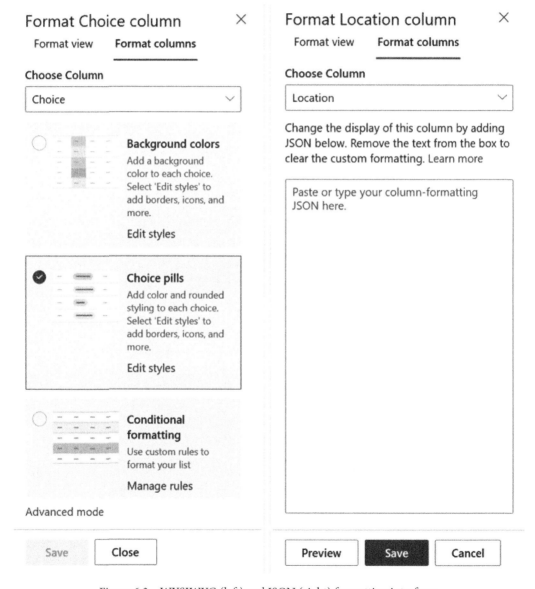

Figure 6.3 – WYSIWYG (left) and JSON (right) formatting interfaces

Once in the formatting pane, you will have the option to change the column you are applying custom styles to. The **Choose Column** dropdown will show you all the columns that support column formatting:

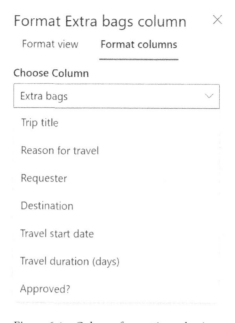

Figure 6.4 – Column formatting selection

WYSIWYG formatting options

There are six different WYSIWYG formatting options for list columns. However, not all of them are available to all column types. The following table shows the names of the formatting options and the column type that they are available for:

Formatting Name and Icon	Column Type
Conditional Formatting	Single line of text, Choice, Date and Time, Person, Number, Yes/No, Hyperlink, Currency, Calculated, Lookup
Background Colors	Choice
Choice Pills	Choice
Format Dates	Date and Time
Data Bars	Number
Format Yes/No	Yes/No

Let's look at the formatting options in detail.

Conditional formatting

Conditional formatting allows you use custom rules to format your columns. To create a new condition for one of the supported column types, do the following:

1. Select **Conditional formatting** from the list of available options. The available options on this screen will depend on the column type you are formatting:

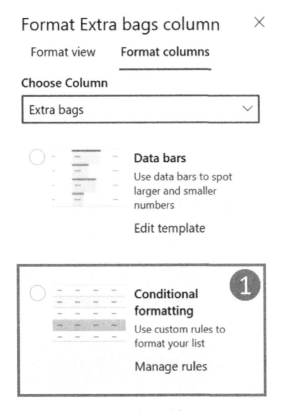

Figure 6.5 – Conditional formatting

2. If this is the first conditional formatting you are defining, by default, you will see a gray background being applied to the column, which means that no custom condition was created yet. To modify it, click on ....

3. From the menu, click on **Edit rule**:

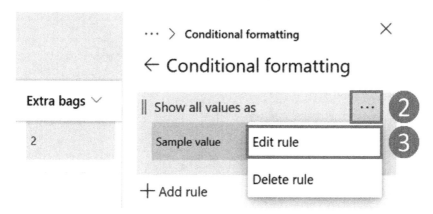

Figure 6.6 – Edit rule

4. From the **If** dropdown, select the column you want to use to build your condition.

5. Choose a comparison for the column.

6. Define the value that will be compared:

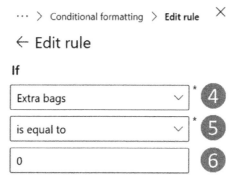

Figure 6.7 – Defining a condition

7. From the **Show list item as** section, click on the **Edit style** button.

8. Select the color you want to apply from the list provided.

9. To customize the column further, click on **More styles**:

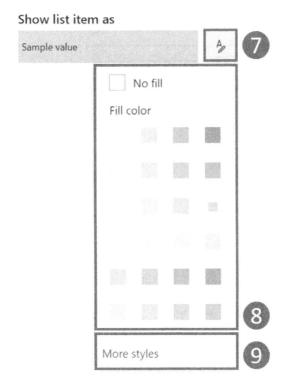

Figure 6.8 – Formatting the column condition

10. From the **Change style** pane of the column, you can select the fill color, format the font, define a custom icon and its alignment, and define borders around the column value:

Figure 6.9 – Changing the column formatting style

11. A formatted column can have multiple conditions applied to it. To create more conditions, click the **Add condition** link.

12. Select the column to be used as a comparison, the comparison, and the value.

13. While you are formatting the column, everything you do in the user interface is reflected immediately in the list. However, this is only published for others to see when you click the **Save** button:

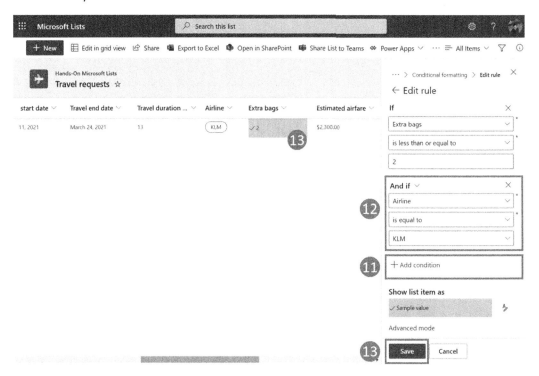

Figure 6.10 – Conditional formatting – second rule in preview mode

14. When formatting a column, you can apply multiple conditions that will format each column. After saving the formatting, click **Conditional formatting** from the top breadcrumb; alternatively, you can go to **Column settings** and click on the **Format this column** option. Once you're on the format pane, click the **Manage rules** link:

Figure 6.11 – Manage rules

15. Repeat *Steps 4* to *13* to create your new condition.

16. To view, edit, delete, or change the order of any existing conditional formatting, open the **Manage rules** pane, as explained in step 14. Here, you will see all the existing rules that have been applied to the column.

17. Click on **…** to open the context menu.

18. Select the desired option:

Figure 6.12 – Managing the conditional formatting rules

When creating conditional formatting rule, you will notice that not all the column types are available to be formatted, and that the comparison options are different for each column type.

The following table shows the supported column types and the comparison condition for each:

Column Type	Comparison Conditions
Choice	Is equal to
	Is not equal to
Data and Time	Is equal to
	Is not equal to
	Is after
	Is before
	Is on or after
	Is on or before
	Is between
Person	Is equal to
	Is not equal to
Number	Is equal to
	Is not equal to
	Is greater than
	Is less than
	Is greater than or equal to
	Is less than or equal to
	Is between
Yes/No	Is equal to
	Is not equal to
Calculated value	Is equal to
	Is not equal to
Single line of text	Is equal to
	Is not equal to

Background colors

Background colors is only available on choice columns and allows you to format the background of each choice that has been defined for the column. To use this type of formatting, do the following:

1.   From the choice of column formatting options, select **Background colors** from the list of available options and click the **Edit styles** link:

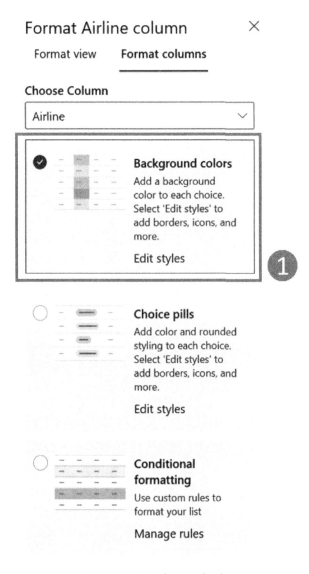

Figure 6.13 – Background colors

2. Select a background color for each choice:

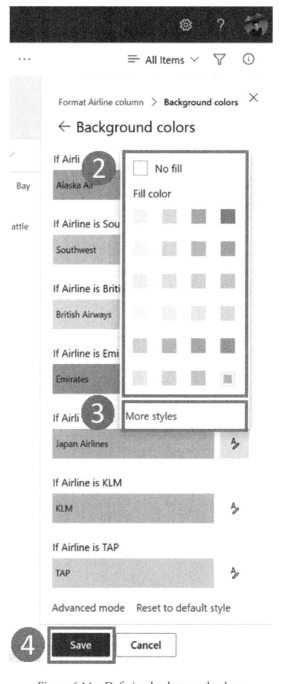

Figure 6.14 – Defining background colors

3.   To further customize the item, click **Edit styles**. From the **Change style** pane, you can define the fill color, format the font, define a custom icon and its alignment, and define the borders of the column value:

Figure 6.15 – Background colors – extra formatting styles

4.   Once these have been defined, click **Save**.

Choice pills

Choice pills are very similar to the background color formatting and is only available to the choice columns. It displays the choices with a rounded border.

To format a choice column using choice pills, do the following:

1. From the choice column formatting options, select **Choice pills** from the list of available options and click the **Edit styles** link:

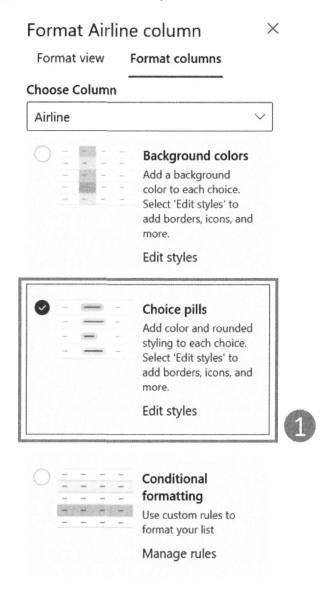

Figure 6.16 – Choice pills

2. Select a background color for each choice:

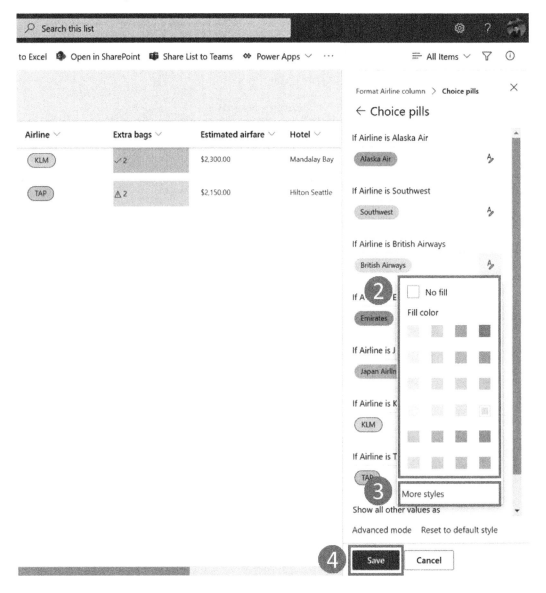

Figure 6.17 – Defining background colors

3. To further customize the item, click **Edit styles**. From the **Change style** pane, you
    can define the fill color, format the font, define a custom icon and its alignment, and
    define the borders of the column value:

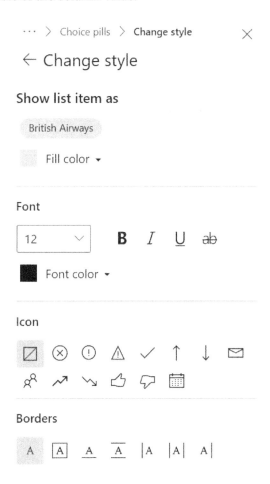

Figure 6.18 – Background color extra formatting styles

4. Once these have been defined, click **Save**.

Format dates

Format dates allows you to add colors, borders, and icons to your Date and Time column type. This formatting helps you easily build conditions using dates. To use this type of format, do the following:

1. From the Date and Time column formatting options, select **Format dates** from the list of available options and click the **Edit styles** link:

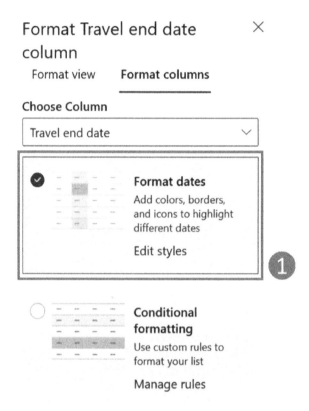

Figure 6.19 – Format dates

2. By default, you will find three conditions that have already been formatted, comparing the column date with today:

*   **If [Column Name] is before today**: Formatted with a yellow background

*   **If [Column Name] is today**: Formatted with a green background

*   **If [Column Name] is after today**: Formatted with a red background:

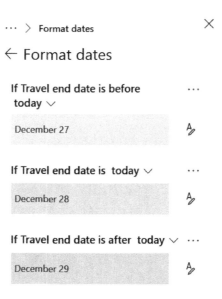

Figure 6.20 – Format dates condition

3. To modify the condition, click the arrow next to **today**. From the menu, you can select **Today**, relative to the day the user is viewing the list, or **A specific date**, which is fixed to a value defined by the user:

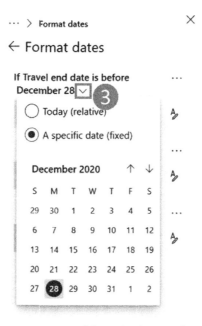

Figure 6.21 – Modifying the date condition

4. To further customize the date column with colors, click the **Edit Style** button and select a color:

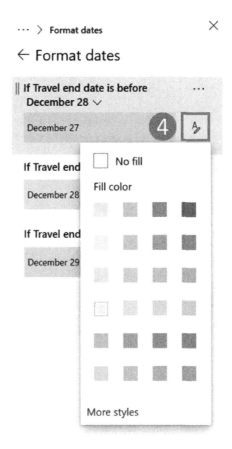

Figure 6.22 – Defining the date condition's color

5. To further customize the item, click **Edit styles**. From the **Change style** pane, you can define the fill color, format the font, define a custom icon and its alignment, and define the borders of the column value:

Figure 6.23 – Date formatting – extra styles

6. Once you have defined these three conditions for your date column, click **Save**:

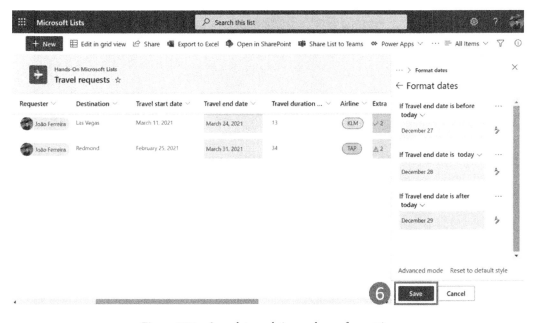

Figure 6.24 – Save date and time column formatting

Data bars

Data bars allow you to format numbers with a bar layout, thus creating a graphic effect in your lists. It only supports numbers and can be used with positive and negative values.

To use data bars formatting, do the following:

1. From the number column formatting options, select **Data bars** from the list of available options and click the **Edit template** link:

Figure 6.25 – Data bars

2. Define a **Minimum value** and **Maximum value** for your bars.

3. Define the colors for the **Positive values** and **Negative values**. The negative option will only be enabled if your range includes negative numbers.

4. Click **Save**:

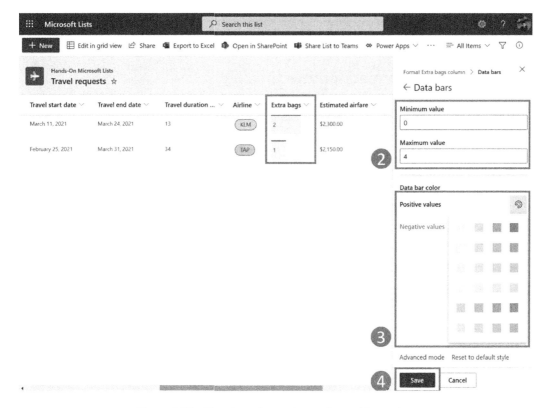

Figure 6.26 – Data bars formatting options with preview

Format yes and no

The yes and no formatting option is only available to the Yes/No columns and allows you to easily define styles of the binary column type.

To use the Yes/No column formatting, do the following:

1.   From the Yes/No column formatting options, select **Format yes and no** from the list of available options and click the **Edit styles** link:

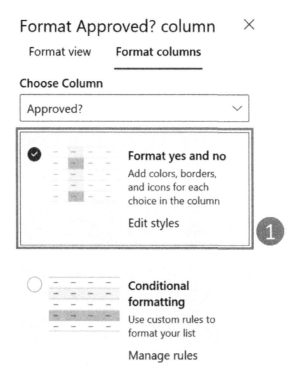

Figure 6.27 – Format yes and no

2. Click the **Edit styles** button to format the background colors for the Yes and No values:

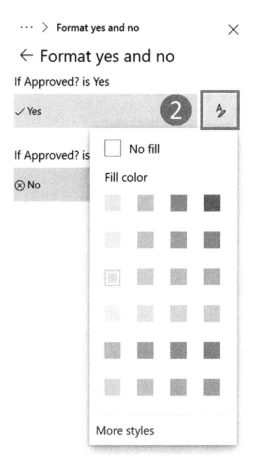

Figure 6.28 – Defining Yes and No background colors

3. To further customize the column, click the **More styles** link. From the **Change style** pane, you can define the fill color, format the font, define a custom icon and its alignment, and define the borders for the column value:

Figure 6.29 – Format yes and no – extra styles

4. Once these have been defined, click **Save**.

Advanced mode

For each of the WYSIWYG formatting options, there is an **Advanced mode** that allows you to access to the JSON formatting that's been automatically generated for the column.

The option to access Advanced mode is located at the bottom of the formatting pane. To open it, click on the **Advanced mode** link.

To switch back to design mode, you must click the **Switch to design mode** link at the bottom of the formatting pane. Any modifications that have been made to the JSON file will be discarded, but Microsoft Lists gives you the option to download a JSON file that contains your latest modifications:

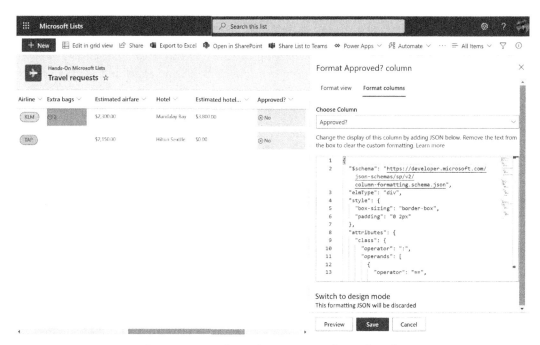

Figure 6.30 – Column formatting – Advanced mode

We will learn more about Advanced mode in the next subsection, where the JSON format will be explained in detail and with examples.

JSON formatting

JSON formatting allows you to format columns beyond what the design mode and the WYSIWYG interface allows you to do.

Before we start digging into the examples and into the more complex customizations, you must become familiar with the JSON schema supported by column formatting. We'll look at this in the following subsections.

HTML elements

As we mentioned previously, JSON format is a mix of a JSON object with custom properties and HTML. This section shows all the supported HTML elements and a brief description of what you should use them for in the context of column formatting:

HTML Element	Common Use in the Context of Column Formatting
div	A div is a generic container for your column that is used to wrap other elements inside it. A div can contain the child of another div.
span	A span is a form of inline phrasing content that you must use to display text or numbers. It can be also used to group elements and apply different styles to the same sentence as text colors.
a	a is the element you must use to create hyperlinks that will allow you to navigate from your list column to somewhere else upon being clicked.
img	img is the HTML tag you must use to represent an image.
svg	svg is the tag you must use to define vector-based graphics. The end result will be similar to an image defined by an img tag.
path	A path tag is used to complement the svg tag and is used to define a path inside an svg graphic.
button	The button tag defines a clickable element in a button format that has actions attached to it in the context of the list column.

The following image is a generic representation of how each of the HTML tags can be used to format your column:

Figure 6.31 – HTML generic tag representation

Let's look at this in more detail:

1. The div element is wrapping all the HTML elements.

2. span showing text.

3. img or svg representing an image.

4. button with an action.

5. a with a hyperlink.

Despite the existence of even more HTML tags, any other tag being used in the context of column formatting will cause an error, and the customizations will not be applied.

HTML element attributes

When using HTML, each element is defined by the attributes specified in the element tag. The following table shows all the attributes supported by column formatting, what HTML elements are applied, and a brief description of their functionality:

HTML Attribute	HTML Tag	Description
href	a	Defines the URL in the `link` tag.
rel	a	Defines the relationship between the link defined in the `href` attribute and the current site.
src	img	Defines the URL for the image to be displayed in the `img` tag.
class	div, span, a, img, svg, path, button	Defines a class for the HTML tag. In the context of column formatting, it is used to format the elements. Column formatting allows you to use predefined classes to format your columns. You can learn more about them in the *Predefined CSS classes* subsection.
target	a	Defines where the URL in the link will open: • `_blank`: Opens the URL in a new tab or window. • `_self`: Opens the URL in the same window where it was clicked. This is the default value when the attribute is not defined.
title	div, span, a, img, svg, button	Provides more information about the `html` element. This extra information is provided as a tooltip when the user hovers over the element.
d	path	Defines the path to be drawn inside in an `svg` graphic.
aria	div, span, a, img, svg, button	Provides accessibility information to users with disabilities using tools such as screen readers.
data-interception	a	Allows you to control the behavior of a link when it is clicked. This attribute is necessary to open SharePoint pages in a new tab as the target option tends to be ignored by the modern SharePoint page router; for example, `data-interception="off"`.
viewBox	svg	Used to scale and position an `svg` graphic.

HTML Attribute	HTML Tag	Description
preserveAspectRatio	svg	Used to define the aspect ratio of an svg element.
style	div, span, a, img, svg, button	Provides a customization of your HTML element with the use of inline CSS attributes. You will learn more about the CSS styles in the *CSS properties* subsection.
role	div, span, a, img, svg, button	Specifies the role attribute, which is used for accessibility.
alt	img	Specifies the alt attribute in an image.

Despite the existence of far more HTML attributes, if any other attribute is used in the context of column formatting, this will cause an error, and the customizations will not be applied.

CSS properties

To customize your columns even further, you can use CSS to apply your own custom styles to the HTML elements using the style attribute. The following table shows all the CSS properties supported by the column formatting, divided into groups:

Text Formatting		
color	direction	letter-spacing
line-height	text-align	text-decoration
text-indent	text-transform	unicode-bidi
vertical-align	white-space	word-spacing
hanging-punctuation	punctuation-trim	text-align-last
text-justify	text-outline	text-overflow
text-shadow	text-wrap	word-break
word-wrap	font	font- family
font-size	font-style	font-variant
font-weight	font-size-adjust	font-stretch

Margin and Padding		
margin	margin-bottom	margin-left
margin-right	margin-top	padding
padding-bottom	padding-left	padding-right
padding-top		

Positioning and Display		
bottom	clear	clip
display	float	left
overflow	position	right
top	visibility	z-index

Backgrounds, Borders, and Shadows		
background-color	fill	background-image
border	border-bottom	border-bottom-color
border-bottom-style	border-bottom-width	border-color
border-left	border-left-color	border-left-style
border-left-width	border-right	border-right-color
border-right-style	border-right-width	border-width
outline	outline-color	outline-style
outline-width	border-bottom-left-radius	border-bottom-right-radius
border-radius	border-top-left-radius	border-top-right-radius
box-decoration-break	box-shadow	box-sizing
opacity		

Scroll Overflow and Mouse Cursor		
overflow-x	overflow-y	overflow-style
cursor		

Size		
height	max-height	max-width
min-height	min-width	width

Flexbox Layout		
flex-grow	flex-shrink	flex-flow
flex-direction	flex-wrap	flex
justify-content	align-items	

Box Alignments		
box-align	box-direction	box-flex
box-flex-group	box-lines	box-ordinal-group
box-orient	box-pack	

Grid Layout		
grid-columns	grid-row	

Column Layout		
column-count	column-fill	column-gap
column-rule	column-rule-color	column-rule-style
column-rule-width	column-span	column-width
columns		

> **Note**
>
> If you are not familiar with CSS and you want to know about each of the properties supported by column formatting, we recommend that you have a look at *Professional CSS 3* by *Piotr Sikora, Packt Publishing*.

Predefined CSS classes

When formatting a column, you can take advantage of the pre-existing CSS classes provided. This being said, you can format HTML elements with backgrounds, colors, and text colors by using the following class names:

Class Name	Behavior
sp-field-severity--good	Applies a green background to the element.
sp-field-severity--low	Applies a light white background to the element.
sp-field-severity--warning	Applies a yellow background to the element.
sp-field-severity--severeWarning	Applies an orange background to the element.
sp-field-severity--blocked	Applies a red background to the element.
sp-field-dataBars	Creates the bar effect we saw earlier in this chapter for data bar formatting.
sp-field-trending--up	Sets the text color of the element to green.
sp-field-trending--down	Sets the text color of the element to red.
sp-field-quickActions	Sets the text color of the actions to the link color defined on the site.

Other than the colors, you can also format the typography for each HTML element using Microsoft predefined classes. The following table shows all the class names available for formatting text:

Class Name	Behavior
ms-fontWeight-light	Sets the font weight to 100
ms-fontWeight-semilight	Sets the font weight to 300
ms-fontWeight-regular	Sets the font weight to 400
ms-fontWeight-semibold	Sets the font weight to 700
ms-fontSize-su	Sets the font size to 42 px
ms-fontSize-xxl	Sets the font size to 28 px
ms-fontSize-xl	Sets the font size to 21 px
ms-fontSize-l	Sets the font size to 17 px
ms-fontSize-mPlus	Sets the font size to 15 px
ms-fontSize-m	Sets the font size to 14 px
ms-fontSize-sPlus	Sets the font size to 13 px
ms-fontSize-s	Sets the font size to 12 px
ms-fontSize-xs	Sets the font size to 11 px
ms-fontSize-mi	Sets the font size to 10 px

When formatting a list, you can take advantage of the SharePoint theme that's been applied to the site where the list is being rendered. This means that you can use predefined CSS classes that apply background colors and text colors to your HTML elements, adjusted to the branding of the site where the list is being rendered.

> **Scenario**
>
> You have created formatting for a travel request list that is used in multiple departments of your company, and it is displayed in the specific department's SharePoint sites. Each department has its own branding that's applied to the SharePoint site, and you want to make sure that your formatting looks good with the branding colors of the site. Instead of using static colors and the predefined classes of Microsoft Lists, you will take advantage of the SharePoint theme default classes, which change dynamically, depending on the theme that's applied to the site.

Each of the 26 SharePoint theme colors can be used for text, background, and border formatting and applied on mouse hover in the following format:

- **ms-fontColor-themePrimary**: Applies the color to the text

- **ms-fontColor-themeSecondary--hover**: Applies the color to the text on mouse hover

- **ms-bgColor-themePrimary**: Applies the color to the background

- **ms-bgColor-themeSecondary—hover**: Applies the color to the background on mouse hover

- **ms-borderColor-themePrimary**: Applies the color to the border of an HTML element

The following table shows all the available color names that you can use, along with their class prefixes and suffixes. Color descriptions have not been provided as they change from theme to theme:

SharePoint Theme Colors		
themeDarker	themeDark	themeDarkAlt
themePrimary	themeSecondary	themeTertiary
themeLight	themeLighter	themeLighterAlt
black	neutralDark	neutralPrimary
neutralPrimaryAlt	neutralSecondary	neutralTertiary
neutralTertiaryAlt	neutralLight	neutralLighter
neutralLighterAlt	white	neutralQuaternaryAlt
neutralQuaternary	neutralSecondaryAlt	primaryBackground
primaryText	accent	

You can also take advantage of the accent colors included in the Microsoft UX framework, called Fluent UI. Each of the 24 colors can be used for text, background, and border formatting, and they are applied on mouse hover in the following format:

- **ms-fontColor-blue**: Applies the color to the text

- **ms-fontColor-blue--hover**: Applies the color to the text on mouse hover

- **ms-bgColor-blue**: Applies the color to the background

- **ms-bgColor-blue--hover**: Applies the color to the background on mouse hover

- **ms-borderColor-blue**: Applies the color to the border of an HTML element

The following table shows all the available color names that you can use, along with their class prefixes and suffixes:

Fluent UI Colors		
`yellowDark`	`yellow`	`yellowLight`
`orange`	`orangeLight`	`orangeLighter`
`redDark`	`red`	`magentaDark`
`magenta`	`magentaLight`	`purpleDark`
`purple`	`purpleLight`	`blueDark`
`blueMid`	`blue`	`blueLight`
`tealDark`	`teal`	`tealLight`
`greenDark`	`green`	`greenLight`

Column formatting properties and attributes

As a combination of HTML and JSON, column formatting has its own properties that are used along with the HTML. The following table shows the specific properties you can use when formatting your columns:

Property	Behavior
`txtContent`	This is the property used to define the text inside an HTML element.
`iconName`	Specifies the Fabric UI icon to display in the HTML element.
`children`	This property is used to create nested HTML elements.
`debugMode`	Optional property used to debug the JSON file while formatting the column.
`forEach`	This property loops through the elements of a multi-value column.
`customAction`	Action applied to a `html` button.
`action`	Type of action applied to the button: • `defautlClick`: This property has the same behavior as a user clicking the list item. • `executeFlow`: This property will trigger the execution of a custom flow defined in Microsoft Power Automate. • `share`: This property will open the default sharing dialog for the item. • `delete`: This property opens a confirmation dialog for item deletion. • `editProps`: This property opens the edit properties pane for the item.

Property	Behavior
customCardProps	This is the property where the HTML for cards will be defined.
formatter	This property is the wrapper for the HTML defined for the card. It is used inside customCardProps.
openOnEvent	A property that defines when a card opens: • Click • Hover
directionalHint	Specifies the direction relative to the target in which a card will be positioned.
isBeakVisible	Specifies if the beak is to be shown or not in the card.
beakStyle	Specifies the style object for the card's beak.
operator	This is a custom expression operator. You will learn more about the available operators in the *Operators* subsection.
operantds	Custom expression operand.
attributes	Additional attributes to be added to an HTML element.
defaultHoverField	This is a property that can be used to format people column types. When defined, it opens the person profile card on hover.

Column formatting supports the use of Fabric UI icons via the use of the iconName property. At the time of writing this book, the gallery of icons contains 1,800 elements.

To gain access to a detailed list that shows these icons, access the official documentation from Microsoft for the Fluent UI at https://developer.microsoft.com/en-us/fluentui#/styles/web/icons.

To find the name of the icon to wish to use in your column formatting, all you have to do is hover over the icon and copy its name, as highlighted in the following screenshot:

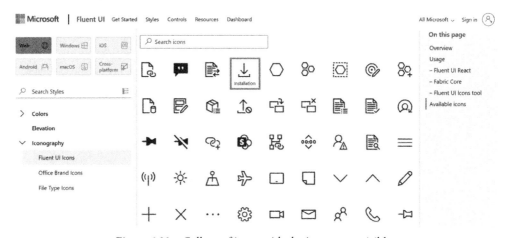

Figure 6.32 – Gallery of icons with the icon name visible

Operators and operands

Operators and operands allow you to compare, calculate, and define values in expressions while formatting your column items. The following table shows all the supported operators in Microsoft Lists:

Operator	Description
+	Addition
-	Subtraction
/	Division
*	Multiplication
<	Less than
>	Greater than
%	Modulus; returns the remainder of a division
==	Equal
!=	Different
<=	Less than or equal
>=	Greater than or equal
||	Or
&&	And
?	Ternary operator if
:	Ternary operator else

Functions

Functions allow you to calculate values in expressions while formatting your column items. The following table contains all the functions in Microsoft Lists with a brief description of each one, followed by an excerpt of the function's usage for column formatting:

Function	Description
toString()	Converts an object into a string: `"txtContent":"=toString(12)"` Results in 12.
Number()	Returns the numeric value of an object. If the object is not a number it, returns NaN: `"txtContent":"=Number('12')"` Results in 12.

Function	Description
Date()	Returns the current date and time: `"txtContent":"=Date('12/12/2020')"` Results in 12/12/2020, 12:00:00 A.M.
cos()	Returns the cosine of a number: `"txtContent":"=cos(12)"` Results in 0.97814760073.
sin()	Returns the sine of a number: `"txtContent":"=sin(12)"` Results in 0.20791169081.
toLocaleDateString()	Returns a string with a date in the local language representation: `"txtContent":"=toLocaleString(@now)"` Results in 12/29/2020.
toLocaleTimeString()	Returns a string with a time in the local language representation: `"txtContent":"=toLocaleTimeString(@now)"` Results in 2:12:24 P.M.
indexOf()	Returns the index of the first occurrence of the object: `"txtContent":"=indexOf('List','s')"` Results in 2.
toLowerCase()	Converts a string into lowercase: `"txtContent":"=toLowerCase('Lists')"` Results in lists.
join()	Returns a string concatenation of an array with a string separator: `"txtContent":"=join(@currentField, '|')"` Results in Ferrari|BMW|Volkswagen.
length	Returns the number of members in a multi-value field.

Function	Description
abs()	Returns the absolute number of an object: `"txtContent":"=abs(-12)"` Results in 12.
loopIndex	Used with the forEach iterator, it provides the index of the loop.
floor()	Rounds the given decimal number to the previous integer number: `"txtContent":"=floor(12.5)"` Results in 12.
ceiling()	Rounds the given decimal number to the next integer number: `"txtContent":"=ceiling(12.5)"` Results in 13.
pow()	Returns the calculated value of a power raised to its base value: `"txtContent":"=pow(2,3)"` Results in 8.
substring()	Returns a substring between a start and end index: `"txtContent":"=substring('Lists',0,3)"` Results in List.
getDate()	Returns the day of the month of a provided date: `"txtContent":"=getDate(Date('12/12/2020'))"` Results in 12.
getMonth()	Returns the month index of a provided date: `"txtContent":"=getMonth(Date('12/12/2020')"` Results in 11.
getYear()	Returns the year of a provided date: `"txtContent":"=getYear(Date('12/12/2020')"` Results in 2020.
toUpperCase()	Returns a string converted into uppercase: `"txtContent":"=toUpperCase('Lists')"` Results in LISTS.

How to access column values

When formatting a column, you will need to access the values stored in the column you are formatting, as well as possibly add the values from other columns to the column formatting process.

To access the value of the current field, you must use the `@currentField` special string, while to access to the value of any other column in the list, you must use the `[$ColumnName]` special string. You will learn more about special string values in the *Special strings* subsection:

```
E.g.
 "txtContent": "@currentField"
 "txtContent": "[$Author]"
```

Depending on the column type you are formatting, you may find complex fields with multiple properties inside them. The following subsections explain all the default objects that exist in Microsoft Lists, with more than one property represented in a JSON format showing all the available properties.

To access the properties of a field, do the following:

```
E.g.
 "txtContent": "@currentField.title"
 "txtContent": "[$Address].Address.City"
```

People

A `people` field in Microsoft Lists has the following properties:

```
{
    "id": "12",
    "title": "João Ferreira",
    "email": "joaoferreira@handsontek.net",
    "sip": "joaoferreira@handsontek.net",
    "picture": "https://contoso.sharepoint.com/joaoferreira_
                contoso_com_MThumb.jpg?t=4589307654",
    "department":"Development",
    "jobTitle":"Teck Lead"
}
```

Location

A location field in Microsoft Lists has the following properties:

```
{
    "Address": {
        "City": "Porto",
        "CountryOrRegion": "Portugal",
        "State": "Portugal Continental",
        "Street": "Rua Sá da Bandeira 8r"
    },
    "Coordinates": {
        "Latitude": "41.14670944213867",
        "Longitude": "-8.609251022338867"
    },
    "DisplayName": "Porto Bay Hotel",
    "LocationUri": "https://www.bingapis.com/api/v6/
        localbusinesses/YN8149x9892130515080188409?setLang=en"
}
```

Lookup

A lookup field in Microsoft Lists has the following properties:

```
{
    "lookupId": "12",
    "lookupValue": "Portugal"
}
```

Hyperlink

A hyperlink field in Microsoft Lists has the following properties:

```
{
    "desc": "Hands-on Microsoft Lists"
}
```

Image

An `image` field in Microsoft Lists has the following properties:

```
{
  "fileName": "image.png",
  "id": "2626d838-e5d3-4333-85d2-d61070c57c82",
  "serverRelativeUrl": "/sites/handsonlists/SiteAssets/Lists/
    2f0c090a-31c3-4bd2-a6e5-7474a2e928a7/image.png",
  "serverUrl": "https://contoso.sharepoint.com"
}
```

Yes and No

A `yes` and `no` field in Microsoft Lists has the following properties:

```
{
    "displayValue": "Yes"
}
```

Currency

A `currency` field in Microsoft Lists has the following properties:

```
{
    "displayValue": "$12.12"
}
```

Number

A `number` field in Microsoft Lists has the following properties:

```
{
    "displayValue": "58.9%"
}
```

Date and Time, Single Line of Text, and Choice

Accessing the values of these three column types is straightforward as they only store a single value. You can access them using the `@currentField` special string.

Special strings

Microsoft Lists formatting makes use of special strings that give you access to direct properties and values in the context of the fields you are formatting. The following table shows all the available special strings:

String	Description
@currentField	This is the string that allows you to access the field being formatted.
[$FieldName]	This is the string that allows you to access other fields while you're customizing a column using the internal name of a field.
[!FieldName]	This string allows you to access any field metadata by using the internal name of the column: `[!NumberOfCopies.DisplayName]` This returns the display name of the field.
@CurrentWeb	Use this string to get the absolute URL of the SharePoint site where the list is stored.
@me	Use this string to get the email of the logged-in user.
@now	Use this string to get the current date and time.
@window.innerHeight	Use this string to get the window's height when the list is being rendered.
@window.innerWidth	Use this string to get the window's width when the list is being rendered.
@currentFiled.displayValue	This string, via its displayValue property, allows you to directly access the value being displayed in the list for the item being formatted. It is only available for the Date/Time, Number, Yes/No, and Currency fields.
[$FieldName].displayValue	This string, via its displayValue property, allows you to directly access the value being displayed in the list for the column being used for formatting. It is only available for the Date/Time, Number, Yes/No, and Currency fields.

> **Quick Tip**
>
> While creating a list, it's normal to change your mind and rename a column once it has been created. When you do this, you are only modifying the display name of a field; the internal name remain the same. While formatting a column, you must reference the internal name of the field and to access it, you must do the following:
>
> 1. Go to the list settings of the list you are formatting.
>
> 2. Hover over the name of the column that has a different display name than the internal name.
>
> 3. Hover over the column name. At the bottom of the browser window, you will see the internal name of the field:
>
>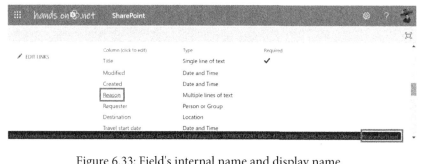
>
> Figure 6.33: Field's internal name and display name

Expressions

Expressions in the column format can be used to define an HTML tag's `textContent` property, style properties, and attribute properties. Expressions are evaluated at runtime when the user is viewing the list.

If you are familiar with Excel formulas, you will be glad to know that expressions can be written with the same syntax used by the Microsoft spreadsheet application.

In the following example, you can see an expression in Excel format in a column formatting a JSON file. We write the name of a user in a `person` field in red if the user is logged in and in blue if it is any other user:

```
{
    "$schema": "https://developer.microsoft.com/json-
               schemas/sp/v2/column-formatting.schema.json",
    "elmType": "div",
    "txtContent": "@currentField.title",
    "style": {
```

```
        "color": "=if(@me == @currentField.email, 'red', 'blue')"
    }
}
```

Alternatively, you can use Abstract Syntax Tree expressions to create your expressions., The following JSON code applies the same formatting but using a more complex syntax than the Excel version. The ternary condition can be translated into Microsoft Lists by using the ? operator with the == operand:

```
(@currentField.title == @me) ? 'red' : 'blue'
```

The following code does the same thing as the preceding code; that is, by using the ? operator with the == operand:

```
{
    "$schema": "https://developer.microsoft.com/json-
                schemas/sp/v2/column-formatting.schema.json",
    "elmType": "div",
    "txtContent": "@currentField.title",
    "style": {
        "color": {
            "operator": "?",
            "operands": [
                {
                    "operator": "==",
                    "operands": [
                        "@me",
                        "@currentField.email"
                    ]
                },
                "red",
                "blue"
            ]
        }
    }
}
```

How to create and apply your own JSON column formatting

Microsoft Lists advanced formatting includes the Monaco source code editor. By default, it will highlight your code, identify syntax errors in the JSON, and validate if the properties you are using are allowed by the formatting schema.

Despite providing these features, there is one thing that the Monaco editor does not provide: the ability to save the formatting locally in a file. To avoid losing your customizations, we recommend that you use a source code editor such as **Visual Studio Code**. To get started, do the following:

1. Download and install Visual Studio Code from the following link. It is available for Windows, macOS, and Linux: `https://code.visualstudio.com/Download`.

2. Open Visual Studio Code. Then, click on **File** and then **New File**.

3. Save the file with the `.json` extension.

4. Start writing your column formatting. You will learn how to do this in the *Learning from examples* subsection:

Figure 6.34 – Visual Studio Code – JSON column formatting

Once you have written your code, you need to add it to your list column by doing the following:

1. Open the column formatting pane. If it does not open in code mode, click on the **Advanced mode** link located at the bottom of the pane.

2. Paste your code in the text box.

3. Click on **Preview** to see how it will be applied before publishing it.

4. If the formatting looks as expected, click **Save**:

Figure 6.35 – Column formatting – custom code

> **Important**
>
> If you decide to use the Monaco editor exclusively, make sure you save a copy of your customizations. Clicking the **Switch to design mode** option will make any custom code disappear.

Learning from examples

Now that you have look at the Microsoft List column formatting schema, as well as all the available options, it is time to start learning about how to build your own JSON formatting. There is nothing better than learning from real examples that have been described and then exemplified.

> **Quick Tip**
>
> In the Microsoft 365 **Patterns and Practices** (**PnP**) open source repository, you can find numerous templates that you can use in your own lists or use them as a starting point to build your own column formatting. The column samples repository is available at `https://github.com/pnp/sp-dev-list-formatting/tree/master/column-samples`.

Simplest column formatting

The simplest column formatting you can do is display an item value inside an HTML `div` or `span` tag. The following example is being applied to a number column. As shown in the following screenshot, there is a minimal alignment difference being caused by the `div` tag wrapping the text:

```
{
    "$schema": "https://developer.microsoft.com/json-
                schemas/sp/v2/column-formatting.schema.json",
    "elmType": "div",
    "txtContent": "@currentField"
}
```

This template is valid for the **date and time**, **choice**, **number**, and **single line of text** fields. To access the values of more complex fields, review the *How to access column values* subsection of this chapter:

Figure 6.36 – Unformatted and formatted number columns

As the visual difference is almost imperceptible to the human eye, we have decided to include an image that contains an excerpt of the HTML source of both columns, highlighting the differences between them:

1. Unformatted number

2. Formatted number:

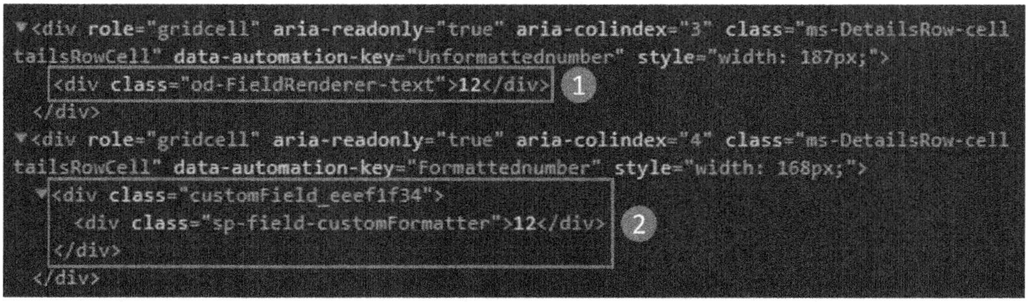

Figure 6.37 – HTML source for the unformatted and formatted number columns

Conditional formatting

Conditional formatting allows you to format a column based on a range of values. Using conditions, you can apply different styles to each column.

Scenario

Peter wants to register the exam grades of his students in a list. Once all the grades have been registered, Peter wants to format the grade column to show the following:

- An icon representing a pass or fail.

- The grade value as a percentage.

- Some text saying if the student has passed or failed the exam.

- Apply a green color for grades higher than 50%.

- Apply a red color for grades below 49%.

The following JSON code addresses all the requirements for the number column that can be used to store the grade values:

```
{
    "$schema": "https://developer.microsoft.com/json-
               schemas/sp/v2/column-formatting.schema.json",
    "elmType": "div",
    "attributes": {
        "class": "=if(@currentField <= 0.49, 'sp-field-severity-
                 blocked', if(@currentField >= 0.50,
                 'sp-field-severity--good', ''))"
    },
    "children": [
        {
            "elmType": "span",
            "style": {
                "display": "inline-block",
                "padding": "0 4px"
            },
            "attributes": {
                "iconName": "=if(@currentField <= 0.49, 'Cancel',
                            if(@currentField >= 0.50, 'CheckMark', ''))"
```

```
            }
        },
        {
            "elmType": "span",
            "txtContent": "=if(@currentField <= 0.49, 'Failed - ',
                           if(@currentField >= 0.50, 'Approved - ',
                           '')) + @currentField.displayValue"
        }
    ]
}
```

https://github.com/PacktPublishing/Hands-On-Microsoft-Lists/blob/main/Chapter06/conditionalFormatting.json

In this example, you can observe the following:

- How to apply a CSS class conditionally to format the background color of a column based on its value.

- How to create a child HTML tag to display an icon.

- How to create a child HTML tag to concatenate a conditional string with the value of the column:

Figure 6.38 – Conditional formatting

Format dates

Dates can be used in multiple contexts inside an organization and with the **Data and Time** field, the date functions, and the @now special string, you can create value and add extra information to your fields, as shown in the following example:

> **Scenario**
>
> The HR department has a list that contains all the employees who have joined the company. Dates are used to keep track of all their work anniversaries. Using this list, via their internal newsletter, the HR department specifies all the employees that are celebrating their work anniversary in the current month.
>
> To avoid forgetting an employee, the HR department wants to format the column so that it highlights the monthly work anniversaries, including the following:
>
> - An icon representing the anniversary
>
> - A green background for the monthly anniversaries
>
> - The number of years the employee has been with the company

```
{
   "$schema": "https://developer.microsoft.com/json-
               schemas/sp/v2/column-formatting.schema.json",
   "elmType": "div",
   "attributes": {
     "class": "=if(getMonth(@currentField) == getMonth(@now),
               'sp-field-severity--good', '')"
   },
   "children": [
     {
       "elmType": "span",
       "style": {
         "display": "inline-block",
         "padding": "0 4px"
       },
       "attributes": {
         "iconName": "=if(getMonth(@currentField) ==
                      getMonth(@now), 'BirthdayCake', '')"
```

```
    }
  ...
```

https://github.com/PacktPublishing/Hands-On-Microsoft-Lists/blob/main/Chapter06/formattingDates.json

In this example, you can observe the following:

- How to work with dates using the `getMonth()` and `getYear()` functions.

- How to work with the `@now` custom string to get the current date.

- How to create a child HTML tag to display an icon.

- How to create a child HTML tag to display the result of an arithmetic operation, concatenated with a string:

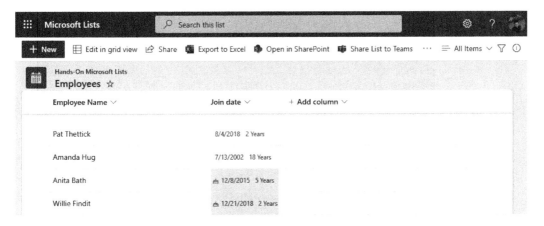

Figure 6.39 – Formatting dates

Creating custom row actions

Custom row actions can be attached to buttons and allow you to easily **view**, **share**, **edit**, or **delete** an item and **execute a flow**:

Scenario

To manage the employees list, the HR department has decided to create an extra column for the list that includes the following actions:

- View item details.

- Share the item with another user.

- Edit the item.

- Delete the item.

- Execute a custom flow to send the anniversary by email to the HR distribution list.

```json
{
    "$schema": "https://developer.microsoft.com/json-
                schemas/sp/v2/column-formatting.schema.json",
    "elmType": "div",
    "children": [
        {
            "elmType": "button",
            "customRowAction": {
                "action": "defaultClick"
            },
            "style": {
                "margin-right": "5px"
            },
            "children": [
                {
                    "elmType": "span",
                    "style": {
                        "display": "inline-block",
                        "padding": "0 4px"
                    },
                    "attributes": {
                        "iconName": "RedEye"
                    }
                },
...
```

https://github.com/PacktPublishing/Hands-On-Microsoft-Lists/blob/main/Chapter06/actions.JSON

In this example, you can observe the following:

- How to create row actions using buttons
- How to create buttons with text and icons

Each of these actions has its own interface. The following screenshots show what happens when a user clicks each of these buttons:

- On default action click:

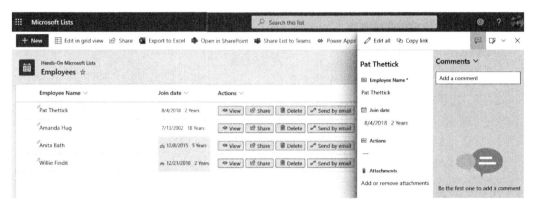

Figure 6.40 – View item detail shown on the default action click

- On share action click:

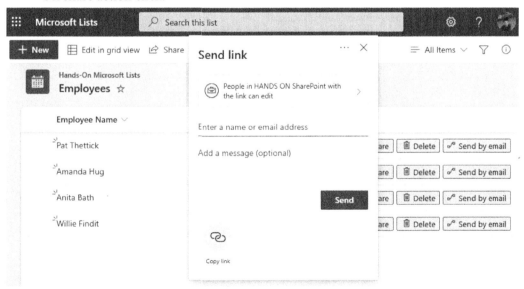

Figure 6.41 – Share item interface shown on the share action click

- On delete action click:

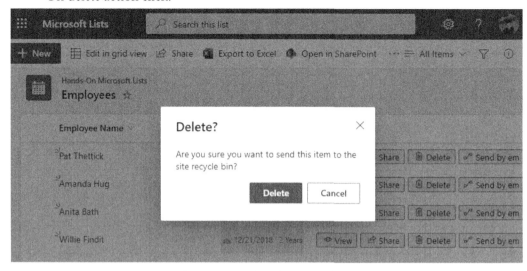

Figure 6.42 – Delete item interface shown on the delete action click

- On send by email action click:

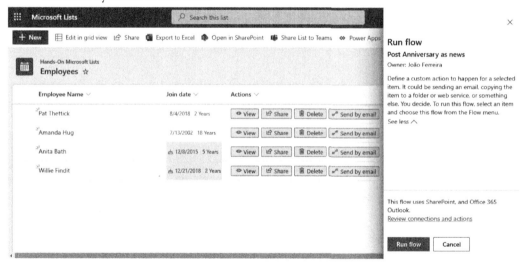

Figure 6.43 – Execute flow interface shown on the send by email action click

Cards

Cards allow you to display more information when the user hovers over a column. The information inside the card is created and formatted using the same syntax we saw for regular column formatting:

Scenario

The IT department keeps track of the new feature releases for a piece of software using a list. This list contains information about the features and their statuses. The IT department wants to customize the list so that they can do the following:

- View the date when the item was added to the list

- View the date when the item was modified

- Display this information when a user hovers over the title of a feature

```
{
    "$schema": "https://developer.microsoft.com/json-
               schemas/sp/v2/column-formatting.schema.json",
    "elmType": "div",
    "style": {
        "font-size": "12px"
    },
    "txtContent": "@currentField",
    "customCardProps": {
        "formatter": {
            "elmType": "div",
            "style": {
                "padding": "15px 45px 15px 15px"
            },
            "children": [{
                "elmType": "div",
                "children": [{
                    "elmType": "span",
                    "txtContent": "Created",
                    "style": {
                        "position": "relative",
...
```

https://github.com/PacktPublishing/Hands-On-Microsoft-Lists/blob/main/Chapter06/cards.JSON

In this example, you can observe the following:

- How to create a card that opens on mouse hover
- How to access other list columns in the context of the column formatting:

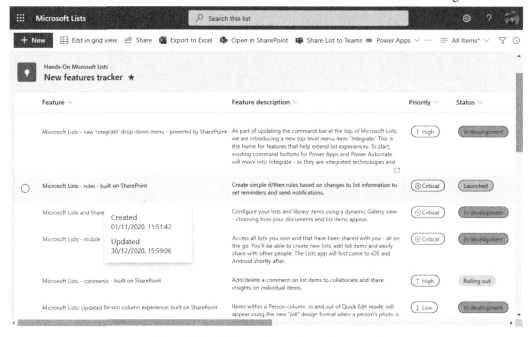

Figure 6.44 – Column formatting using a card

Foreach

A `foreach` loop in the column formatting allows you to format different elements on multi-value fields, such as `choice`, `lookup`, or `people` fields:

> **Scenario**
>
> Each time an employee needs to travel, they may fill in a form that registers the travel request for future approval in a list. The travel request list has a choice field where the user must select the destination country or any layover countries. Once a new request has been submitted, the submitter and the approver must see the following:
>
> - The countries that require a special visa, marked with a yellow background
>
> - All the other countries, marked with a green background

```
{
    "$schema": "https://developer.microsoft.com/json-
              schemas/sp/v2/column-formatting.schema.json",
    "elmType": "div",
    "debugMode": true,
    "children": [{
        "elmType": "span",
        "forEach": "country in @currentField",
        "txtContent": "[$country]",
        "style": {
            "padding": "4px"
        },
        "attributes": {
            "class": {
                "operator": "?",
                "operands": [{
                        "operator": "==",
                        "operands": [
                            "[$country]",
                            "United States"
                        ]
                    },
                    "sp-field-severity--warning",
                    "sp-field-severity--good"
...
```

https://github.com/PacktPublishing/Hands-On-Microsoft-Lists/blob/main/Chapter06/forEach.json

In this example, you can observe the following:

- How to loop through multi-value fields
- How to use abstract syntax tree expressions to compare strings and apply CSS classes:

Figure 6.45 – Foreach formatting applied to a choice column

Debugging JSON formatting

It's possible that, while formatting a column with JSON, you end up with an empty field. This usually means that even though the structure of your JSON is correct, an error has occurred while you were formatting your column.

To see the error message, you can add the `debugMode` attribute to your JSON with the property set to `true`, as shown in the following example:

```
{
    "$schema": "https://developer.microsoft.com/json-
                schemas/sp/v2/column-formatting.schema.json",
    "elmType": "div",
    "debugMode": true,
    "forEach": "country in @currentField",
    "txtContent": "[$country]"
}
```

When this property is defined, if an error occurs, you will see the error message in the column you are trying to format, as shown in the following screenshot:

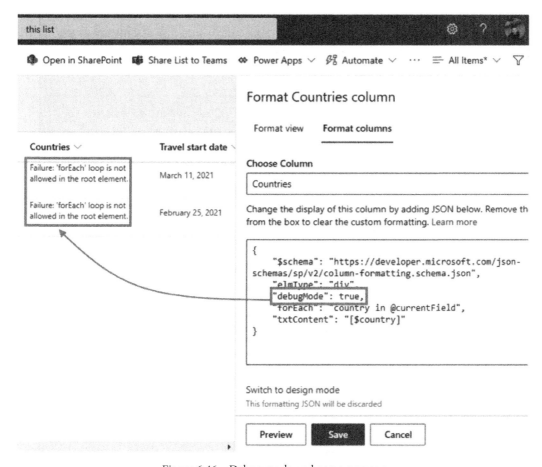

Figure 6.46 – Debug mode and error message

With the formatting options you have learned about in this chapter, you can transform how data is displayed in your lists. We've also covered all the basic concepts we can use to customize our lists even further by using custom view formatting. This will be explained in more detail in the next chapter.

Summary

In this chapter, you learned how to customize a list column using the tools built into the browser and using an advanced combination of JSON and HTML. With the learnings from this chapter, you can easily transform the data in your columns into something else making it easier to understand and more adjusted to your organization. Ultimately, this feature will help with the user adoption of Microsoft Lists as users will be able to better relate with Microsoft Lists.

The JSON schema that's available for column formatting is the base foundation for making code customizations in Microsoft Lists. In the next chapter, we'll learn how the same syntax can be reused to customize list views and list forms.

7
Customizing Microsoft Lists Views

Similar to column formatting, Microsoft Lists allows you to tailor list views to your own business needs via custom formatting. This way, you can create unique business scenarios that can be filtered automatically with the click of a button.

In this chapter, you will learn how to take your lists to the next level by covering the following main topics:

- Understanding Microsoft Lists formatting
- Learning from examples

Technical requirements

You can find the code files present in this chapter on GitHub at https://github.com/PacktPublishing/Hands-On-Microsoft-Lists/tree/main/Chapter07.

Understanding Microsoft Lists view formatting

With Microsoft Lists, you can take customizations to the next level and format the entire view instead of just the columns.

View formatting supports the same formatting methods we saw in the Column formatting section of this book; that is, WYSIWYG and JSON formatting.

In this section, we will explain how to format a view in Microsoft Lists without having to explain the HTML and JSON syntax. If you need help remembering the options that are available for formatting, please check out the *Column formatting* section of this book.

How to format a list view

Before we start exploring the more technical areas of view formatting, you must know how to format a view.

To gain access to the customization interface, do the following:

1. Open your list.

2. Click the **View selection** option.

3. From the **View selection** menu, click on **Format current view**:

Figure 7.1 – Microsoft Lists view formatting

4. Upon clicking the format view, the customization pane will open, which contains the options that are available for the current view type.

WYSIWYG formatting options

Like column formatting, view formatting also includes a WYSIWYG design mode that allows you to format your view and see your changes in real time.

The following table shows the available formatting options for the default list layouts:

List Layout	View Formatting
List	Alternating row styles
List	Conditional formatting
Gallery	Card designer

Alternating row styles

The alternating row styles allow you to define a background color and text styles for the odd rows so that they are different to the even rows. To format your view with alternating row styles, do the following:

1. Select **Alternating row styles** from the list of available options.

2. Click the **Edit row styles** link:

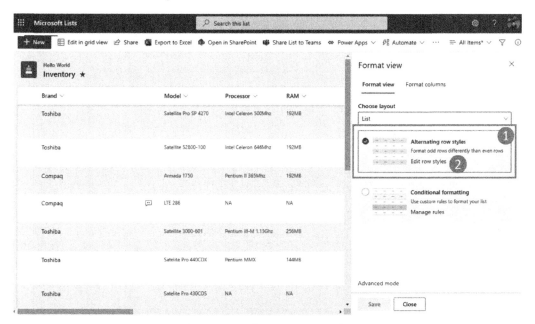

Figure 7.2 – Alternating row styles

3.   On **Odd rows**, click the **Edit style** button.

4.   Select the fill color for your row:

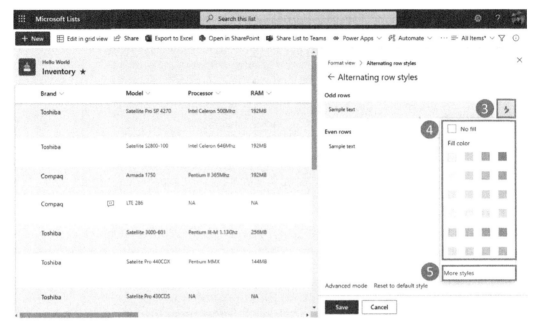

Figure 7.3 – Odd row configuration

5.   To format the text further, click on the **More styles** link. Here, you can format the font and the borders for your rows:

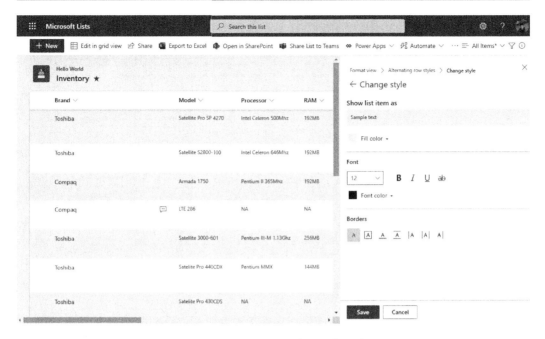

Figure 7.4 – Alternating rows advanced configuration

6.   Repeat *steps 3* to *5* for **Even rows**.

Conditional formatting

Conditional formatting allows you to define conditions so that you can apply background colors and text formatting to your rows. To format your view with conditional formatting, do the following:

1.   Select **Conditional formatting** from the list of available options.

2. Click the **Manage rules** link:

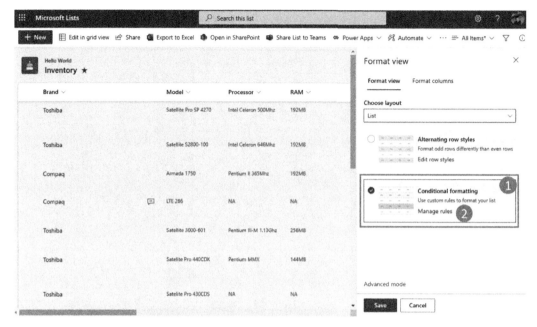

Figure 7.5 – List view conditional formatting

3. If this is the first conditional formatting you are defining, by default, you will see a gray background for all the rows. This means that a custom condition hasn't been created yet. To modify it, click on **…** next to **Show all values as**.

4. From the menu, click **Edit rule**:

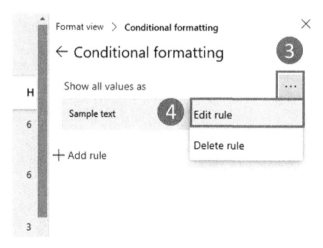

Figure 7.6 – Edit rule

5. From the **If** dropdown, select the column you want to use to build your condition.

6. Choose a comparison for the row.

7. Define the value that will be compared.

8. From the **Show list item as** section, click on the **Edit style** button.

9. Select the color you want to apply from the list provided.

10. To customize the row further, click on **More styles**:

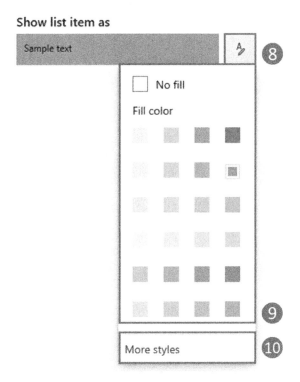

Figure 7.7 – Format row condition

11. From the **Change style** pane for the row, you can define the fill color, format the font, and define borders around the row value:

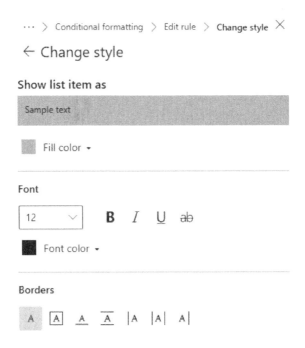

Figure 7.8 – Conditional view formatting advanced styles

12. A formatted view can have multiple conditions applied to it. To create more conditions, click on the **Add condition** link.

13. Define your new condition for the view by selecting the column to be used as a comparison, the comparison, and the value.

14. While you are formatting the view, everything you do in the user interface is reflected immediately in the list. However, this is only published for others to see when you click the **Save** button:

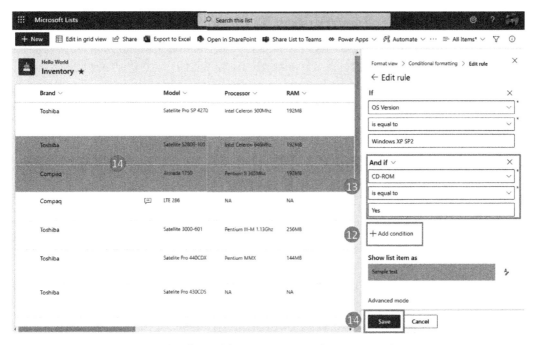

Figure 7.9 – Conditional formatting – extra formatting and preview

15. When formatting a view, you can apply multiple conditions that will be applied differently to each row. After saving the formatting, click **Conditional formatting** in the top breadcrumb:

Figure 7.10 – Edit rule

16. Repeat *steps 4* to *14* to create your new condition.

17. To **view**, **edit**, **delete**, or **change the order** of any existing conditional formatting, open the manage rules pane, as explained in *step 15*. Here, you will see all the rules that have been applied to the column.

18. Click on **…** to open the context menu.

19. Select the desired option:

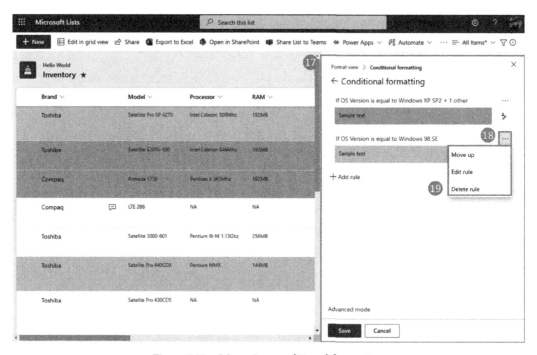

Figure 7.11 – Managing conditional formatting

Card Designer

The Card Designer allows you to modify the card that's applied to the Gallery view. To select which columns must appear in the card, do the following:

1. Select the **Gallery** layout.

2. From the list of available options, select **Card Designer**.

3.   Click on **Edit card**:

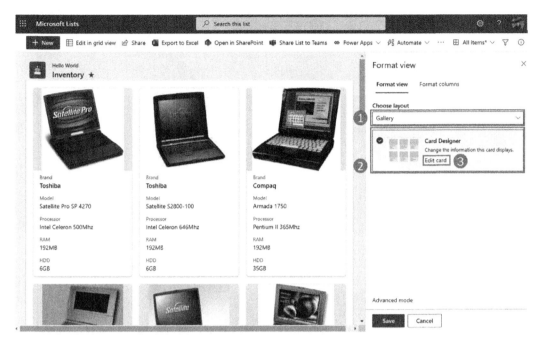

Figure 7.12 – Card Designer

4.   Select the columns you want to apply to the card. By default, the layout has six columns selected and displays a picture or person field as the first column if one is available.

5.   You can rearrange the position of your columns by clicking **...** and then choosing **Move up** or **Move down**.

6. Once you have created your card, click **Save** to publish the view to all the users:

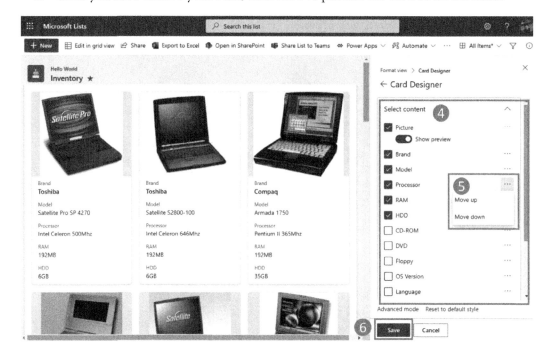

Figure 7.13 – Card Designer column selection

JSON formatting

JSON formatting allows you to customize views beyond what the design mode and the WYSIWYG interface allow you to do.

Before we start digging into the examples and into the more complex customizations, you must become familiar with the JSON properties that are specific to Microsoft Lists views, combined with the HTML and JSON properties we saw in the *Column formatting* section so that you can build list view custom layouts.

View formatting properties and attributes

As a combination of HTML and JSON, view formatting has its own properties that are used along with the HTML. The following table shows the specific properties you should use when formatting views:

Property	Behavior
rowFormatter	A JSON object that defines how a row is formatted. In this object, you must use the properties, functions, and conditions we saw in the *Column formatting* section.
additionalRowClass	A CSS class that is applied to the entire row. It supports expressions and is only valid for List and Compact List layouts.
hideSelection	If true, then the selection UX in the List and Compact List layouts will be disabled. It will be ignored if no rowFormatter has been defined.
hideColumnHeader	If true, then the list column header UX in the List and Compact List layouts will be hidden.
tileProps	A JSON object that defines the tiles in the Tiles layout. It has the following properties: • height: Height of the tile in pixels. • width: Width of the tile in pixels. • hideSelection: If true, then the selection UX in the Tiles layout will be disabled. • formatter: A JSON object that defines how a tile is formatted. In this object, you must use the properties, functions, and conditions we saw in the *Column formatting* section.
groupProps	A JSON object that defines the formatting of a view group.
headerFormatter	A JSON object that defines the formatting for the header of a view group.
footerFormatter	A JSON object that defines the formatting for the footer of a view group.
hideFooter	An optional property that allows you to hide the footer in a view group.

Predefined CSS classes

When formatting a view, you can take advantage of the pre-existing CSS styles provided by Microsoft default classes. The following table shows the specific CSS classes that can be applied to the view formatting. These can then be complemented by the CSS classes we saw in the *Column formatting* section:

Class name	Behavior
sp-row-card	Creates a card effect that gives the HTML element a background color and a shadow
sp-row-title	Formats the HTML element in bold
sp-row-listPadding	Creates padding in the HTML element
sp-row-button	Formats the button HTML element

Special strings

Microsoft Lists view formatting makes use of special strings that will give you access to direct properties and values in the context of the view you are formatting. The following table shows all the available special strings. All the custom strings we saw in the *Column formatting* section can be used for view formatting:

String	Description
@currentField	This is the same string we saw in the *Column formatting* section; however, in the view formatting context, it will always return the title column.
@rowIndex	Returns the index of each row in the view.
@group	Gives access to the group data for the list column. The group gives access to the following properties: • fieldData: The value shown in the group • columnDisplayName: The name of the column used to build the group • count: The number of elements currently in the group
@columnAggregate	Gives access to the aggregation value for the column in the view. The column aggregate has the following properties: • value: The value shown for the aggregation • columnDisplayName: The name of the column used to build the group • type: The type of aggregation selected for the column
@aggregates	Gives access to all the columns and respective values that are aggregated in the view.

How to create and apply your own JSON view formatting

Microsoft Lists advanced formatting includes the Monaco source code editor. By default, it will highlight your code, identify syntax errors in the JSON, and validate whether the properties you are using are allowed by the formatting schema.

Despite providing these features, there is one thing that the Monaco editor does not provide: the ability to save the formatting locally in a file. To avoid losing your customizations, we recommend that you use a source code editor such as **Visual Studio Code**. To get started, follow these steps:

1. Download and install Visual Studio Code from the following link. It is available for Windows, macOS, and Linux: `https://code.visualstudio.com/Download`.

2. Open Visual Studio Code. Then, click on **File** and then **New File**.

3. Save the file with the `.json` extension.

4. Start writing your view formatting. You will learn how to do this in the *Learning from examples* subsection:

Figure 7.14 – Visual Studio Code – view formatting JSON

Once you have written the code, you need to add it to your list column by doing the following:

1. Open the **View formatting** pane and click on **Advanced mode**, which is located at the bottom of the pane.

2. Paste your code into the text box.

3. Click on **Preview** to see how it will be applied before publishing it.

4.   If the formatting looks as expected, click **Save**:

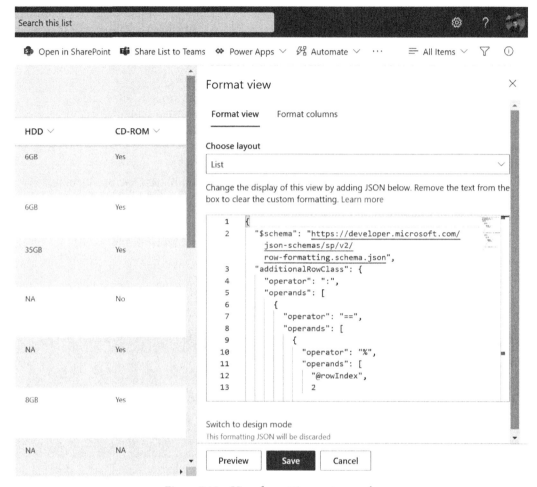

Figure 7.15 – View formatting custom code

> **Important**
>
> If you decide to use the Monaco editor exclusively, make sure you save a copy of your customizations. Clicking the **Switch to design mode** option will make any custom code disappear.

Learning from examples

Now that you have looked at the Microsoft List column formatting and view formatting schemas, it's time to start learning how to build your own JSON. There is nothing better than learning from real examples that are described and then exemplified.

Quick Tip

In the Microsoft 365 **Patterns and Practices** (**PnP**) open source repository, you can find numerous templates that you can use in your own lists or use as a starting point to build your own view formatting.

The column samples repository is available at `https://github.com/pnp/sp-dev-list-formatting/tree/master/view-samples`.

Conditional view formatting

One of the simplest view formattings you can do is create a custom alternate row formatting. The following code formats the even rows with a background color.

This example can also be achieved in design mode. However, by using JSON, you can customize it even further:

```
{
    "$schema": "https://developer.microsoft.com/json-
                schemas/sp/view-formatting.schema.json",
    "additionalRowClass": "=if(@rowIndex%2==0,'ms-bgColor-
        magenta ms-fontColor-black ms-fontColor-white--hover ms-
        bgColor-redDark--hover','')"
}
```

The following screenshot shows the result of applying the code to the view:

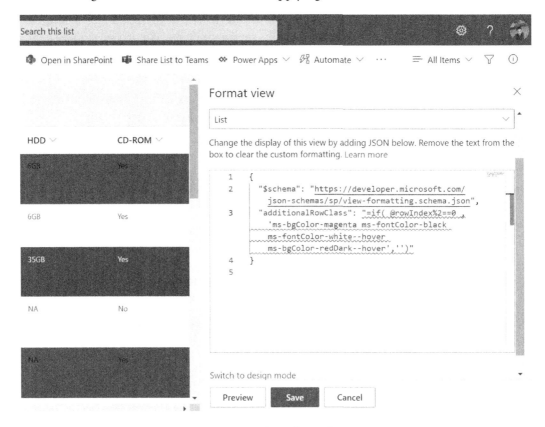

Figure 7.16 – Conditional view formatting

In this example, you can observe the following:

- How to access the index of a row using the custom @rowIndex string
- How to format a row conditionally
- How to apply background colors and text colors
- How to apply background colors and text colors on mouse hover

Tile layout

Tile layout formatting allows you to format each column row as a tile, which allows you to use any HTML structure to display the content.

Scenario

John has a Microsoft List connected to Microsoft Power Automate that's being used to store the daily forecast for the company's office locations. Inspired by the Microsoft Windows weather tiles, John has decided to format his list to display the weather information for each of the cities in tile format:

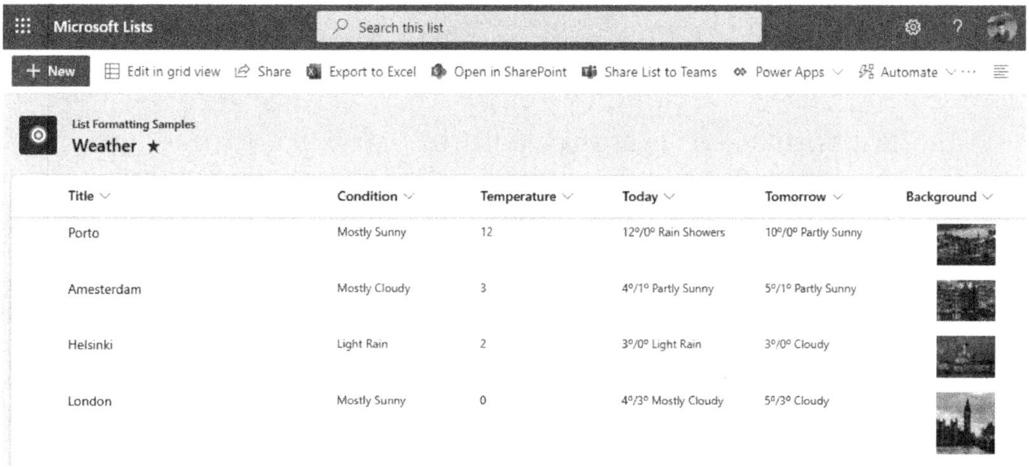

Figure 7.17 – Weather list

The following code snippet will transform the weather data stored in the list into a tile view:

```
{
    "$schema": "https://developer.microsoft.com/json-
                schemas/sp/view-formatting.schema.json",
    "hideSelection": true,
    "width": "250",
    "height": "250",
    "formatter": {
        "elmType": "div",
        "children": [{
            "elmType": "div",
            "style": {
                "display": "inline-block",
                "min-width": "250px",
                "min-height": "250px",
```

```
            "margin-right": "10px",
            "box-shadow": "2px 2px 4px darkgrey"
        },
    ...
```

https://github.com/PacktPublishing/Hands-On-Microsoft-Lists/blob/main/Chapter07/weather.json

In this example, you can observe the following:

- How to define the height and width of a tile
- How to create a custom tile structure using the formatter property
- How to use custom CSS with the style property:

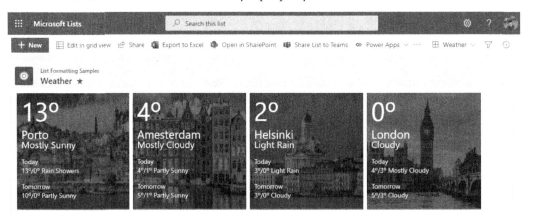

Figure 7.18 – Weather tile format

This example shows how flexible the tile layout can be and how it can be used as a starting point for other scenarios.

Formatting a view group header and footer

List views can be grouped and aggregated by the columns containing all the information that have the same value aggregate inside an accordion.

With view formatting, you can go a step further and also customize the headers and the footers of your groups, as shown in the following screenshot:

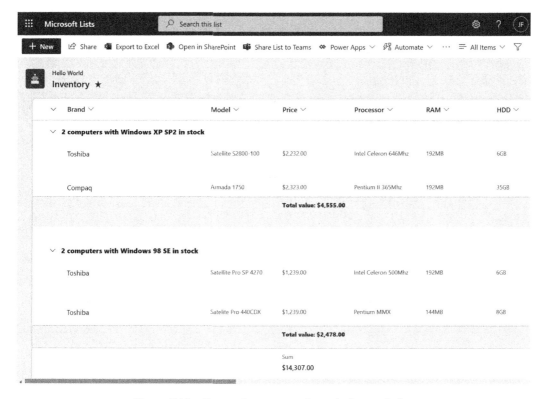

Figure 7.19 – Formatting a group view – before and after

In this example, you can observe the following:

- How to format the group header
- How to use the value from an aggregation in the header
- How to format the group footer:

```
{
    "$schema": "https://developer.microsoft.com/json-
                schemas/sp/v2/row-formatting.schema.json",
    "groupProps": {
        "headerFormatter": {
            "elmType": "div",
            "style": {
```

```
              "font-weight": "800"
          },
            "txtContent": "= @group.count + if(@group.count > '1',
                          ' computers', ' computer') + ' with ' +
                          @group.fieldData.displayValue + ' in
                          stock'"
      },
        "footerFormatter": {
        "elmType": "div",
        "style": {
          "font-weight": "800"
        },
            "txtContent": "= 'Total value: ' +
                          @columnAggregate.value"
      }
    }
  }
```

https://github.com/PacktPublishing/Hands-On-Microsoft-Lists/blob/main/Chapter07/groups.json

With that, we have learned how to format lists using column formatting and view formatting. Use the examples provided to get started and then adjust them to your own needs.

Summary

In this chapter, you learned how to customize a list view using the built-in tools and using a combination of JSON and HTML.

The JSON schema, which we covered in the column formatting and view formatting chapters of this book, is the foundation for making code customizations in Microsoft Lists. As we'll see in the next chapter, the same syntax can be reused to customize list forms.

8
Customizing Microsoft Lists Forms

In the previous chapter, you learned how to customize Microsoft Lists columns and views, and in this chapter, you will learn how to customize the forms used by the application to display list items and to create new items in a list.

This type of customization helps you to consume and to insert the information in a list in a more structured way, making the consumption of data easier and the introduction of new values less prone to errors.

In this chapter, you will learn how to take your list forms to the next level by going through the following main topics:

- What is a Microsoft Lists form?

- How to customize a Microsoft Lists form

- How to create a custom Microsoft Lists form using Power Apps

Technical Requirement

You can find the code files present in this chapter on GitHub at `https://github.com/PacktPublishing/Hands-On-Microsoft-Lists/tree/main/Chapter08`.

What is a Microsoft Lists form?

In Microsoft Lists, you will have to deal with two different types of forms and in this chapter, we will teach you how to customize each one. But before we dig into the technical areas of the chapter, we want you to have a clear vision of the differences between both types:

- **New item form** – This is the type of form that is used to introduce new data into lists. It is generated by default based on list columns and the content types you have in lists. In this chapter, you will learn how to customize it to match your own business needs. The same form is also used to edit the information stored in a list item. When an item is edited, the user is presented with the same form with the textboxes already filled with the existent information.

- **List item detail form** – The list item detail form is used to view all the list item columns. It is shown when you click on a list item to open it and is also the form a user sees when a list item is shared. In this chapter, you will learn how to customize, organize, and highlight the information with more value in an item.

In the following screenshot, you can see a new item form and a list item detail form without customizations side by side. You can see that the main difference between both forms is in the input elements:

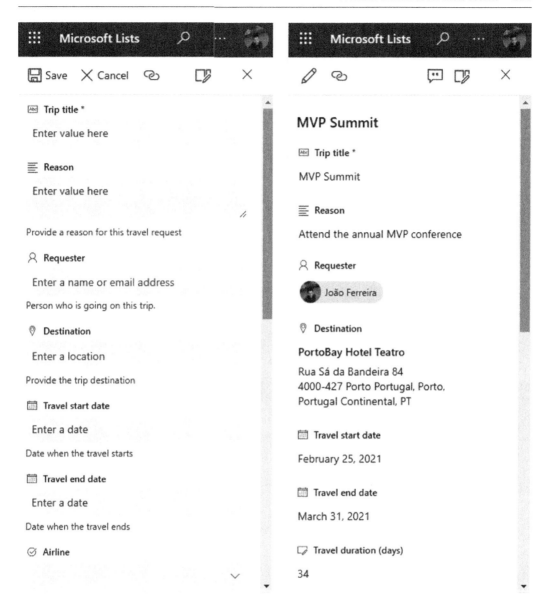

Figure 8.1 – Microsoft Lists form types

Now that you know what Microsoft Lists forms look like, let's see in the next section how you can customize them.

How to customize a Microsoft Lists form

The customization of Microsoft Lists forms gives you the possibility to highlight the important data that you want to stand out for each list item or the possibility to hide, show, or group columns that will help users to better consume the information based on your business processes.

Showing or hiding columns in a form

In Microsoft Lists, you can show and hide columns from your list without deleting them. This functionality becomes extremely handy when you have columns in the list that you do not want to display when a user expands the item detail or creates a new item.

Any user with permissions to create or manage views will be able to show or hide columns in a list. To format a form for a list item, you must do the following:

1. From the list you want to modify, click on one of the items to open the item detail form. Alternatively, if your list does not have content yet, click on the **New** button.

2. From the item detail pane, click on the **Edit form** button.

3. From the dropdown, click on **Edit columns**:

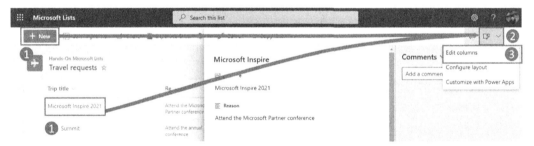

Figure 8.2 – Editing a Microsoft Lists form

4. Select the columns you want to include in the item detail form – check a column to show it and uncheck it to hide it.

5. To reorder the columns, you must hover over the item with the mouse and click on the vertical **...** located on the right.

6. Select **Move Up** or **Move Down** according to your needs. Alternatively, you can click on the item and drag it to the desired position:

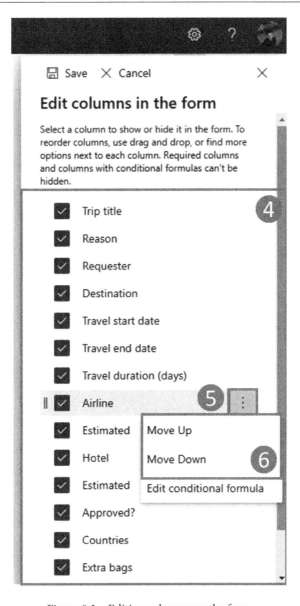

Figure 8.3 – Editing columns on the form

Once you choose the columns for your form, all the unselected columns will disappear from both forms, however, you will continue to see them in the list view as the columns that are displayed there are defined by the list view itself.

Showing or hiding form columns conditionally

The form formatting does not need to be all or nothing, and you can choose to hide or show columns conditionally based on the data stored in the list for each column.

Conditional formulas use the same Excel syntax we saw in *Chapter 6, Customizing Microsoft Lists*, in the *Column formatting* section. With an `if` condition, you can define whether the column is visible or hidden:

```
=if([$Extra_x0020_Bags]==0,'true', 'false')
```

A conditional formula starts with an equal signal followed by a condition and by the attributes `true` and `false`, which define the visibility for the column depending on the outcome of the condition.

The condition must reference a column by its **internal name**, and it could be the column being formatted or any other column in the list. **Operators**, **operands**, **functions**, and **special strings**, which we saw in *Chapter 6, Customizing Microsoft Lists*, in the *Column formatting* section, can be used to conditionally format a column.

Quick tip

If your column name has *spaces* in the internal name, you must replace them with the space representation `_x0020_`.

If you have renamed your column and you need to know the original internal name to use in the formatting, you can do the following:

1. Go to the list settings of the list you are formatting.

2. Hover over the name of the column that has a display name different than the internal name.

3. Hover over the column name and at the bottom of the browser window you will see the internal name of the field:

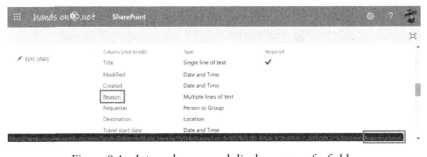

Figure 8.4 – Internal name and display name of a field

You will be able to conditionally format the following column types:

- A single line of text
- Multiple lines of text
- Choice – only supported for single values
- Number
- Yes/No
- Date and time
- Person or group – only supported for multiple values
- Hyperlink
- Image
- Lookup

Despite supporting most of the column types, the following are not supported by Microsoft Lists:

- Person or group – does not support multiple values
- Choice – does not support multiple values
- Currency
- Location
- Calculated
- Managed metadata

To apply conditional formatting to the form columns, you must do the following:

1. Open the edit columns pane as explained in the previous section.
2. Click in the vertical ... to open the column context menu.

3. Click on **Edit conditional formula**:

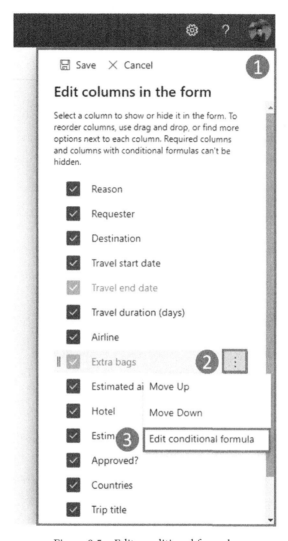

Figure 8.5 – Edit conditional formula

4. In the pop-up window, type your formula.

5. Click on **Save** to apply the formula.

6. A column formatted conditionally will be displayed disabled in the form as its visibility depends on the data:

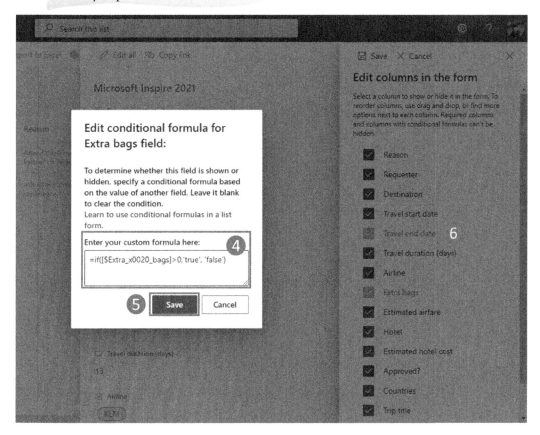

Figure 8.6 – Apply conditional formula

Now that you know the theory, let's see how you can conditionally format a column with the examples in the next subsection.

Learn by examples

To understand the conditional column formatting in this section, you have a few examples that show how you can use it with multiple column types making use of **operators**, **operands**, **functions**, and **special strings**.

Text columns

```
=if([$Destination]=='Las Vegas','true', 'false')
```

In this example, you can observe the following:

- How a text column comparison can be made.
- How to define a string for the comparison – the text value is always defined between apostrophes.

Number columns

```
=if([$Hotel]<3000,'true', 'false')
```

In this example, you can observe the following:

- How to compare number columns – the value used in the comparison is defined **without** using the apostrophes.

```
=if(([$Flight]+[$Hotel])<4000,'true', 'false')
```

In this example, you can observe the following:

- How to compare a number doing an arithmetic operation between two columns – operations must be defined between parentheses.

Date columns

```
=if([$TravelStartDate]>@now,'true', 'false')
```

In this example, you can observe the following:

- How to compare a date column with the current day using the special string @now.

```
=if([$TravelStartDate]>@now && [$EndDate] <=
Date('24/3/2021'),'true', 'false')
```

In this example, you can observe the following:

- How to compare a date column with the current day using the special string @now.
- How to use the function Date() to convert a string to a date.
- How to compare a date range using the operand &&.

Person columns

```
=if([$Requester.email]=='joaoferreira@handsontek.net','true',
'false')
```

In this example, you can observe the following:

- How to compare a user with a given email.
- How to access the properties of complex column types.

Yes/No columns

```
=if([$Approved]==true,'true', 'false')
```

In this example, you can observe the following:

- How to compare Yes/No columns. The comparison value in this column formatting can only be `true` or `false` and must be used without apostrophes.

Use the preceding examples as a starting point to format your columns in a list.

Formatting a list form's header and footer

Microsoft Lists allows you to further customize a list item detail form by applying custom formatting to the header and footer of each item detail.

The formatting of the header and footer is created using the same syntax we saw in *Chapter 6*, *Customizing Microsoft Lists*. Using JSON and HTML, you will be able to create custom structures using the column values available in the item.

Despite using the same syntax and schema, the type of columns available to be used to format the header and the footer are restricted to the following column types:

- A single line of text
- Multiple lines of text
- Hyperlink
- Number
- Currency
- Picture

Any other column type referenced in the header and footer formatting will be ignored and will return an empty value.

To format the header and footer of a detail list item form, you must do the following:

1. Open the list item detail form.
2. Click on the **Edit form** button.

3. From the menu, click on **Configure layout**:

Figure 8.7 – Configure form layout

4. From the **Apply formatting to** dropdown, select the location where you want to apply the formatting.

5. Paste the JSON formatting in the textbox.

6. Click on **Preview** to see the formatting applied.

7. Once you are happy with it, click on **Save** to make it available to all users with access to the list:

Figure 8.8 – Form formatting

Now that you know what the available options are to format the header and the footer, have a look at the following examples and use them as a starting point for your new customization.

Learning by examples

To better understand how to build header and footers for your forms, here is an example that can be used in both locations. The following code creates an HTML structure with a static icon and a partial static title that is complemented by the value stored in the title column:

```json
{
    "elmType": "div",
    "attributes": {
        "class": "ms-borderColor-themePrimary"
    },
    "style": {
        "width": "99%",
        "border-top-width":"0px",
        "border-bottom-width": "2px",
        "border-left-width": "0px",
        "border-right-width": "0px",
        "border-style": "solid",
        "margin-bottom": "16px"
    },
...
```

https://github.com/PacktPublishing/Hands-On-Microsoft-Lists/blob/main/Chapter08/Header.json

In this example, you can observe the following:

- How to create a custom header/footer for the list form
- How to add a custom icon to the form
- How to concatenate a string using the + operator
- How to format the typography using the Fabric UI predefined classes for themes

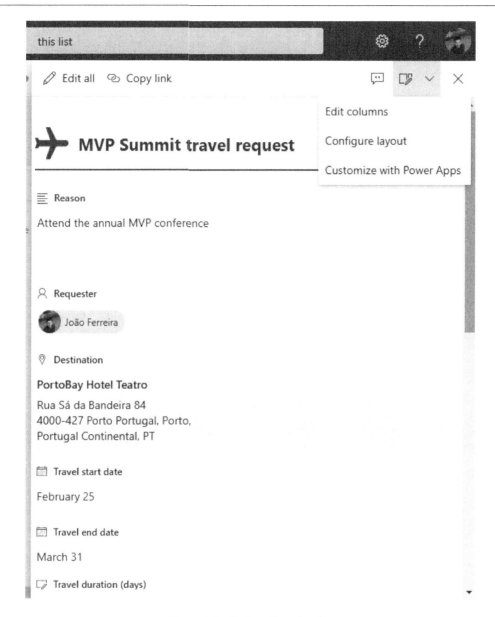

Figure 8.9 – Custom form header

Formatting the form body

One of the big disadvantages of the autogenerated list forms is the scrolling that is necessary to do to view all the list columns. The form formatting allows you to address this issue by displaying columns side by side horizontally instead of arranging them vertically.

Form body formatting is available for you to make a list form more readable by grouping columns inside custom groups that only exist on the list item detail form.

Unlike all the other formatting options, the body format does not follow the same JSON schema and syntax and it does not support the use of HTML. Instead, it has its own JSON schema that is generically represented as follows:

```
{
    "sections":[
        {
            "displayname":"Section 1",
            "fields":[
                "fieldName",
                "fieldName1"
            ]
        }
    ]
}
```

In this schema, you just need to define the following fields:

- `displayname` – The string that will be displayed as the title of the group.
- `fields` – The display name of the column – unlike the other formatting options, the body formatting does not make use of the internal column name.

Columns are automatically organized alphabetically, disregarding the definition order inside the group, and cannot be repeated in multiple groups. All the previous column formats defined for the list are kept inside the body format.

To format the body of a detail list item form, you must do the following:

1. Open the list item detail form.
2. Click on the **Edit form** button.

3. From the menu, click on **Configure layout**:

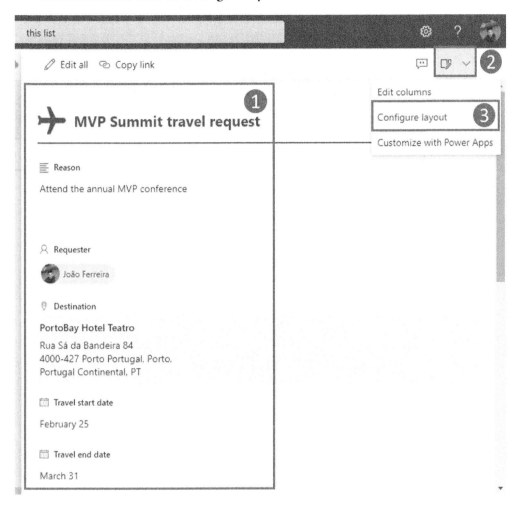

Figure 8.10 – Configure form body layout

4. From the **Apply formatting to** dropdown, select **Body**.

5. Paste the JSON formatting in the textbox.

6. Click on **Preview** to see the formatting applied.

7. Once you are happy with it, click on **Save** to make it available to all users with access to the list:

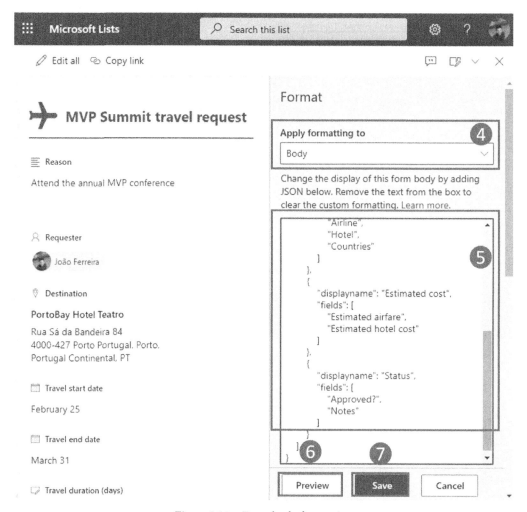

Figure 8.11 – Form body formatting

Learning by examples

To better understand how to customize the body of your form, here is an example. The following code creates groups for the columns of a travel request list:

```
{
    "sections": [{
        "displayname": "Personal Information",
```

```
        "fields": [
            "Trip title",
            "Requester",
            "Reason"
        ]
    },
    {
        "displayname": "Details",
        "fields": [
            "Destination",
            "Travel start date",
            "Travel end date",
            "Travel duration (days)",
            "Airline",
            "Hotel",
            "Countries"
        ]
    },
    {
        "displayname": "Estimated cost",
        "fields": [
            "Estimated airfare",
            "Estimated hotel cost"
        ]
    },
    {
        "displayname": "Status",
        "fields": [
            "Approved?",
            "Notes"
        ]
    }
  ]
}
```

https://github.com/PacktPublishing/Hands-On-Microsoft-Lists/blob/main/Chapter08/Body.json

In this example, you can observe the following:

- How to create multiple groups in the form body
- How to add multiple columns to each group

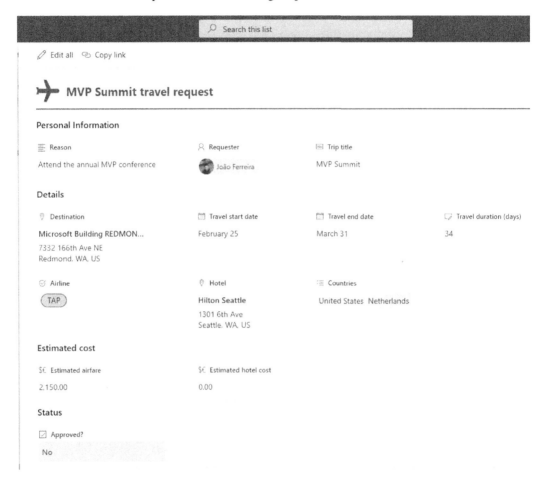

Figure 8.12 – Body formatting applied

In this screenshot, you can see how the form looks different and how the information is easily consumed immediately without the need to scroll to see all the information about an item.

How to create a Microsoft Lists custom form using Power Apps

You can extend your Microsoft Lists custom forms beyond the default options that are provided by the application with the use of Power Apps.

Power Apps is a platform from Microsoft that makes rapid application development through a browser accessible to any power user and it does not require development skills.

The custom business apps built with the Power Apps platform are designed to be responsive and to run natively on browsers and mobile devices.

> **Note**
>
> The following section does not cover all the options included in Power Apps. It aims to give you the basic knowledge to build forms for Microsoft Lists using an alternative platform. If you want to learn in detail about all the possibilities available in PowerApps, we recommend you take a look at the *Learn Microsoft PowerApps* book from Packt at `https://www.packtpub.com/product/learn-microsoft-powerapps/9781789805826`.

To create a custom form for your list using Power Apps, you must do the following:

1. On the Lists command bar, click on the **Power Apps** application.

2. From the menu, click on **Customize forms**:

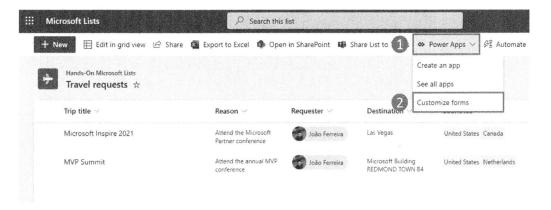

Figure 8.13 – Customize Power Apps forms

3. After a few seconds, you will land in the Power Apps application with a premade form for your list.

4. To modify the form properties, select the form by clicking on it. A selected form is shown with a blue border.

5. To add/remove extra fields to/from the form, from the left pane, click on the **Edit fields** link:

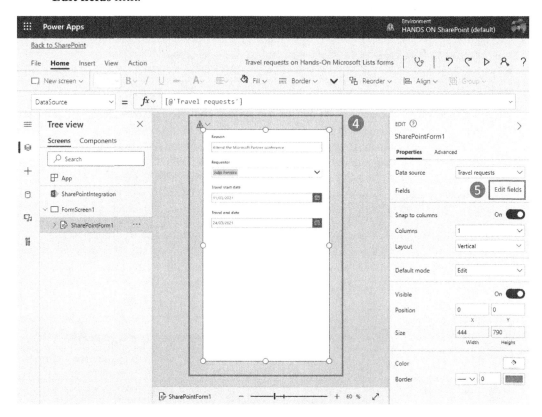

Figure 8.14 – Power Apps builder

6. Select the columns that you want to make visible in your form. As you can see in the following screenshot, complex columns are represented by multiple fields in Power Apps, for example, the **Destination** column.

7. Click on **Add**.

8. Format the form according to your needs:

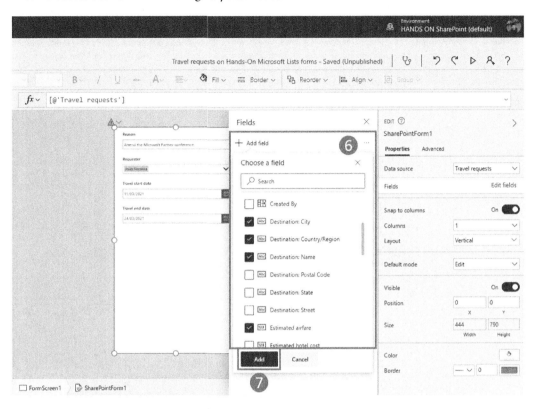

Figure 8.15 – Add columns to a PowerApps form

Publishing the Power Apps form to your list

Once you are happy with your custom form, it's time to publish it to your list by doing the following:

1. From the Power Apps application, click on **File**.

2.   On the vertical menu, click on **Save** and then click on the **Save** button:

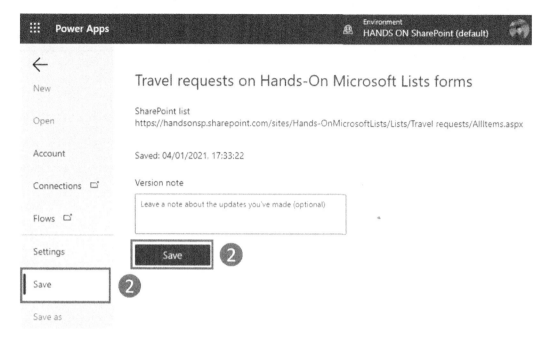

Figure 8.16 – Save the PowerApps custom form

3.   Once the form is saved, click on the **Publish to SharePoint** button:

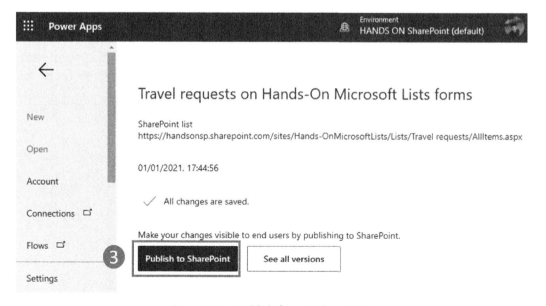

Figure 8.17 – Publish form to SharePoint

4. To make it visible to all your users, from the pop-up window click on **Publish to SharePoint** again.

5. From your list on Microsoft Lists, click on **New**. The new form will be revealed in the right pane as a default Microsoft Lists form. The Power Apps form will be used to create, edit, and view Lists items in the list:

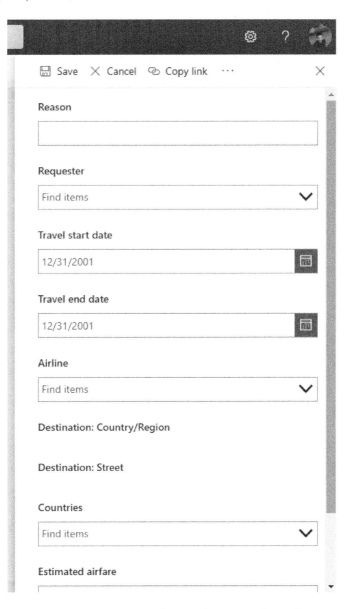

Figure 8.18 – PowerApps form in the Microsoft Lists list

Modifying the form applied to the list

After applying a Power Apps form to your list, you have the possibility to revert it back to the original list form. To do this, follow these steps:

1. From your list, click on the **cog** icon.

2. From the **Settings** pane, click on **List settings**.

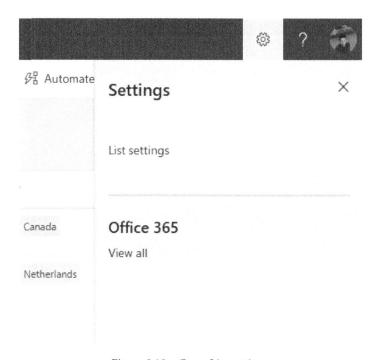

Figure 8.19 – Open List settings

3. Under **General Settings**, click on **Form Settings**.

4. From Form Settings, you have the option to select the following:

    *   Use the custom list form.

    *   **Use a custom form created in PowerApps** – This option is only available in the modern list experience.

- **Use a custom form created in InfoPath** – InfoPath is deprecated, and we do not recommend that you use it:

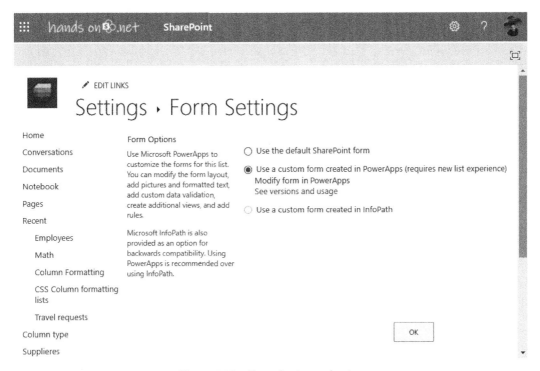

Figure 8.20 – Form Settings selection

With the use of Power Apps forms, you have learned all the currently supported methods from Microsoft to customize Lists forms.

Summary

This chapter closes the Microsoft Lists customizations. With everything you have learned so far, you will be able to customize your list forms, making them unique and adjusted to your business needs.

This chapter ended with a reference to Microsoft Power Apps, bridging the Power Platform and the further integration we will see in the next chapter.

9
Integrating Microsoft Lists with the Power Platform

In the previous chapters of this book, we learned how to use Microsoft Lists to store and consume data in an effective way.

In this chapter, you will start to learn how Microsoft Lists can be extended, and how the content stored by the application can be used to create business processes or dashboards, which will give you a different perspective on the data that is stored in the platform.

Microsoft Power Platform is composed by 4 different applications that allow you to build custom applications based on your business logic using a low-code programing language making it accessible to most power users.

To introduce you to the Power Platform, we will cover the following topics:

- Exploring the Power Platform
- Power Automate and Microsoft Lists
- Power BI and Microsoft Lists
- Power Virtual Agents and Microsoft Lists

Exploring the Power Platform

The Microsoft Power Platform is a set of applications that allows power users without developer skills to automate business processes and to build business applications.

The Power Platform is currently constituted by four different applications:

- **Power Apps**: Transforms any power user in an app builder. We have seen Power Apps in the previous chapter and how you are able to build custom forms for Microsoft Lists. While Power Apps are an integral part of the Power Platform, we will not cover them any further in this chapter, and rather provide more information on the other applications.

- **Power Automate**: Allows you to automate processes and repetitive tasks by creating so-called flows. With more than 400 connectors, you can connect to multiple applications from different providers.

- **Power BI**: Highlights the information that matters with custom reports. You will be able to find virtually anything that is hidden at first glance in your data.

- **Power Virtual Agents**: Allows you to build bots without writing code, in a natural and intuitive way:

Figure 9.1 – Power Platform representation

In this chapter, we will cover Power Automate in detail and will learn how to use Power BI and Power Virtual Agents through scenarios that you can adjust and adapt to your reality.

Learning Power Automate and Microsoft Lists

Power Automate allows you to create workflows in Microsoft 365 and automate processes and respond to actions and events. This includes cloud flows, which we will cover in this section, as well as desktop flows, which are used to perform repetitive actions on actual devices. Any flow mentioned within this chapter is a cloud flow, and we will refer to them as flows only.

Power Automate uses so-called connectors to connect to the various offerings within the Microsoft cloud, such as SharePoint, Outlook, Azure, and others, as well as external systems. When using Power Automate, you will not find any connector specific to Microsoft Lists. Instead, you will need to use the connectors built for SharePoint that allow you to connect to any list, team, or personnel.

> **What is a Power Automate connector?**
>
> A Power Automate connector allows you to read or write information from a Microsoft or third-party solution without writing code, allowing you to create all operations from a graphical user interface.

To start using Power Automate with Microsoft Lists, you can observe one of the following approaches:

- From the list itself, by clicking the **Power Automate** option located in the **Integrate** menu in the command bar, as shown in the following screenshot. This option allows you to create a flow from one of the templates provided, and acts as a shortcut to the template you select:

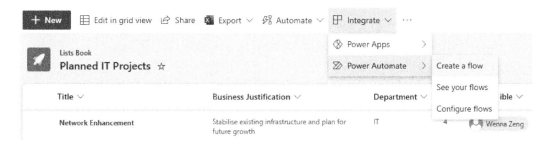

Figure 9.2 – Creating a flow from a list context

- Start a flow from scratch or based on an existing template from the Power Automate portal located at `https://flow.microsoft.com`. From here, you then need to define which list you want to connect to, something that is already taken care of in the aforementioned approach:

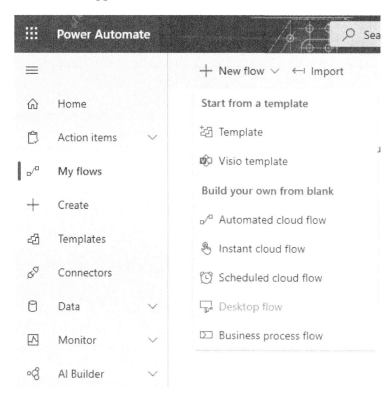

Figure 9.3 – Creating a flow from the Power Automate portal

There is no difference in the available functionality of the flow that gets created in these two approaches, so you can use either of them. Furthermore, whether you start with a completely blank flow or use one of the templates provided, it does not impact what you can do within the workflow. You can still customize it according to your needs after you have started setting it up.

> **Learn more about Power Automate**
>
> Within this book, we are only scratching the surface of what can be done with Power Automate. It is highly recommended that you check the available online training offerings from Microsoft for more information and training material. To get started, visit the **Power Automate** portal at `https://flow.microsoft.com` and select the **Learn** option in the navigation. Selecting the Documentation option from this list will bring you to the central homepage of the existing Microsoft Power Automate documentation, where you can find all relevant in-depth information on everything related to Power Automate, including how to create different kinds of flows, how to use the different connectors, and more.

Another important thing to know is that there are different types of flows that you can create, which help with different scenarios:

- **Automated flows** run automatically once a specific event has occurred. For example, this can be used when a new item has been added to a list.

- **Instant flows** run when a manual action is undertaken, such as clicking a specific button. This can be a button added to a list via column formatting or a button clicked in a Power App. Additionally, instant flows can be started from a list item directly.

- Lastly, **Scheduled flows** run on a defined schedule. As an example, you can run a flow on a daily basis to archive list items to another list.

A flow contains a trigger, which indicates when the workflow should get started, as well as actions, which are the steps that get performed as part of the workflow. Both of these components will be explored in the context of Microsoft Lists in the following subsections.

Understanding Power Automate triggers

When you create a new flow in Power Automate, you need to define when the flow should start, as indicated by a trigger. Depending on the type of flow you create, different triggers are available. For a scheduled flow, the trigger is based on a defined recurrence, such as daily at a specific time, every 5 minutes, and similar. For instant flows, the trigger will be a specific action performed outside of Power Automate, such as clicking a button. Automated flows respond to events that occur in a specified system that the flow is connected to.

When you create an automated flow, there is a range of triggers available for the SharePoint connector. You can easily see them by creating a new automated flow, and then entering *SharePoint* into the trigger search box:

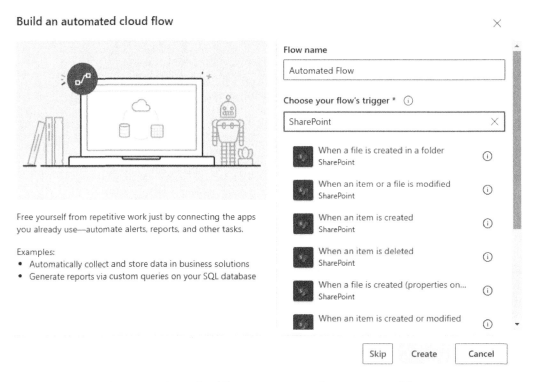

Figure 9.4 – Example of SharePoint triggers for an automated flow

The triggers listed include triggers both for lists and libraries, with the difference being that all triggers work for libraries, whereas the triggers that mention a *file* work for libraries only, and not for lists.

For Microsoft Lists, you can therefore make use of the following triggers:

- **When an item or a file is modified** runs when changes to an existing item are made. As an example, this can be used when you want to receive an immediate email notification regarding changes.

- **When an item is created** gets started whenever a new item gets created in your list. You could use this to start an approval process for new entries.

- **When an item is created or modified** is a combination of the two previous triggers and gets executed for both scenarios.

- **When an item is deleted** could be used to monitor whether entries get removed.

By comparison, for an instant flow, there is only one trigger directly related to Microsoft Lists, which is called **For a selected item**:

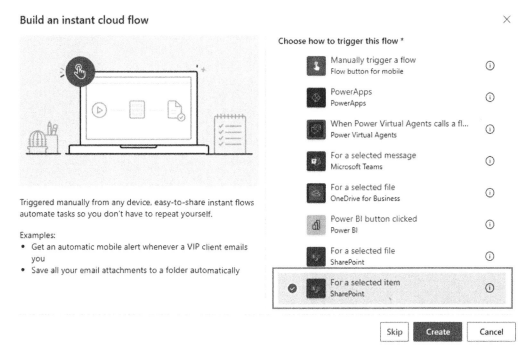

Figure 9.5 – For a selected item

As instant flows get executed manually, this trigger simply helps to start the workflow from a selected item in a list. After you set up one or more instant flows on a list, they are shown in the **Automate** menu of your list and can be started from there after you have selected an item:

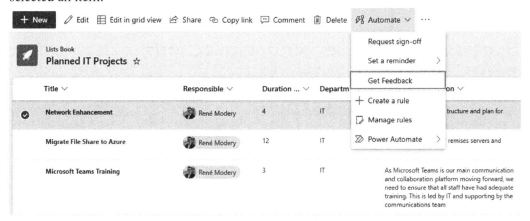

Figure 9.6 – Starting an instant flow called Get Feedback on the selected list item

Lastly, scheduled flows can be created to run regularly on a defined time pattern. When you create one, you select at what time you want to start the flow, and how often it should be repeated. You can define any schedule, from running every second up to running every month:

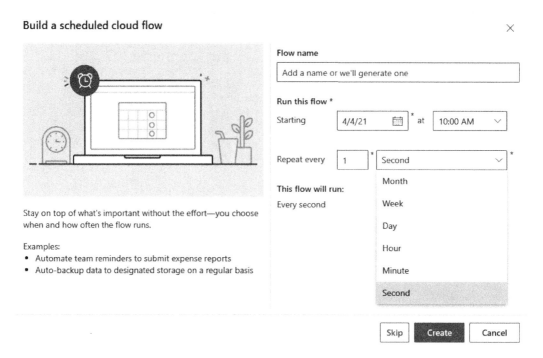

Figure 9.7 – Setting up a scheduled flow to run periodically

Once you have defined the type of flow you want to create and the corresponding trigger action, as a next step, you will want to perform various actions as part of it.

Understanding Power Automate actions

Actions in Power Automate are used to perform individual steps in your workflow. As mentioned, you can use a large range of connectors to connect to different systems, with each connector providing different actions.

For Microsoft Lists, the SharePoint connector gives you the following actions:

- **Get item** can be used to retrieve a single item with its details. For example, when you execute an instant flow on a list item, this action will be needed to retrieve the selected item's details.

- **Get items** helps you to retrieve a list of items. You would usually use this in combination with a filter that you provide, such as when you want to retrieve all items that were created within a specific timeframe.

- **Create item** allows you to create a new item in the specified list.

  To remove a specific item from a list, use the **Delete item** action.

- **Update item** gives you the option to make changes to an existing item.

- If you want to attach a file to a list item, you can make use of the **Add attachment** action.

- To see a list of changes that were made to an item during a specific period, the **Get changes for an item or a file (properties only)** action can be used.

- **Get Lists** gives you the possibility to retrieve all lists from a selected SharePoint site.

- **Get List views** helps to retrieve all views for a given list.

- If you want to share an item with someone else and grant them permissions, the **Grant access to an item or a folder** action is available, which allows you to also specify a custom message that can be sent to the people you share the item with.

- Lastly, **Stop sharing an item or a file** removes any sharing links to a list item.

Referencing Microsoft Lists in Power Automate triggers and actions

When you use the SharePoint connector, the available triggers and actions ask you to provide a SharePoint site where your list is stored. While it tries to recommend previously used sites to you, the suggestion list may not include the site in which your list is located. In such a scenario, you can use the following URLs (replace the examples below accordingly with your own site's URL):

For a SharePoint site, copy and paste the full URL to it. It will look similar to `https://contoso.sharepoint.com/sites/sitename`.

For personal lists that are located in your own OneDrive, use the OneDrive URL similar to `https://contoso-my.sharepoint.com/personal/username_contoso_com`.

These actions alone are naturally not sufficient to create useful workflows. There is a large range of additional actions available from the other connectors, which can be combined with the actions above. A list of currently available connectors can be found on `https://docs.microsoft.com/en-us/connectors`. As Microsoft and other companies regularly update the available connectors and actions, it is recommended to review them from time to time to see whether there are new, useful functionalities available.

Implementing a sample notification flow

Now that you have learned how triggers and actions work, we will look at how they can be combined to create a full, useful workflow. The scenario we are trying to achieve is to send a daily summary of projects from the *Planned IT Projects* list, which shows any projects that were added in the past 24 hours, any projects that start in the next 7 days, and any projects that are currently in progress. This summary should be sent every morning to a predefined list of recipients:

1. To get started, navigate to `https://flow.microsoft.com`.

2. Select **My flows** from the navigation, and choose **Scheduled cloud flow** from the **New flow** dropdown:

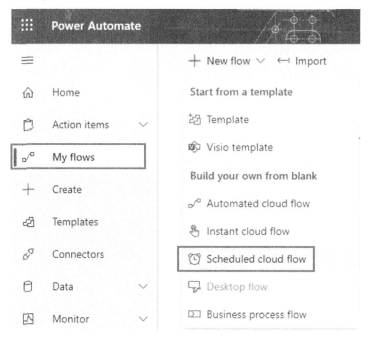

Figure 9.8 – Creating a new scheduled cloud flow

3. Give your flow a name, and schedule it to be run daily at 8 A.M:

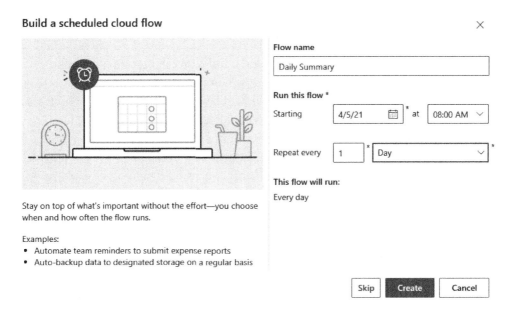

Figure 9.9 – Scheduling the Daily Summary flow to run every day at 8 A.M.

4.   Click **Create** to create your flow. On the next screen, select **New Step** to add a new action. Find the **Get items** action from the SharePoint connector, as we want to retrieve the items in the *Planned IT Projects* list that were created in the past 24 hours:

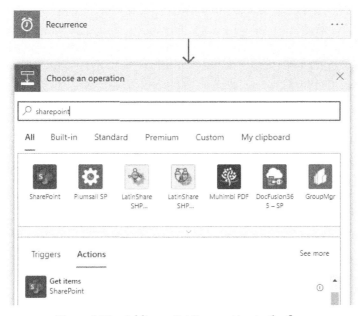

Figure 9.10 – Adding a Get items action to the flow

5. Once added, you need to select the SharePoint site where your list is located, as well as the list itself.

6. Clicking on **Show advanced options**, some additional configuration options are shown. Here, you can add some filters to the **Get items** action, which allow us to add the required date filter. In the **Filter Query** field, we can provide an appropriate *OData* filter to only retrieve items where the **Created** field lies within the past 24 hours. *OData* is a standard protocol that is also used in SharePoint to help with querying and filtering data. You can find more detailed information in the Microsoft documentation. Within this book, we will keep its usage short and provide appropriate explanations.

    In the field, type in `Created ge`. *Created* refers to the list column that stores the timestamp when the item was created, and *ge* means "greater than or equal to." Next, click on **Add dynamic content**. In the new dialog that appears, you have the option to reference a range of expressions, including calculations. As we want to do a date calculation, we simply ascertain the current time via the `utcNow()` expression and subtract one day from it. The corresponding full expression is `addDays(utcNow(),-1)`. Click on **OK** to add your expression to the **Filter Query** field. Lastly, put the dynamic expression you just added within single quotes. This means that after the expression has been evaluated, its value will be put within single quotation marks, and is thus a valid term within the *OData* filter.

    Note that when you copy the full field, including the dynamic expression, you will retrieve a code snippet that looks like this: `Created ge '@{addDays(utcNow(),-1)}'`. `@{ }` indicates that a dynamic expression follows. If you need to use similar filter values for multiple actions, you can thus easily copy and paste them as well as modify them when required:

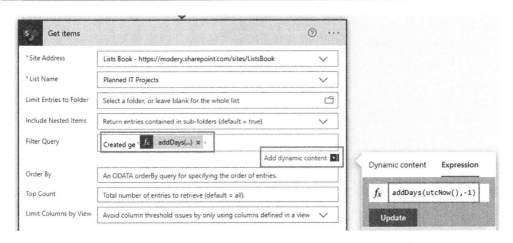

Figure 9.11 – Applying a date filter to get the Get items action

7. Next, we want to retrieve all projects that start in the next 7 days. Again, add a
    Get items action and update the **Filter Query** field. This time, we are restricting
    the items to all those that have a **Project Start** date between now and 7 days in the
    future. Similar to the previous filter, we can create an *OData* filter to restrict the data
    range: `ProjectStart ge '@{utcNow()}' and ProjectStart le '@{addDays(utcNow(),7)}'`.

8. Lastly, we want to get a list of all running projects, which we know have a start
    date in the past, as well as an end date in the future. Thus, our OData filter
    is `ProjectStart le '@{utcNow()}' and ProjectEnd ge '@{utcNow() }'`.

9. When you add multiple actions of the same type, they will use the same name with
    an incremental number behind them, such as *Get items 2*. You can click on the
    ellipsis in the top-right corner of an action and select **Rename** to provide a more
    descriptive name.

10. Now that we have retrieved the data, we want to select specific fields and create some tables from them. Find the **Select** action, which allows you to take an array or a list, such as what we have retrieved, and map parts of its data to new values. What we will simply do is to select specific fields only for each item retrieved, and have them shown in a table. When you click in the **From** field, the **Dynamic content** dialog is shown, from where you can select an output from a previous step. For example, you can select the value from a previous *Get items* step, which translates into the actual list of projects retrieved during that step. Additionally, when you select an **Enter value** field for the **Map** options, you can also select the corresponding columns from your list, or even create composites or other data transformations. We will show both the project start and end dates in the same table column here. In the **Enter key** field, enter an appropriate new name to be used in your table. For example, while the **Title** field is used internally within SharePoint, we want to display it as *Project Name* here:

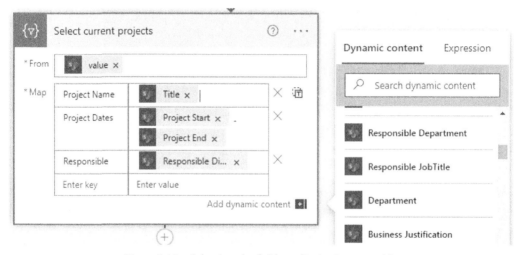

Figure 9.12 – Selecting the fields to display in your table

11. Add similar **Select** steps for our three different sets of data that we retrieved.

12. Next, add three **Create HTML table** actions. This action will take an array as input, and turn it into an HTML table. For each action, select one of the three previously created **Select** actions as input.

13. Now that we have retrieved the relevant data and formatted it, we want to send it out as an email. We can use the **Send an email (V2)** action from the **Office 365 Outlook** connector. Enter a subject and recipients, and create an email body. As before, you can make use of previously generated output from other actions as part of the dynamic content. In our scenario, we use the generated HTML tables to place them in the email body:

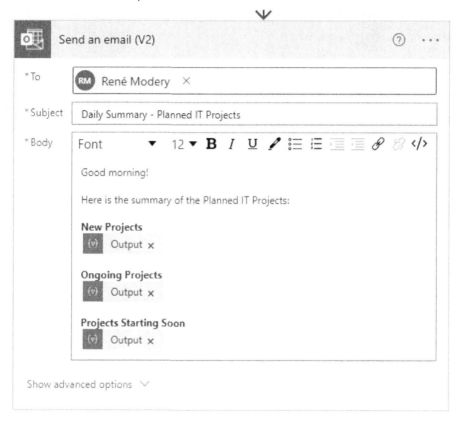

Figure 9.13 – Configuring the Send an email (V2) action

14. Any time during the development of your flow, you can use the **Test flow** functionality to verify whether it is working as expected. Once you have completed the full setup as per the preceding steps, it is recommended to confirm that the email gets sent successfully with the right data. Click on **Test** in the top-right corner, and in the following dialog, select **Manually** and then click the **Test** button. Confirm via the **Run flow** button to run a manual execution of your flow:

Figure 9.14 – Overview of the Daily Summary flow

You can rearrange the steps performed within your flow at any time. Steps that make use of an output from a previous step will naturally have to start only after the referenced step is complete, but other steps can be done in different orders. *Figure 9.14* shows an overview of all the steps in our Daily Summary flow, and how you can rearrange them according to the data that is being transformed. We first retrieve the data for new projects, select the fields, and then create a table, followed by the projects that are starting soon and those that are running currently.

Regardless of the order of these hypothetical groups of steps, the email that gets generated in the end will always contain the same structure and components based on the content you created:

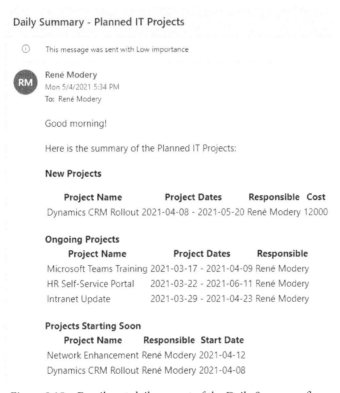

Figure 9.15 – Email sent daily as part of the Daily Summary flow

Another option in terms of receiving notifications is through Microsoft Teams. You can easily set up a flow that posts a new message to a specific person or inside a specific channel. Let's assume that you have an IT Steering Committee that is regularly reviewing new projects, and which uses Teams to collaborate on any related activities. A simple example that can be implemented is to have a so-called adaptive card posted into the IT Steering Committee Team whenever a new project is added to the list, so that the members of this team get notified without having to receive yet another email.

Adaptive cards provide a way of sharing and displaying information by providing structure and content in JSON format, without having to define the corresponding HTML and CSS rendering. This way, when posted to Microsoft Teams, for example, Teams will manage the rendering and allow a consistent UI pattern. To learn more about adaptive cards and using a designer to create your own, visit `https://adaptivecards.io/`.

For the example mentioned, you can set up a new automatic flow that gets triggered whenever a new item gets added to the *Planned IT Projects* list. The only other action required is called **Post adaptive card in a chat or channel** from the Microsoft Teams connector. Within this action, you select the Team and Channel where you want to post the adaptive card and provide the relevant JSON content. *Figure 9.16* shows a sample adaptive card with dynamic content coming from our list:

Figure 9.16 – Posting an adaptive card to a Microsoft Teams channel

Once a new project has been added, the flow runs and posts the corresponding content into the Channel, where Teams members will receive a corresponding notification and can reply to the post if they wish:

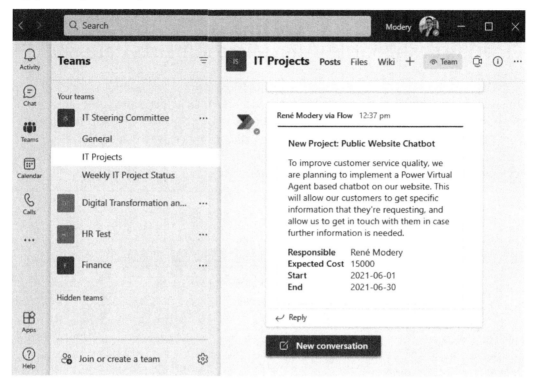

Figure 9.17 – Adaptive card posted in Microsoft Teams via Power Automate

As can be seen, we can get a useful summary email with just a few actions in a flow, and even post updates directly into Microsoft Teams with very little effort. Depending on requirements, more could be done here, such as a better formatting of the email, a dynamic list of recipients, or even a copy of the email itself getting posted to a Teams channel. More information on how to leverage Power Automate better can be found in Microsoft's documentation, to which a reference was provided at the beginning of this section.

Exploring Power BI and Microsoft Lists

Power BI is Microsoft's business intelligence solution to connect to, model, and visualize data. It allows you to connect to different data sources, transform your data, and create models from it, and finally visualize it in appropriate and appealing dashboards for your audience. You can use it to get further insights into your existing data and make decisions based on the information obtained.

It should be noted that Power BI is not available as a free version and requires a license. Depending on your existing Office 365 licensing, this may or may not be available to you. However, to get started with exploring it and its possibilities, you can use the free trial option.

Creating dashboards using Microsoft Lists data and Power BI

The best way to quickly understand what Power BI can offer to get more value out of Microsoft Lists is through an example. To get started, open the Power BI Desktop application. You then have the option to retrieve data from a range of data sources, including Microsoft Lists. In the **Get data** dialog, under the **Online Services** category, you will find the **SharePoint Online List** connector:

Figure 9.18 – Getting data from a SharePoint online list in Power BI

Once you click the **Connect** button, you will need to provide a SharePoint site URL in which your list and its data reside, as well as Microsoft account credentials to connect to the site:

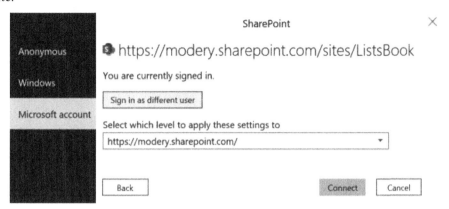

Figure 9.19 – Connecting to the SharePoint site from Power BI

After you have connected successfully, the **Navigator** dialog will show you all the available lists and libraries and the site you provided. This includes backend lists such as **appdata** or **appfiles**, but also any Microsoft list that you created. Once you select a list, a preview will be shown on the right-hand side so that you can first verify that the data inside is relevant for your Power BI report, and can then proceed with loading the data into it:

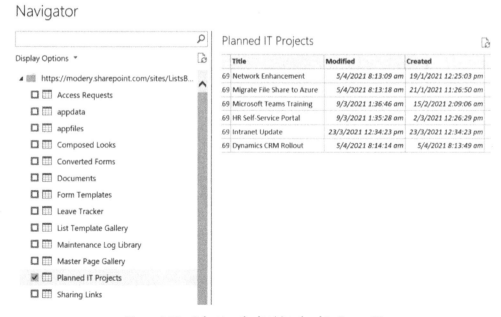

Figure 9.20 – Selecting the list(s) to load in Power BI

The data from your list is loaded into a table in your Power BI report. It is important to know that after you have loaded data into Power BI, you can do further transformations. For example, you could change the data type, create new columns with additional information, format your data, and more. A common transformation is to change the data type of an imported column from a string to an integer, so that you can perform calculations with it. To extend the existing data further, we can use calculated columns to create new data based on a formula. The value of a calculated column is evaluated per row in the data. For our *Planned IT Projects* list, we add a calculated column to compute the average weekly project cost, which is defined as the total project cost divided by the duration of the project in weeks:

```
AverageWeeklyCost = ROUND('Planned IT
Projects'[ExpectedCost]/'Planned IT
Projects'[Durationinweeks],0)
```

If you want to perform calculations across all of your data, or a filtered range of your data, you can use measures. An example of a measure is the calculation of the total cost of your projects. You define it as the sum of all expected costs, but when you apply filters within your dashboard, such as showing only projects from the IT department, meaning less of your data is shown, only the filtered values are used for the calculation:

```
TotalProjectCost = sum('Planned IT Projects'[ExpectedCost])
```

> **Transform, shape, and model data in Power BI**
>
> The information provided in this chapter about how to transform your data in Power BI is kept relatively short. To learn more about the possibilities available to you, including how to create your own measures and calculated columns, visit https://docs.microsoft.com/en-us/power-bi/transform-model/.

After you have transformed your data and created some data models accordingly, you can add various visualizations to the dashboard in your report. Visualization is a way to display your data graphically in a report. Examples of this include pie charts, line charts, cards, and more. Besides a large number of out-of-the-box visualizations available directly in Power BI, you can also easily add additional visualizations provided by Microsoft and other companies through AppSource. Additionally, you can also add filters to a report, for example, through visualizations that are called slicers.

With these visualization capabilities and the data from your list, you can create a dashboard to provide further insights:

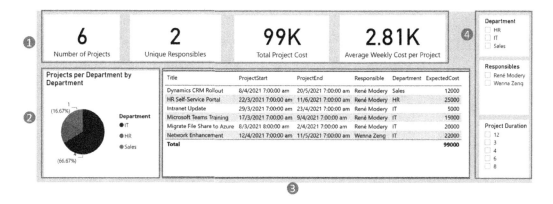

Figure 9.21 – Sample Power BI dashboard with data from a list

Figure 9.21 shows a sample dashboard with data from the *Planned IT Projects* list and various visualizations:

1. A couple of cards were added at the top to provide some quick overall insights into the data, such as the number of projects and responsibles, as well as the total project cost and average weekly cost per project.

2. A pie chart is used to show the distribution of the projects across the departments.

3. A table is used to show some relevant data extracts in a table format.

4. Lastly, a couple of slicers were added to provide filtering capabilities.

When you use a slicer, the data in the dashboard will be filtered accordingly. Selecting the **IT** option from the **Department** slicer, the dashboard will then only show the data for the projects that were categorized as IT projects, and all visualizations will be updated, as shown in *Figure 9.22*:

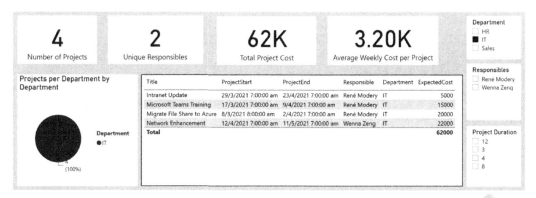

Figure 9.22 – Power BI dashboard showing a filtered view

You can also add an additional dashboard to a report to create different screens for different purposes. For example, to show more financial-related information, you could set up a dashboard as shown in *Figure 9.23*. Here, the amount of text is kept to a minimum, and the focus is more on visually appealing visualizations. These visualizations will help the viewer to get a better understanding of the financial impact of the projects, which projects are relatively short, but with relatively high costs, and other things besides:

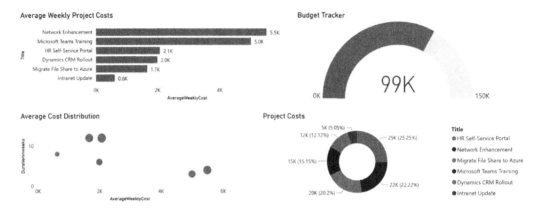

Figure 9.23 – Power BI dashboard showing different visualizations

While the creation of a simple dashboard can be done relatively quickly, it should be noted that the main purpose of the dashboard should be defined first – what should be achieved with the dashboard, who will consume the information, and how will this benefit the individual, the team, or the organization?

We still encourage you to explore Power BI further to learn more about its capabilities and possibilities and suggest the official Microsoft documentation as a starting point: `https://docs.microsoft.com/en-us/power-bi/`.

Learning about Power Virtual Agents and Microsoft Lists

With Power Virtual Agents, you can create bots that use information stored in Microsoft Lists to reply to users. The integrations between Microsoft Lists, Power Virtual Agents, and Power Automate make the interaction with the list data a breeze.

> **Note**
>
> Power Virtual Agents is not included in the Microsoft 365 plans, and it requires a separate license in order for it to work. More information about prices can be found on the Power Virtual Agents website: `https://powervirtualagents.microsoft.com/`.

In this section, you will learn how to create a bot that replies to the end user with the information that is stored in the list. Although the process described does not cover all the Power Virtual Agents features in detail, it rather focuses on integration with Microsoft Lists.

Scenario

Diane is responsible for all the new hires in the HR department, and to make her work easier, she has created a list in Microsoft Lists to track the status of new recruitments. Diane wants to be able to get the recruitment status of a candidate from a bot, instead of looking for it in the list.

The scenario described above can be achieved using the Recruitment tracker list template, provided in Microsoft Lists, connected to Power Virtual Agents by doing the following:

1. Start by opening Power Virtual Agents: `https://powerva.microsoft.com/`.

2. Once inside the web application, click on the robot icon to open the **Bots** menu, as shown in *Figure 9.24*.

3. On the vertical pane, click on **New bot** as follows:

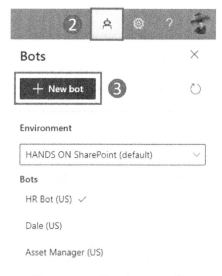

Figure 9.24 – Creating a new bot

4. In the **Create a new bot** popup (as shown in *Figure 9.25*), provide a name, language, and select the environment where you want to create it.

5. Click on **Create**, as shown in the following screenshot:

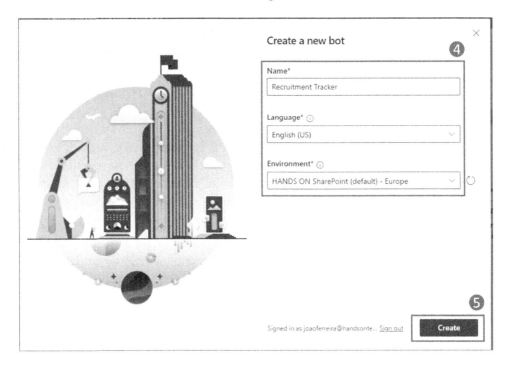

Figure 9.25 – Defining bot details

6. On the bot home page, click on **Topics** in the vertical menu.

7. Click on **New Topic**.

8. Provide a couple of trigger phrases that you would like to use.

9. Click on **Go to authoring canvas**, as shown in the following screenshot:

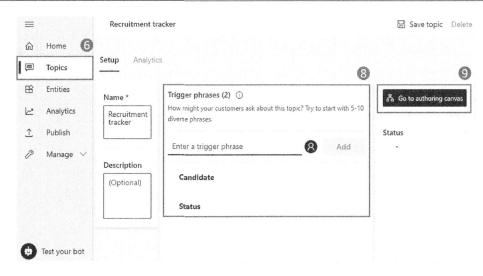

Figure 9.26 – Creating trigger phrases

10. In the **Message** box (as shown in *Figure 9.27*), type a greeting message that you would like the bot to say when you ask a question.

11. Click on the plus (**+**) icon and then click in the **Ask a question** field, as shown in the following screenshot:

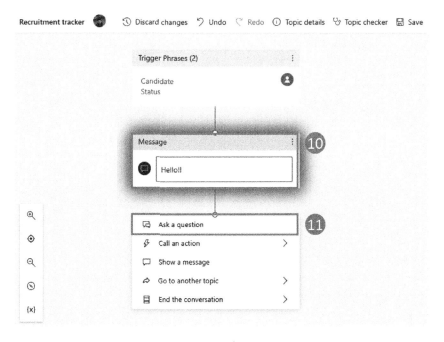

Figure 9.27 – Ask a question

12. Type the question that the user will see when the bot is triggered.

13. In the **Identify** dropdown (as shown in *Figure 9.28*), select **User's entire response**.

14. In the **Save response as** field (as shown in *Figure 9.28*), provide a name for the variable where the reply will be stored.

15. Click on the plus (+) icon and then click in the **Add a condition** field, as shown in the following screenshot:

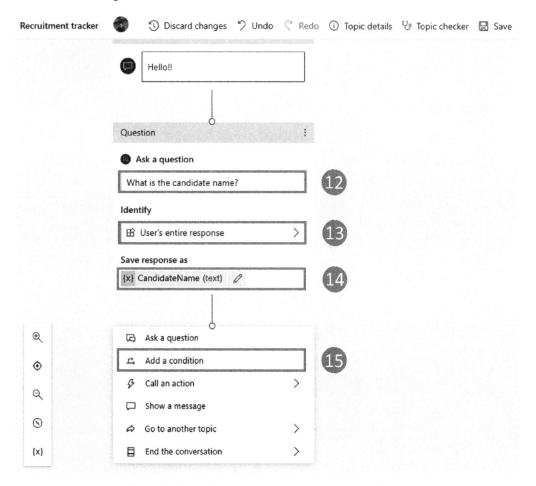

Figure 9.28 – Asking a question and creating a condition

16. In the left condition, select the **CandidateName** variable (as shown in *Figure 9.29*), and then in the dropdown, select **has value**.

17. Click on the plus (+) icon and then click in the **Call an action** field (as shown in *Figure 9.29*).

18. On the menu, click on **Create a flow**, as shown in the following screenshot:

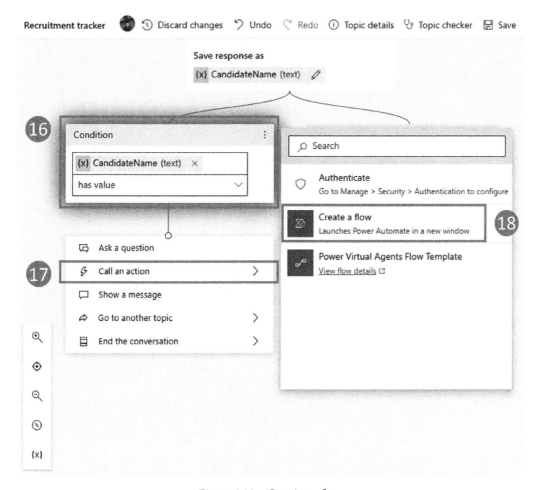

Figure 9.29 – Creating a flow

This action will open Power Automate in a new tab with the Power Virtual Agents connector already added.

19. Click on **Add an input**, select **Text**, and then provide a name.

20. Click on the plus (+) icon between both steps and then click in the **Add an action** field as follows:

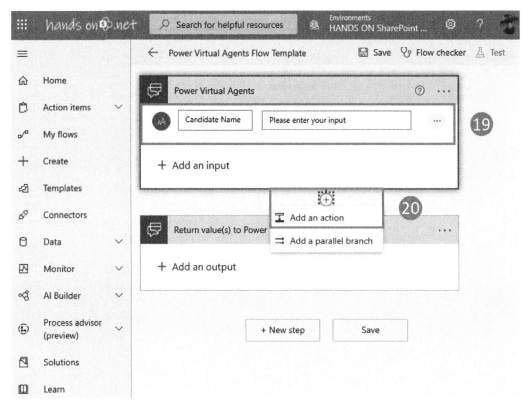

Figure 9.30 – Adding an action

21. Select the **SharePoint Get items** action.

22. Provide the site address of the site where the list is stored, as shown in *Figure 9.31*.

23. Select the **List name** field, as shown in *Figure 9.31*.

24. Click on **Show advanced options**.

25. In the **Filter Query** field, type `Title eq ''`, as shown in *Figure 9.31*.

26. Click between the apostrophes and select the **Dynamic content** list. Then, select the **Candidate Name** field as follows:

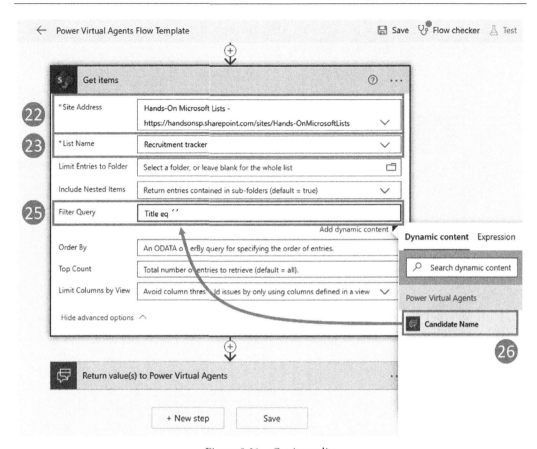

Figure 9.31 – Get items list

27. Click on the plus (+) icon between both steps and then click in the **Add an action** field.

28. Select **Initialize variable**, as shown in *Figure 9.32*.

29. Provide a name and select the **String** type, as shown in *Figure 9.32*.

30. Click on the plus (+) icon between both steps and then click in the **Add an action** field, as shown in *Figure 9.32*.

31. Select **Set variable** (as shown in *Figure 9.32*). As SharePoint gets items, an action can return more than one result, so **Apply to each** is added automatically to the set variable.

32. Select the variable you initialized in the previous step, and then select **Progress Value** in the **Value** field, as follows:

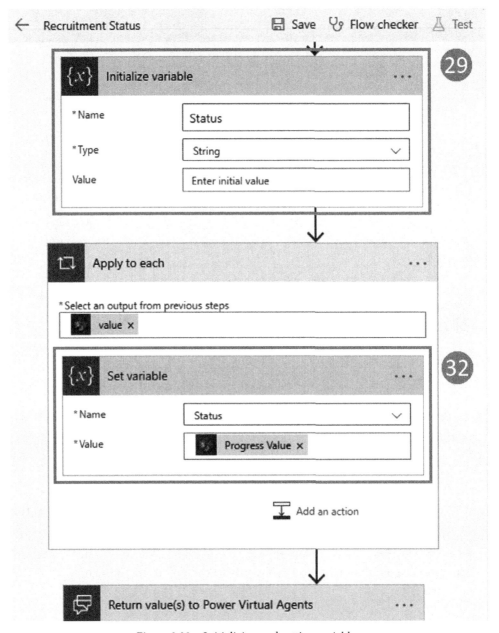

Figure 9.32 – Initializing and setting variables

33. Expand the **Return value(s) to Power Virtual Agents** field, as shown in *Figure 9.33*.

34. Click in the **Add an output** field, as shown in *Figure 9.33*.

35. Provide a name and select the variable defined previously:

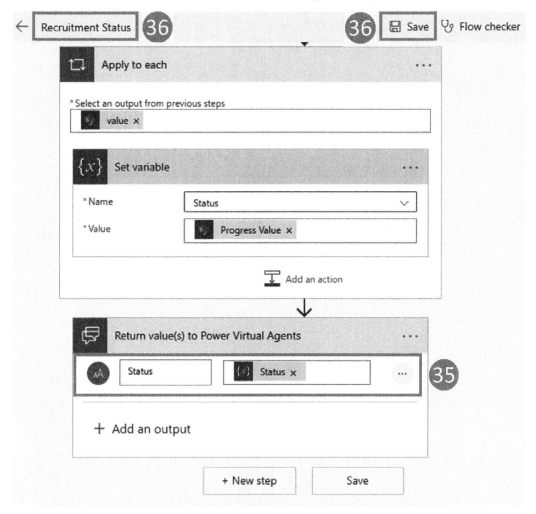

Figure 9.33 – Returning a value to Power Virtual Agents

36. Provide a name to the flow and hit **Save**, as shown in *Figure 9.34*.

37. Return to Power Virtual Agents.

38. Click on the plus (+) icon and then click in the **Call an action** field, as shown in *Figure 9.34*.

39. On the menu, select the flow (in our **Recruitment Status** scenario) you have just created, which is shown as follows:

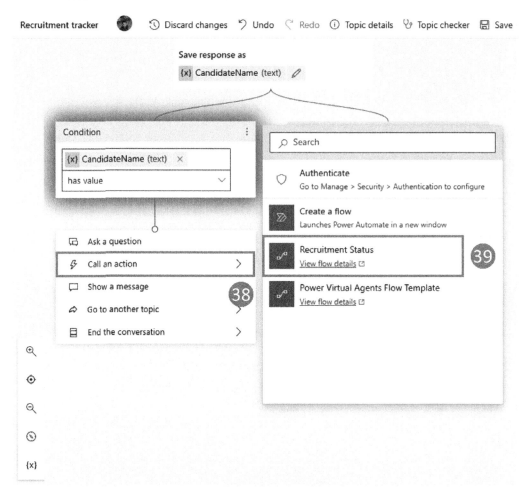

Figure 9.34 – Selecting a flow

40. Select the variable, for example, **CandidateName**, as shown in *Figure 9.35*.

41. Click on the plus (+) icon, and then click in the **Show a message** field.

42. Type the message with the reply from the list as follows:

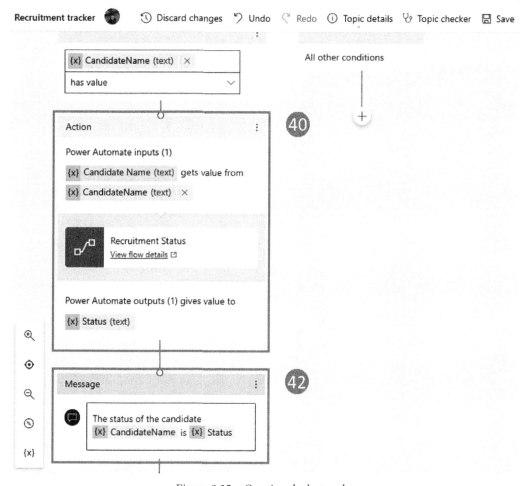

Figure 9.35 – Creating the bot reply

43. Click in the **Test bot** field and start using it as follows:

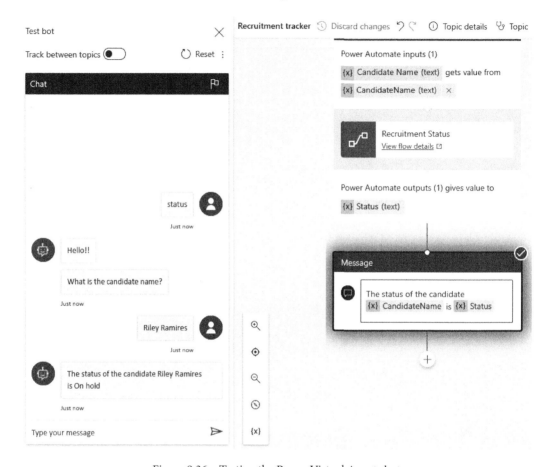

Figure 9.36 – Testing the Power Virtual Agents bot

As you can see in the preceding screenshot, the bot can follow the flow you have defined and obtain data from the list. Certainly, there were a few clicks involved in the process, but everything was built without using a single line of code.

If you want to embed your bot in other applications, we recommend that you take a look at this site: `https://docs.microsoft.com/en-us/power-virtual-agents/publication-connect-bot-to-web-channels`.

Summary

In this chapter, we explored how you can use the Power Platform, specifically Power Automate, Power BI, and Power Virtual Agents, to get more value out of your Microsoft Lists. You should now be equipped with a high-level overview of the capabilities of each of the offerings, and be able to start using them in combination with Microsoft Lists.

In the next chapter, we will further explore what kinds of options are available to manage Microsoft Lists programmatically through PowerShell including configuring tenant-wide settings, and managing list data in batches.

10
Microsoft Lists for Admins and Advanced Users

So far, we have covered how you can create your own lists, including creating them based on a template, how to enhance them visually, and how to integrate them with the Power Platform.

If you are an administrator in your organization or an advanced user, this chapter will give you more information on the tools needed to manage global Microsoft Lists settings in your tenant, how to manage list content via PowerShell, and more.

This chapter will cover the following topics:

- How to manage global Microsoft Lists settings as an administrator
- Using PnP PowerShell to manage Microsoft Lists and content
- Creating Microsoft Lists templates via PnP PowerShell

Technical requirements

You can find the code files present in this chapter on GitHub at `https://github.com/PacktPublishing/Hands-On-Microsoft-Lists/tree/main/Chapter10`.

How to manage Microsoft Lists as an administrator

As a **Global Administrator** or **SharePoint Administrator** in your tenant, you are able to manage two general Microsoft Lists configuration settings. These are only configurable via PowerShell and not through the browser, and you will thus need to install the **SharePoint Online Management Shell** module for PowerShell, through which the corresponding commands are provided.

> **SharePoint Online Management Shell**
>
> The PowerShell commands in this section require the SharePoint Online Management Shell module, which is provided by Microsoft. It can easily be installed on a Windows computer, but to run the different cmdlets, you will require either SharePoint Administrator rights or Global Administrator rights in your Office 365 tenants.
>
> Information on how to install the module can be found here: `https://docs.microsoft.com/en-us/powershell/sharepoint/sharepoint-online/connect-sharepoint-online`.

The first setting that you can manage allows you to control whether members of your tenant can create personal lists. If enabled, when someone creates a new list, the list creation dialog will only show SharePoint sites in the **Save to** section; the **My lists** option will be removed.

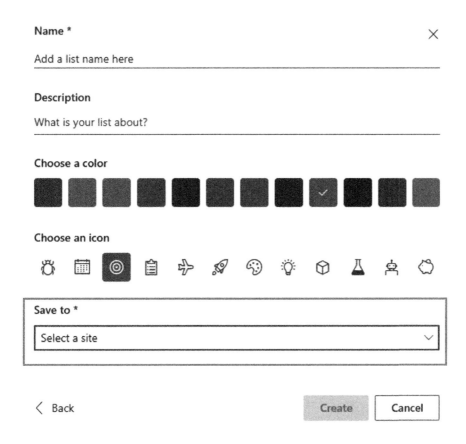

Figure 10.1 – List creation dialog with personal list creation turned off

While, by default, you have the option to create a list either in a SharePoint site or in your OneDrive, there may be reasons why you want to restrict creation in the latter. If you want to do so, you can disable this by opening a PowerShell window and executing the following code:

```
Connect-SPOService -Url https://mytenant-admin.sharepoint.com
Set-SPOTenant -DisablePersonalListCreation $true
```

The Connect-SPOService cmdlet requires the Url parameter where you need to provide your tenant's SharePoint Admin Center URL. This is the first command you need to run in order to connect to your tenant. The Set-SPOTenant command allows you to manage some general settings of your tenant, among them the mentioned functionality to define whether personal lists can be created through the DisablePersonalListCreation property. Setting this property to $true will disable it, whereas setting it to $false will re-enable it.

If you want to check your tenant's current setting, you can run the following command:

```
Get-SPOTenant | select DisablePersonalListCreation
```

The second setting that is currently available allows you to manage the available out-of-the-box templates that can be selected during list creation, as seen in *Chapter 3, Microsoft Lists Core Features.*

If you want to disable a specific template, you can provide the template's ID as part of the `DisableModernListTemplateIds` parameter while executing `Set-SPOTenant`. The IDs for the templates are listed in the following table:

Template	Template ID
Issue tracker	'C147E310-FFB3-0CDF-B9A3-F427EE0FF1CE'
Employee onboarding	'D4C4DAA7-1A90-00C6-8D20-242ACB0FF1CE'
Event itinerary	'3465A758-99E6-048B-AB94-7E24CA0FF1CE'
Asset manager	'D2EDA86E-6F3C-0700-BE3B-A408F10FF1CE'
Recruitment tracker	'3A7C53BE-A128-0FF9-9F97-7B6F700FF1CE'
Travel requests	'C51CF376-87CF-0E8F-97FF-546BC60FF1CE'
Work progress tracker	'B117A022-9F8B-002D-BDA8-FA266F0FF1CE'
Content scheduler	'9A429811-2AB5-07BC-B5A0-2DE9590FF1CE'
Incidents	'E3BEEF0B-B3B5-0698-ABB2-6A8E910FF1CE'
Patient care coordination	'0134C13D-E537-065B-97D1-6BC46D0FF1CE'
Loans	'7C920B56-2D7A-02DA-94B2-57B46E0FF1CE'

For example, to turn off the Issue tracker template, you would run the following command:

```
Set-SPOTenant -DisableModernListTemplateIds 'C147E310-FFB3-
0CDF-B9A3-F427EE0FF1CE'
```

The list creation dialog will then be updated accordingly and only show those list templates that are still enabled:

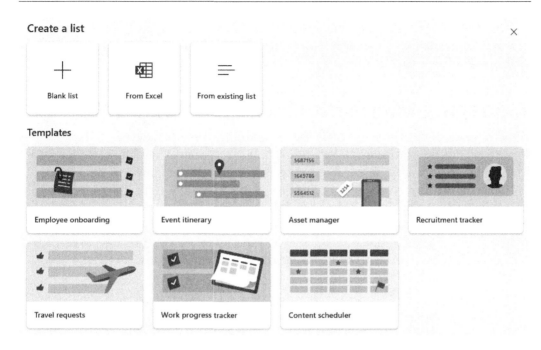

Figure 10.2 – List creation dialog with the Issue tracker template disabled

To turn a template back on again, simply use the `EnableModernListTemplateIds` parameter with the corresponding ID:

```
Set-SPOTenant -EnableModernListTemplateIds 'C147E310-FFB3-0CDF-
B9A3-F427EE0FF1CE'
```

And to get an overview of all templates that are currently disabled, you can run the following command:

```
Get-SPOTenant | select DisabledModernListTemplateIds
```

The following screenshot shows the currently disabled list templates:

```
Administrator: Windows PowerShell                    —    □    ×
PS C:\> Get-SPOTenant | select DisabledModernListTemplateIds

DisabledModernListTemplateIds
-----------------------------
{c147e310-ffb3-0cdf-b9a3-f427ee0ff1ce}


PS C:\>
```

Figure 10.3 – PowerShell window showing all currently disabled list templates

Generally, these two settings are likely to be managed only in rare situations. The majority of organizations will keep the default configuration and allow personal list creation as well as the usage of all available templates.

Managing Microsoft Lists via PowerShell

As we have seen just now, you can use the **SharePoint Online Management Shell** PowerShell module to manage two specific settings on the tenant level for Microsoft Lists. When it comes to managing lists directly via PowerShell, this module does not provide you with any functionality. However, there is a separate module available called **PnP PowerShell** that gets maintained by Microsoft as well as active community members, which allows you to manage Microsoft 365 environments, and specifically SharePoint Online, Teams, Planner, and Power Automate. The cmdlets that are provided to manage SharePoint lists naturally also work with Microsoft Lists and will be explained in more detail in this section.

> **More information on PnP PowerShell**
>
> More information on the PnP PowerShell module, including how to install it, how to connect to SharePoint Online, and a list of all available cmdlets provided through it, is available at `https://pnp.github.io/powershell`.

With the PnP PowerShell module, you are able to access Microsoft Lists programmatically, and thus automate processes instead of performing them manually. While this may sound similar to using Power Automate, and you can often perform the same process with either tool, there are some differences between them. Depending on what you are trying to achieve, one of them may be more suitable than the other. A detailed comparison is out of scope for this chapter, and we will focus on some examples of where a PowerShell script makes sense.

Overview of PnP PowerShell cmdlets for Microsoft Lists

While the PnP PowerShell module contains more than 500 cmdlets, there are some that are specific to SharePoint lists and can thus be used with Microsoft Lists. The following table provides an overview of the most commonly used cmdlets to work with lists and list items. It should be noted that these cmdlets run in a site-specific context, and thus only return results from the site you are currently connected to via PowerShell.

Cmdlet	Description
Get-PnPList	This cmdlet retrieves all lists or a specific list from the current site
New-PnPList	You use this cmdlet to create a new list in the current site
Remove-PnPList	This cmdlet allows you to delete a specified list
Set-PnPList	If you want to update the settings or properties of a list, such as the title, this cmdlet can be used
Get-PnPListItem	You can retrieve one or more items from a specified list with this cmdlet
Add-PnPListItem	If you need to create a new list item you can use Add-PnPListItem
Remove-PnPListItem	This cmdlet is used to delete a list item
Set-PnPListItem	Lastly, if you need to update the columns of a list item, you can make use of Set-PnPListItem

The cmdlets that are used to manage list items require you to specify which list you want to operate on to ensure that you are working in the right context. To showcase the possibilities of these examples, let's retrieve our Planned IT Projects list, add a new entry, and update it:

```
Connect-PnPOnline -Url https://examples.sharepoint.com/sites/
ITProjects -Credentials (Get-Credential)

$list = Get-PnPList -Identity "Planned IT Projects"

$item = Add-PnPListItem -List $list -Values @{"Title" =
"PowerShell Training"; "Responsible" = "rene@modery.net";
"ExpectedCost" = 3500}

Set-PnPListItem -List $list -Identity $item -Values @
{"Department" = "IT"; "Durationinweeks" = 1; "ProjectStart"=
"05/03/2021"; "ProjectEnd" = "05/06/2021"}
```

First, we connect to the SharePoint site that contains our list via the Connect-PnPOnline cmdlet. Next, we use Get-PnPList to retrieve our Planned IT Projects list and store it in the variable $list. We then create a new item in this list via Add-PnPListItem and set some of the values, while storing the newly created item reference in the $item variable. Lastly, we update the item we just created via Set-PnPListItem and set a few more column values.

Referencing list columns in PnP PowerShell

List columns have both an internal name, which is a unique name that gets set up when you create the column and cannot be changed, and a display name that can be updated anytime. Usually, when you access a column programmatically such as via PowerShell, you would reference the column via its internal name to ensure that your code still works even after you renamed a column's display name.

There are different ways to determine the internal name. One of them is to sort the column for which you want to find out the internal name in a view and check the URL for the `sortField` parameter's value. For example, if we sort by `Expected Cost` in the `Planned IT Projects` list, the URL will change to something like the following: `https://example.sharepoint.com/sites/ITProjects/Lists/Planned%20IT%20Projects/test.aspx?sortField=ExpectedCost&isAscending=true`.

Based on this, we can determine that the internal name for this column is `ExpectedCost`.

As you can see, with only a few lines of code we are able to create a new item in a list and update its values:

Figure 10.4 – Creating and updating an item in a list via PnP PowerShell

For a single item, this would not make much sense, but imagine you need to create hundreds or thousands of items, for example, as part of an on-time or regular data import. This is where this functionality is most useful.

Using PnP PowerShell to perform a batch import of data

Let's assume you have an Excel spreadsheet with data of all past, current, and future projects that you want to migrate into the `Planned IT Projects` list. You plan to do so by leveraging the PowerShell cmdlets we just saw. You save the spreadsheet in CSV format so that it can easily be read and parsed in a structured manner through a PowerShell script.

	A	B	C	D	E	F	G	H
1	Title	BusinessJ	Departme	Durationi	Responsi	Expected	ProjectStart	ProjectEnd
2	DevOps	Leverage	IT	7	wenna@	17000	20/5/2021	8/7/2021
3	Azure File	Bring to th	IT	9	rene@mo	21000	13/3/2021	15/5/2021
4	Internet	Capitalize	IT	10	rene@mo	21000	17/4/2021	26/6/2021
5	Productio	Objective	HR	3	rene@mo	1000	22/4/2021	13/5/2021
6	Salesforc	Collabora	IT	3	wenna@	14000	4/4/2021	25/4/2021
7	Meeting	Credibly	Sales	2	rene@mo	5000	6/5/2021	20/5/2021
8	Laptop Re	Complete	IT	6	rene@mo	11000	10/6/2021	22/7/2021
9	PowerSh	Proactive	IT	9	wenna@	6000	3/6/2021	5/8/2021

Figure 10.5 – CSV file containing information about projects

Once we have read the preceding data in PowerShell, we can then easily loop through all entries and create a new item in our list with the corresponding data:

```
Connect-PnPOnline -Url https://examples.sharepoint.com/sites/
ITProjects -Credentials (Get-Credential)
$list = Get-PnPList -Identity "Planned IT Projects"
$csv = Import-Csv AllITProjects.csv

foreach($project in $csv) {
    Add-PnPListItem -List $list -Values @{
        "Title" = $project.Title;
        "Responsible" = $project.Responsible;
        "ExpectedCost" = $project.ExpectedCost;
        "Department" = $project.Department;
        "Durationinweeks" = $project.Durationinweeks;
        "ProjectStart"= [datetime]::ParseExact($project.
          ProjectStart,"d/M/yyyy",$null)
        "ProjectEnd" = [datetime]::ParseExact($project.
          ProjectEnd,"d/M/yyyy",$null)
    }
}
```

As before, we connect to our SharePoint site and establish a context to the list. Next, we import the data from our CSV file with the `Import-Csv` cmdlet. Lastly, we loop through all rows from the CSV file via `foreach`, and create new entries in our list with `Add-PnPListItem`. We provide a corresponding mapping for the data in the CSV file and the columns in the list as part of the `Values` parameter.

```
Windows PowerShell                                                    —    □    ✕

PS C:\> foreach($project in $csv) {
>> Add-PnPListItem -List $list -Values @{
>> "Title" = $project.Title;
>> "Responsible" = $project.Responsible;
>> "ExpectedCost" = $project.ExpectedCost;
>> "Department" = $project.Department;
>> "Durationinweeks" = $project.Durationinweeks;
>> "ProjectStart"= [datetime]::ParseExact($project.ProjectStart,"d/M/yyyy",$null)
>> "ProjectEnd" = [datetime]::ParseExact($project.ProjectEnd,"d/M/yyyy",$null)
>> }
>> }

Id    Title                            GUID
--    -----                            ----
10    DevOps Enhancements              0ff6b28f-fb14-4f86-8779-00cb6020b9e9
11    Azure Fileshare Migration        7534b87a-1276-4c53-a387-5fc4fda4dbeb
12    Internet Upgrade                 0644a075-e9ef-4d2c-90e1-f1b916128502
13    Production Planning Tool         d4f4fa93-606f-4b8a-b010-619397dc6a54
14    Salesforce Replacement           b0e0afc5-620c-4a27-ba32-f3fbc7626679
15    Meeting Room AV Equipment        2dc4db5c-cfb8-46bf-8406-44c982aff162
16    Laptop Refresh                   3a3be0d8-8c7b-42db-8ea4-352b4366c0f0
17    PowerShell Training              ca058658-fc36-4ead-8b30-b93298f7e5c6

PS C:\>
```

Figure 10.6 – Importing data from the CSV files via PowerShell

Performing a mass-update of data via PowerShell

Another good example of where using a PowerShell script is useful is updating data in a list in bulk. Imagine you were told that the `Expected Cost` estimates in the `Planned IT Projects` list need to be increased by 10 percent, as it has been discovered previous estimates were usually a bit too low. While you can factor this in easily for any new data, you will also need to update any existing data:

```
Connect-PnPOnline -Url https://examples.sharepoint.com/sites/
ITProjects -Credentials (Get-Credential)
```

```
$list = Get-PnPList -Identity "Planned IT Projects"
```

```
$items = Get-PnPListItem -List $list
```

```
foreach($item in $items) {
```

```
Write-Host "Current Expected Cost:
    $($item["ExpectedCost"])"
Write-Host "New Expected Cost:
    $($item["ExpectedCost"]*1.1)"
Set-PnPListItem -List $list -Identity $item.Id -Values @
    {"ExpectedCost" = $item["ExpectedCost"]*1.1}
}
```

After we connect to our list, we retrieve all current items via `Get-PnPListItem` and then loop through the results. For each item, we write some information on the PowerShell output window and update the item's `ExpectedCost` column by increasing it by 10 percent.

The effort to perform this change is relatively small, and performing this update takes only around 1 second per item. While it will take some run for larger lists, you can keep it running in the background while the script is updating all items.

Creating copies of a Microsoft list

The last example we want to cover in this chapter is how you can create duplicates of a list on another site. While you can create a new list based on an existing template easily directly through the UI in the list creation dialog, this is only useful if it needs to be done once or irregularly. If you need to perform this action multiple times on different sites, or even if you want to do it as part of an automated site provisioning process that involves PnP PowerShell, then the following functionality will be more valuable.

After you connect to a SharePoint site, you can download a template of a list, including all columns, designs, and views, via the `Get-PnPSiteTemplate` cmdlet. The following code shows how the `Planned IT Projects` list can be downloaded to a local file called `PlannedITProjects.pnp`:

```
Get-PnPSiteTemplate -Out PlannedITProjects.pnp -Handlers Lists
-ListsToExtract "Planned IT Projects"
```

If you intend to include existing content in the template, you can have it added to your local file by running the following cmdlet afterward:

```
Add-PnPDataRowsToSiteTemplate -Path PlannedITProjects.pnp -List
"Planned IT Projects"
```

Now that you have the template of this list, you can easily create a new instance of this list with the same name, settings, columns, and so on, on a separate site as follows:

```
Connect-PnPOnline -Url https://examples.sharepoint.com/sites/
PlannedProjects -Credentials (Get-Credential)
Invoke-PnPSiteTemplate -Path .\PlannedITProjects.pnp
```

We simply connect to the target site where the new list should be created, and then run the `Invoke-PnPSiteTemplate` cmdlet and provide it with our previously generated template. A new list based on this template will then be set up.

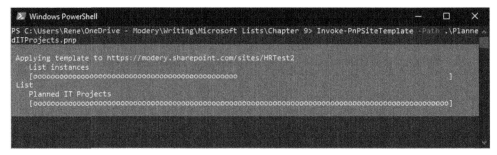

Figure 10.7 – Creating a new list based on the Planned IT Projects template via PnP PowerShell

After the list creation has succeeded, you can verify that the list has been set up correctly by opening your site in the browser. All columns, views, and other configuration elements should be present, and you are able to fill your list with new data.

Figure 10.8 – Newly created list based on the Planned IT Projects template

You could combine all this into a simple process when you are planning to roll out a new standardized list to manage projects in individual departments:

1. Initially, the individual departments provide feedback on what should be included in the list: how the data should be structured, what kind of default views are needed, how content should be formatted, and so on.

2. Once defined, you can set up a new list and demonstrate it to the stakeholders.

3. After a few iterations, and after the list setup has been confirmed, you can proceed with rolling it out to the different department sites by writing a simple PowerShell script:

   - Connect to the site where you created your demo list.

   - Download the list template with the `Get-PnPSiteTemplate` cmdlet.

   - Connect to each department site, for example, by storing the URL in an array and then looping through them, and create a new list there via the `Invoke-PnPSiteTemplate` cmdlet.

The effort required to create and run this script is far lower than creating a copy of the demo list in each target site via the list creation wizards, plus it can be modified and reused easily for additional scenarios when needed.

Summary

In this chapter, we have reviewed how advanced users and administrators can make use of different PowerShell modules and their various cmdlets to automate processes. You saw examples of managing global settings in a tenant that affect Microsoft Lists, as well as how to manage individual lists and their content. Based on this, you are now able to implement simple scripts yourself to simplify and automate activities you need to perform.

In the following, final chapter, you will learn how to extend Microsoft Lists with the SPFx framework.

11
Extending Microsoft Lists Using SPFx

This is the last chapter of the book and the most technical one, which will teach you the basic foundations to extend Microsoft Lists features using SPFx.

With the use of code, you will be able to create new solutions and scenarios that are not possible to achieve with the out-of-the-box features that we covered earlier in the book.

In this chapter, we will cover the following topics:

- Learning about SPFx
- How to create a SharePoint framework extension
- Building a field customizer extension
- Building a view command set extension

Technical requirements

You can find the code files present in this chapter on GitHub at `https://github.com/PacktPublishing/Hands-On-Microsoft-Lists/tree/main/Chapter11`

What SPFx is and how to get started

SPFx is the acronym for the **SharePoint Framework** – the client-side development model to extend SharePoint, which allows developers to extend the Microsoft Lists platform using custom solutions.

As we saw in the first chapter, Microsoft Lists is an evolution of SharePoint lists, and it has inherited everything that was developed for the *parent* platform over the years. This means that with Microsoft Lists, you will be able to use SPFx extensions to bring more functionality to your own lists.

Before we dig into the technical aspects of the development, first you need to prepare your environment and understand the components that together make the SharePoint framework. As the following figure illustrates, the framework is built of several components that, when combined, create the modern development method for SharePoint.

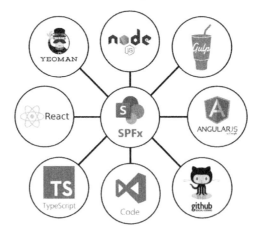

Figure 11.1 – SharePoint Framework components

Let's look at each of these components in detail.

Node.js

Node.js is a runtime environment used to build and execute applications, making them performant and lightweight. With the use of Node.js, developers also get access to npm, the largest ecosystem of open source libraries that make development easier and faster.

To learn more about Node.js and to install it on your device, visit the site `https://nodejs.org/en/`.

Yeoman

Yeoman is a template generator used in the SharePoint Framework to create a project structure, it runs on top of Node.js.

To learn more about Yeoman and to install it on your device, visit the site `https://yeoman.io/`.

TypeScript

TypeScript is an evolution of the original JavaScript containing concepts that are available in more complex languages such as C#. It is an open source language created and maintained by Microsoft that is executed on top of Node.js.

If you know how to develop using JavaScript, you would probably like to know that all JavaScript code is valid TypeScript, and you can start programming immediately without the need to learn a new language.

To learn more about TypeScript and to install it on your device, visit `https://www.typescriptlang.org/`.

React, AngularJS, or any other frontend framework

Though all these frameworks are great to develop web apps, Microsoft has chosen React as the framework for development. But this does not mean that you cannot use others such as Angular.

If you are not familiar with any of these frameworks, you should know that with SPFx, you will be able to create an empty template that only uses TypeScript.

To learn more about React or Angular, and to install it on your device, visit `https://facebook.github.io/react/` and `https://angularjs.org/`.

Gulp

The gulp task runner is used to automate tasks that otherwise have to be done manually.

Gulp is used in the SharePoint framework in a variety of tasks, such as building or bundling the packages for the extensions that will customize Microsoft Lists.

To learn more about TypeScript and to install it on your device, visit `https://gulpjs.com/`.

Visual Studio Code

Visual Studio Code is an open source and multiplatform source code editor made by Microsoft that will help you in the development of your extensions.

To learn more about Visual Studio Code and to install it on your device, visit `https://code.visualstudio.com/`.

Now that you know what the main components of the SharePoint Framework are, let's see how you can use it to extend Microsoft Lists.

Creating a SharePoint Framework extension

Now that you know the components of the SharePoint Framework, it's time to learn how to get started with creating the project to build your first extension.

> **Note**
>
> The SharePoint Framework is multiplatform and can be used on Windows, macOS, and Linux. The examples given in this chapter only use Windows screenshots, but everything is valid for all of the operating systems.

The following instructions are generic for **field customizers** and **view command sets**, as the creation of both project types only differs in one of the steps:

1. Start by opening the terminal window on your operating system.

2. Type the command `yo @microsoft/SharePoint`.

3. Provide a **solution name** for your solution as shown in *Figure 11.2*.

4. For the next question about the SharePoint versions that you want to target, choose **SharePoint Online only (latest)**.

5. Choose whether you want to use the current folder or create a subfolder with the name of the solution.

6. For the deployment question, type **Yes**.

7. For the API permissions question, type **No**. If you are familiar with the Microsoft Graph API and want to use it in your extension, type **Yes**.

8. In the question about the client-side component, choose **Extension**.

9. There are three types of extensions available for SharePoint, but only two of those are applied to Microsoft Lists. Choose accordingly – **Field Customizer** or **List View Command** set.

10. Provide a **Field Customizer name** for the extension.

11. Provide a **Field Customizer description** for the extension.

12. Choose the framework you would like to use to build your solution. The examples provided in this chapter were built using the option **No JavaScript framework**.

13. The creation of the project will start. It might take a few minutes depending on your internet bandwidth. It is shown as follows:

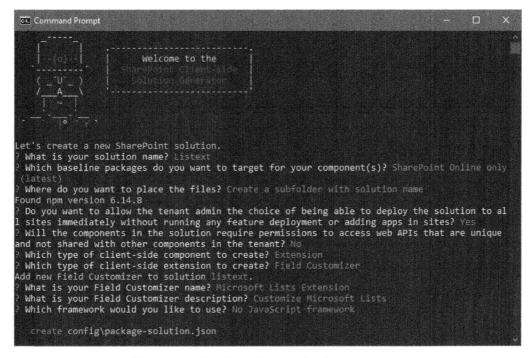

Figure 11.2 – SharePoint Framework solution generator

14. Once the project is created, navigate to the project folder in the terminal and type `code .` to open it with Visual Studio Code.

With your SharePoint Framework project created, in the next sections, you will learn how it is structured and how you can build your custom code.

Building a field customizer extension

Field customizer extensions allow you to customize columns beyond what the JSON and HTML allow you to do with the column formatting. With the use of SPFx, you will be able to format the columns using custom HTML structures, which are not supported by the column formatting. Or, you could go even further and use external APIs to transform the data in your columns.

Let's discuss the following scenario.

John has built a list where he manages all the company offices worldwide. Besides having the typical information that defines an office such as the address, John wanted to go a step further and display the temperature for the city where the office is located, with the temperature being displayed in real time.

To achieve this, John has created a field customizer extension that gets the weather for a specific city using an external API, which is shown as follows:

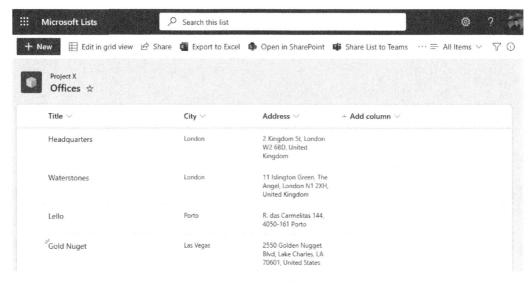

Figure 11.3 – Offices list

When you create a field customizer extension, you will get three default functions that will be executed to customize the column in a list, which are as follows:

- `onInit` – This is the function where you must initialize your extension. Any code that you need to get executed before formatting the column must be defined here.

- `onRenderCell` – This is the function that is executed to transform the column information. From here, you will be able to access the column values and inject your own HTML structure.

- `onDisposeCell` – This function should be used to free any resources that were allocated during rendering.

In the following screenshot, you can see how the three functions look:

```
TS MicrosoftListsExtensionFieldCustomizer.ts ✕

src > extensions > microsoftListsExtension > TS MicrosoftListsExtensionFieldCustomizer.ts > ⚡ MicrosoftListsExtensionFieldCustomizer
21     const LOG_SOURCE: string = 'MicrosoftListsExtensionFieldCustomizer';
22
23     export default class MicrosoftListsExtensionFieldCustomizer
24       extends BaseFieldCustomizer<IMicrosoftListsExtensionFieldCustomizerProperties> {
25
26       @override
27       public onInit(): Promise<void> {
28         // Add your custom initialization to this method.  The framework will wait
29         // for the returned promise to resolve before firing any BaseFieldCustomizer events.
30         Log.info(LOG_SOURCE, 'Activated MicrosoftListsExtensionFieldCustomizer with properties:')
31         Log.info(LOG_SOURCE, JSON.stringify(this.properties, undefined, 2));
32         Log.info(LOG_SOURCE, 'The following string should be equal: "MicrosoftListsExtensionField
33         return Promise.resolve();
34       }
35
36       @override
37       public onRenderCell(event: IFieldCustomizerCellEventParameters): void {
38         // Use this method to perform your custom cell rendering.
39         const text: string = `${this.properties.sampleText}: ${event.fieldValue}`;
40
41         event.domElement.innerText = text;
42
43         event.domElement.classList.add(styles.cell);
44       }
45
46       @override
47       public onDisposeCell(event: IFieldCustomizerCellEventParameters): void {
48         // This method should be used to free any resources that were allocated during rendering.
49         // For example, if your onRenderCell() called ReactDOM.render(), then you should
50         // call ReactDOM.unmountComponentAtNode() here.
51         super.onDisposeCell(event);
52       }
53     }
54
```

Figure 11.4 – Column extension main functions

In order to implement the scenario described, it is necessary to use an external API to get the weather for the city. In this case, we will use the free Open Weather API, and to make the request to the service, we will add a new node module to the SPFx solution.

To prepare your solution to use Open Weather API, do the following:

1. In Visual Studio Code, click on **View**, and then in the menu, click on **Terminal**.

2. In the terminal, type `npm install openweather-apis` and press *Enter*.

If you want to know more about the Open Weather API node module, have a look at this site: https://www.npmjs.com/package/openweather-apis.

Now that you have the module added to the solution, it is time to get the API key that will allow you to use it.

3. To get started, visit https://openweathermap.org/api.

4. Sign up and request the free API.

5. Once you validate your email, the API key will be sent by email. This API allows you to make a million calls per month and a maximum of 60 calls/minute.

With your API key to Open Weather, it's now time to modify the solution to display the weather along with the name of the city.

6. In Visual Studio Code, open the ts source file located in the folder /src/extensions.

7. Replace the onRenderCell function with the following code:

```
@override
  public onRenderCell(event:
    IFieldCustomizerCellEventParameters): void {
    // Use this method to perform your custom cell
    // rendering.
    let city = event.fieldValue;
    var weather = require('openweather-apis');
    (weather as any).setLang('en');
    (weather as any).setCity(city);
    (weather as any).setUnits('metric');
    (weather as any).setAPPID('YOUR API KEY');
    (weather as any).getAllWeather(function(err, temp){
      if(temp!=null){
        let city = temp.name;
        let condition = temp.weather[0].main;
        let icon = `https://openweathermap.org/
          img/w/${temp.weather[0].icon}.png`;
        let temperature = temp.main.temp.toString().
          split('.')[0];
        let html = `
          <div style="position: absolute; left: 8px; top:
            8px; font-size: 31px; font-weight:
            500;">${temperature}°</div>
```

```
        <img src="${icon}" style="position: absolute;
            left: 35px; top: 8px;">
        <div style="position: absolute; top: 10px;
            left: 90px;">${city}</div>
        <div style="position: absolute; top: 30px;
            left: 90px;">${condition}</div>
        `;

        event.domElement.innerHTML = html;

    }
    });
}
```

https://github.com/PacktPublishing/Hands-On-Microsoft-Lists/tree/main/Chap-ter11/Weather%20column

The source code for the solution is quite simple. It gets the value of the city column (`let city = event.fieldValue;`) and makes a request to the API to retrieve the weather for that location.

8. In the preceding code, replace the string YOUR API KEY with your own API key value.

9. In Visual Studio Code, open the `elements.xml` file located in the `./sharepoint/assets/` folder as shown in *Figure 11.5*.

10. Edit the field **Name** and provide a name, and a **DisplayName**.

11. Change **Type** to **Text** and remove the property **Min**. At the end, your file should be similar to the one represented in the following screenshot:

Figure 11.5 – Elements.xml field definition

If you want to use other types of columns, we recommend you have a look at this site:

```
https://docs.microsoft.com/en-us/sharepoint/dev/schema/
field-definitions
```

Now that you have the solution running, it's time to test it live in your own environment.

12. In Visual Studio Code, open the `serve.json` file located in the `config` folder as shown in *Figure 11.6*.

13. Modify the value for the `pageUrl` property to the URL to the list, as shown in *Figure 11.6*.

14. Rename the `InternalFieldName` property with the name of the column, for example, `City`, as follows:

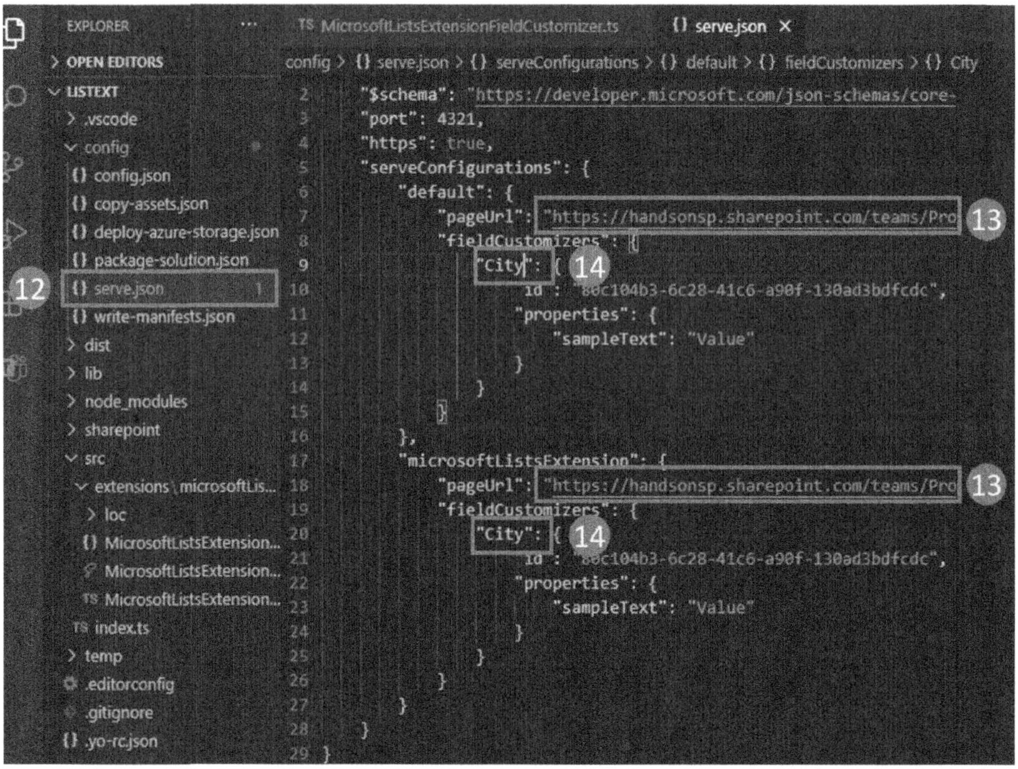

Figure 11.6 – Modified serve.json file

15. From the Visual Studio Code terminal, type `gulp serve`.

16. A new page will open in your browser. Once it opens, click on the **Load debug scripts** button as follows:

Allow debug scripts?

WARNING: This page contains unsafe scripts that, if loaded, could potentially harm your computer. Do not proceed unless you trust the developer and understand the risks.

If you are unsure, click Don't load debug scripts.

Load debug scripts   Don't load debug scripts

Figure 11.7 – Load debug scripts

After a few seconds, you will see the extension appear in the **City** column. The final result will be similar to the one exemplified in the following figure, with the weather being shown alongside a representative image of the condition, the name of the city, and the description of the current condition:

Figure 11.8 – SPFx field customizer

Once you are happy with the final result, you need to install it on your SharePoint, so it becomes visible to all users. To accomplish the instructions described from this point on, you must have permission to install custom applications on SharePoint.

17. From the Visual Studio Code terminal, run the command `gulp bundle -ship`.

18. Once the previous command execution has finished, run the command `gulp package-solution --ship`.

19. After the successful execution of both commands, in your File Explorer, open the project solution folder, and then navigate to `./sharepoint/solution/` where you will find a file with the extension `sppkg`.

20. Open your SharePoint app catalog. If you want to learn more about it, we recommend you have a look at this site: `https://docs.microsoft.com/en-us/sharepoint/use-app-catalog`.

21. Once in the app catalog, click on **Apps for SharePoint** located in the vertical menu.

22. Click on **FILES** and, from the command bar, click on **Upload Document** as follows:

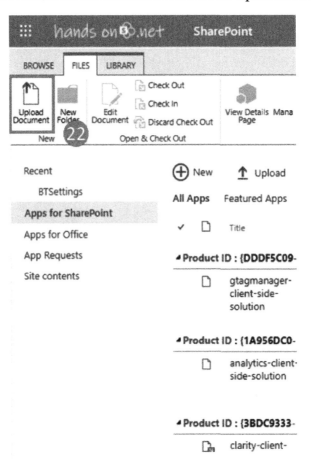

Figure 11.9 – Upload Document

23. Click on the **Choose files** button and select the sppkg file.

24. Click **OK**.

25. On the popup that appears, leave the option **Make this solution available to all sites in the organization** unchecked as follows:

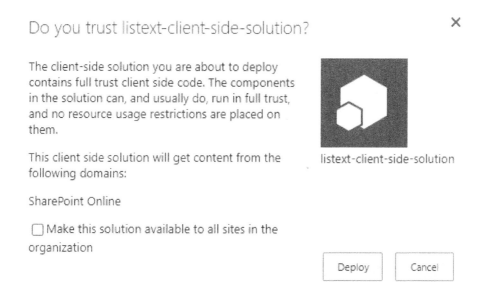

Do you trust listext-client-side-solution?   ✕

The client-side solution you are about to deploy contains full trust client side code. The components in the solution can, and usually do, run in full trust, and no resource usage restrictions are placed on them.

This client side solution will get content from the following domains:

SharePoint Online

☐ Make this solution available to all sites in the organization

listext-client-side-solution

Deploy   Cancel

Figure 11.10 – Click Deploy

Now that the app is installed in the SharePoint tenant, you must add it to the site collections where you want to make use of it.

26. Navigate to the SharePoint site where your list is located.

27. Click on the cog icon, and from the settings pane, click on **Site contents**.

28. Click on **New** and then click on **App** as follows:

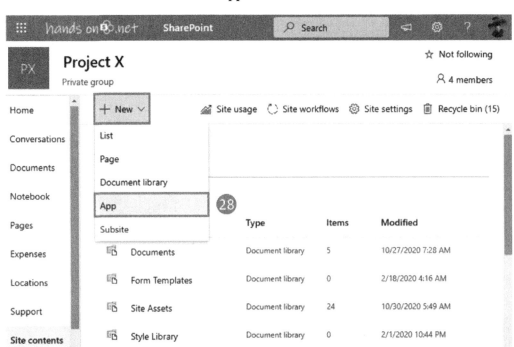

Figure 11.11 – Add an app

29. Search for the name of your custom solution and click on it to install it for the SharePoint site.

   The last step you need to do is add a new site column to the list where you want the customization to be visible. You can reuse the solution in multiple lists by taking the following steps.

30. Open the list where you want to add the column customization.

31. Click on the cog icon, and then in the settings pane, click on **List Settings**.

32. In the **Columns** section, click on **Add from existing site columns** as follows:

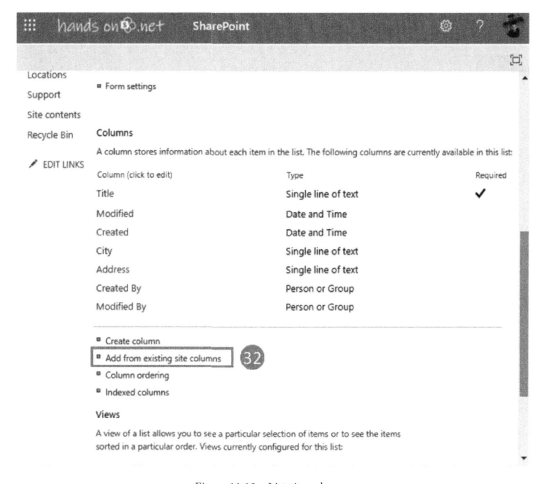

Figure 11.12 – List site columns

33. In the **Available site columns** list, look for the name of your column, for example, **City**.

34. Select **SPFx Columns** from the site columns dropdown.

35. Click on **Add** to move it to the **Columns to add** list.

36. Make sure you have the option **Add to default view** checked.

37. Click **OK** as shown in the following figure:

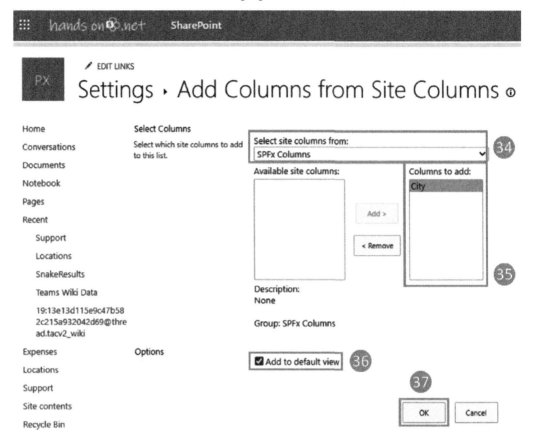

Figure 11.13 – Add a list site column

When you add content to your list, the values inserted in the **City** column will be automatically formatted by the definition made by the field customizer extension.

Despite being built with a specific list in mind, the extension can be reused in other lists as well. All you have to do is repeat *Steps 26* to *37*.

In the following screenshot, you can observe the same extension applied to the **Travel requests** list seen earlier in the book, in *Chapter 6*, *Customizing Microsoft Lists*:

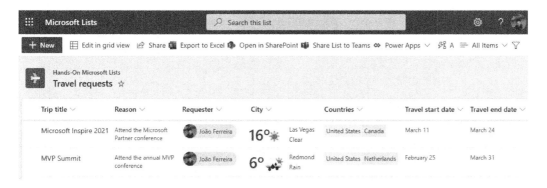

Figure 11.14 – Extension applied to a Travel requests list

With the example described in this chapter, you should be able to start customizing your columns, using it as a starting point for more complex scenarios.

Building a view command set extension

View command set extensions allow you to add extra functionalities to the command bar of a list that can be executed for a single item or for the entire list, allowing you to include your business processes in Microsoft Lists.

Let's discuss the following scenario.

John wants to share lists and list items on Microsoft Teams and wants to automate the copy/paste process between both applications. John wants to implement the **Share to Teams embedded** button that can be used from any application to share a link to Teams. To make this new option available to all the lists in the tenant, John has decided to build a command set extension.

When you create a command set extension, you will get three default methods that are executed to create the command set:

- `onInit` – This is the method where you must initialize your extension. Any code that you need to get executed before creating the command set must be defined in this function.

- `onListViewUpdated` – This method is executed every time something changes in the list, for example, a list item selection.

- `onExecute` – This method is executed when a user clicks on the new command bar option.

In the following screenshot, you can see what the three methods look like:

```typescript
TS ShareItemToTeamsCommandSet.ts ×
src > extensions > shareItemToTeams > TS ShareItemToTeamsCommandSet.ts > ...
20        sampleTextOne: string;
21        sampleTextTwo: string;
22      }
23    |
24    const LOG_SOURCE: string = 'ShareItemToTeamsCommandSet';
25
26    export default class ShareItemToTeamsCommandSet extends BaseListViewCommandSet<IShareItemToTeamsCommandSe
27
28      @override
29      public onInit(): Promise<void> {
30        Log.info(LOG_SOURCE, 'Initialized ShareItemToTeamsCommandSet');
31        return Promise.resolve();
32      }
33
34      @override
35      public onListViewUpdated(event: IListViewCommandSetListViewUpdatedParameters): void {
36        const compareOneCommand: Command = this.tryGetCommand('COMMAND_1');
37        if (compareOneCommand) {
38          // This command should be hidden unless exactly one row is selected.
39          compareOneCommand.visible = event.selectedRows.length === 1;
40        }
41      }
42
43      @override
44      public onExecute(event: IListViewCommandSetExecuteEventParameters): void {
45        switch (event.itemId) {
46          case 'COMMAND_1':
47            Dialog.alert(`${this.properties.sampleTextOne}`);
48            break;
49          case 'COMMAND_2':
50            Dialog.alert(`${this.properties.sampleTextTwo}`);
51            break;
52          default:
53            throw new Error('Unknown command');
54        }
55      }
56    }
```

Figure 11.15 – Command set extension

In order to implement the scenario described, it is necessary to modify the solution and build an extra function that will add the Microsoft Teams share feature to all Microsoft lists.

The embed share button is a script provided by Microsoft. If you want to learn more about it, have a look at this site: https://docs.microsoft.com/en-us/microsoftteams/platform/concepts/build-and-test/share-to-teams.

To prepare your own solution, do the following:

1. In Visual Studio Code, open the `ts` source file located in the folder `/src/extensions`.

2. After the `onExecute` method, paste the following function:

```
private appendShareToTeamsScript(): void{
    //Add Share to Teams script to the page
    var script    = document.createElement("script");
    script.type   = "text/javascript";
    script.src    = "https://teams.microsoft.com/share/
                    launcher.js";
    document.body.appendChild(script);

    //Create a hidden element to make use of the
    //ShareToTeams feature
    var div   = document.createElement("div");
    div.id  = "hiddenShareBTN";
    document.body.appendChild(div);
}
```

https://github.com/PacktPublishing/Hands-On-Microsoft-Lists/tree/main/Chapter11/Share%20item%20to%20Teams

3. In Visual Studio Code, open the `manifest.json` file located in the folder `/src/extensions`.

4. In the `manifest.json` file, replace the elements defined inside the `items` property with the following code:

```
"LISTS_COMMAND": {
    "SHARELISTITEM_COMMAND": {
        "title": { "default": "Share List item to Teams" },
            "iconImageUrl": "",
            "type": "command"
        },
    "SHARELIST_COMMAND": {
        "title": { "default": "Share List to Teams" },
        "iconImageUrl": "",
```

```
        "type": "command"
    }
}
```

This definition creates two buttons for the command bar – one to share list items when a single item is selected, and another one to share the list when no item is selected, or more than one item is selected.

Each button is defined by the following:

- `title` – A string with the text that is displayed in the list command bar.

- `iconImageUrl` – The image that is used next to the command. It can be defined as a JPEG, PNG, or SVG.

- `type` – It will always be `command`.

5. Go back to the `ts` source file located in the folder `/src/extensions`.

6. Replace the `onInit` method with the following code:

```
@override
public onInit(): Promise<void> {      debugger;
    this.appendShareToTeamsScript();
    return Promise.resolve();
}
```

7. Replace `onListViewUpdated` with the following code:

```
@override
public onListViewUpdated(event:
    IListViewCommandSetListViewUpdatedParameters): void {
    const shareListItemCommand: Command = this.
        tryGetCommand('SHARELISTITEM_COMMAND');
    const shareListCommand: Command = this.
        tryGetCommand('SHARELIST_COMMAND');
    //Share to Microsoft Teams
    if (shareListItemCommand && shareListCommand) {
        if(event.selectedRows.length === 1){
        //Share list item
            if(event.selectedRows[0].
                getValueByName("FileLeafRef") != 'Folder'){
                //Share item is not available for folders
```

```
            shareListItemCommand.visible = true;
            shareListCommand.visible = false;
        }else{
            //For selected folder, share the entire list
            shareListItemCommand.visible = false;
            shareListCommand.visible = true;
        }
    }else{
        //share list
        shareListItemCommand.visible = false;
        shareListCommand.visible = true;
    }
  }
}
```

In `onListViewUpdated`, you can find the logic to show the share item or the share list button depending on the number of elements selected.

8. Replace the `onExecute` method with the following code:

```
@override
  public onExecute(event:
    IListViewCommandSetExecuteEventParameters): void {
      switch (event.itemId) {
      case 'SHARELISTITEM_COMMAND':
        var filePath: string = null;
        var datahref: string;
        try{
          filePath = event.selectedRows[0].
            getValueByName("ServerRedirectedEmbedUrl");
        }catch{
          filePath = null;
        }
        //Handle files on document libraries
        if(filePath != null){
          datahref = filePath; // office file with
                                //preview
          if(datahref == ""){
            //file without preview
```

```
            var fileRef = event.selectedRows[0].
                getValueByName("FileLeafRef");

            var tenantURL = document.location.origin;

            var listURL = this.context.pageContext.list.
                serverRelativeUrl;

            datahref =
                `${tenantURL}${listURL}/${fileRef}`;

            datahref = datahref.replace(/ /g,"%20");

        }

    }else{

        var selectedRowID = event.selectedRows[0].
            getValueByName("ID");

        var tenantURL = document.location.origin;

        var listURL = this.context.pageContext.list.
            serverRelativeUrl;

        datahref = `${tenantURL}${listURL}/DispForm.
            aspx?ID=${selectedRowID}`;

        datahref = datahref.replace(/ /g,"%20");

    }


    //prepare the Share To Teams button

    var hiddenBTN = document.
        getElementById('hiddenShareBTN');

    hiddenBTN.innerHTML = `<div
        id="hiddenhareTeamsBTN" style="display:none;"
        class="teams-share-button"
        data-href="${datahref}"></div>`;

    eval('shareToMicrosoftTeams.renderButtons();');

    var hiddenLink = hiddenBTN.
        getElementsByTagName('a');

    hiddenBTN[0].click();

    break;

case 'SHARELIST_COMMAND':

    //prepare the Share To Teams button

    var hiddenBTN = document.
        getElementById('hiddenShareBTN');

    hiddenBTN.innerHTML = `<div
        id="hiddenhareTeamsBTN" style="display:none;"
        class="teams-share-button"
        data-href="${document.location.href}"></div>`;
```

```
eval('shareToMicrosoftTeams.renderButtons();');
var hiddenLink = hiddenBTN.
    getElementsByTagName('a');
hiddenLink[0].click();
break;
    default:
        throw new Error('Unknown command');
    }
}
```

In this method, you can find the logic that is applied to each one of the buttons when the user clicks on them.

Your solution is ready to be tested in your own environment. All you have to do is prepare it to open in your own tenant.

9. In Visual Studio Code, open the `serve.json` file located in the `config` folder.

10. Modify the value for the `pageUrl` property to the URL of the list where you want to test it.

11. In Visual Studio Code, click on **View**, and from the menu, click on **Terminal**.

12. In the terminal, type `gulp serve`.

13. A new page will open in your browser. Once it opens, click on the **Load debug scripts** button, as follows:

Figure 11.16 – Load debug scripts

The new commands will appear in the list. Test them, and refine the behaviors according to your needs. Once you are happy with the solution, it is time to create the installation file to apply it globally to all the lists.

To accomplish the instructions described from this point on, you must have permission to install custom applications on SharePoint.

14. From the Visual Studio Code terminal, run the command `gulp bundle -ship`.

15. Once the previous command execution has finished, run the command `gulp package-solution --ship`.

16. After the successful execution of both commands on your File Explorer, open the project solution folder, and then navigate to `./sharepoint/solution/` where you will find a file with the extension `sppkg`.

17. Open your SharePoint app catalog. If you want to learn more about it, we recommend you have a look at this site: `https://docs.microsoft.com/en-us/sharepoint/use-app-catalog`.

18. Once in the app catalog, click on **Apps for SharePoint** located in the vertical menu.

19. Click on **FILES** and from the command bar, click on **Upload Document**:

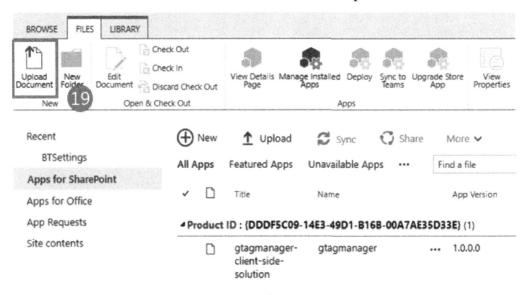

Figure 11.17 – Upload Document

20. Click on the **Choose files** button and select the sppkg file.

21. Click **OK**.

22. On the popup that appears, check the **Make this solution available to all sites in the organization** option and click **Deploy**:

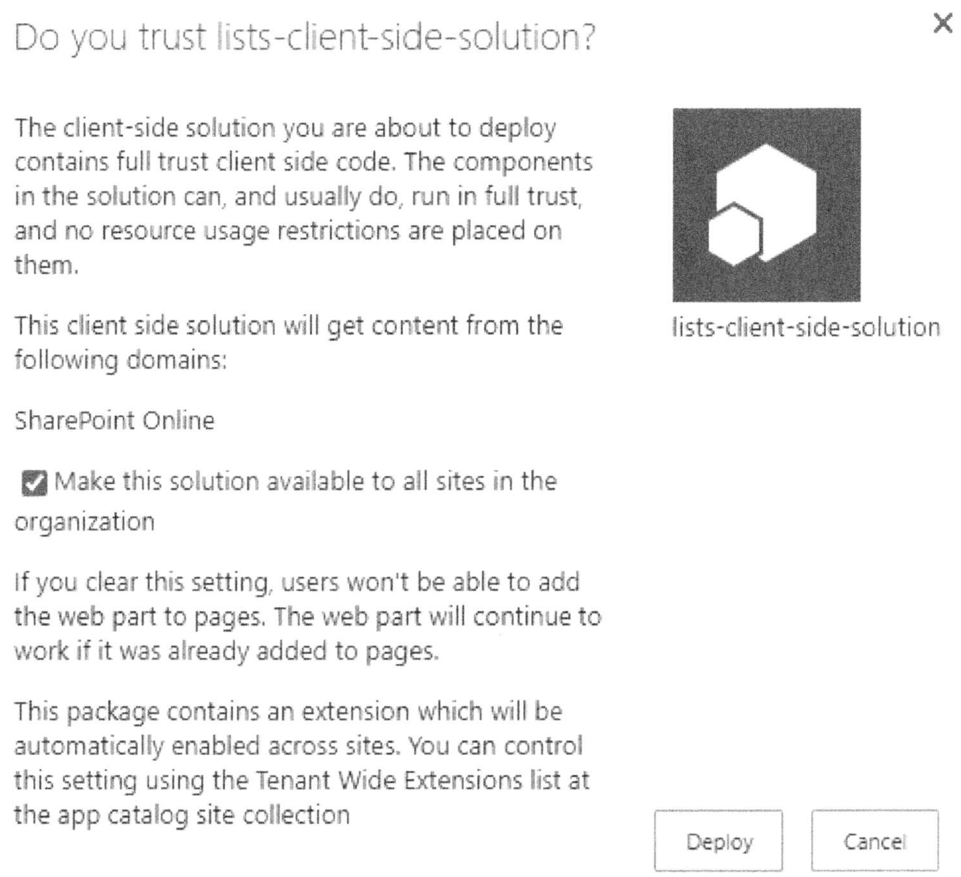

Do you trust lists-client-side-solution?   ✕

The client-side solution you are about to deploy contains full trust client side code. The components in the solution can, and usually do, run in full trust, and no resource usage restrictions are placed on them.

This client side solution will get content from the following domains:

SharePoint Online

☑ Make this solution available to all sites in the organization

If you clear this setting, users won't be able to add the web part to pages. The web part will continue to work if it was already added to pages.

This package contains an extension which will be automatically enabled across sites. You can control this setting using the Tenant Wide Extensions list at the app catalog site collection

lists-client-side-solution

Deploy   Cancel

Figure 11.18 – Click Deploy

Your solution is installed and applied to all lists in the tenant. The end result will be similar to the following screenshot with the **Share List item to Teams** popup opening at the top of the list:

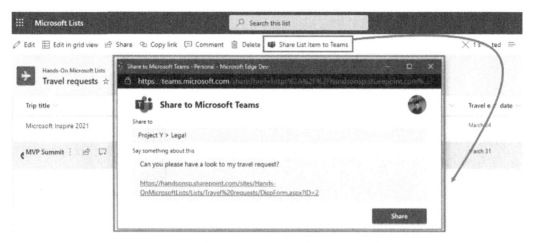

Figure 11.19 – Share item to Teams from Microsoft Lists

This solution allows you to post a message to a Teams channel with a link to the list or to the list item. It will be similar to the example in the following screenshot:

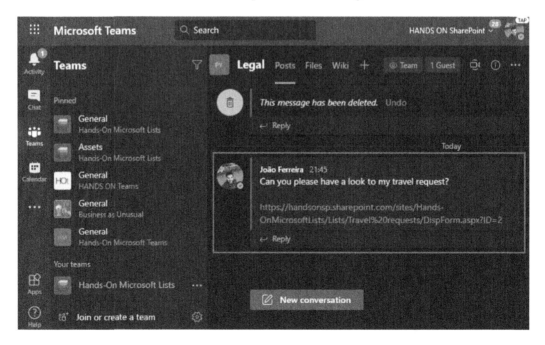

Figure 11.20 – List item shared to Microsoft Teams

You can create multiple extensions and have them applied at the same time to your lists. Use these examples as a starting point, and have fun.

Summary

In this chapter, you have learned how to extend Microsoft Lists beyond what Microsoft provides by default in the application. You've learned about the SharePoint Framework, its main components, and the available options to extend Microsoft Lists using custom field customizers and command sets.

You are now ready to bring your processes and business logic to the context of Microsoft Lists, adding more value to the content stored in lists.

If you have read the entire book by now, you should be the real hero of Microsoft Lists in your organization, ready to empower others to achieve more using this awesome application.

Hi!

We are João and Rene, authors of Hands-On Microsoft Lists. We really hope you enjoyed reading this book and found it useful for increasing your productivity and efficiency in Microsoft Lists. Our goal for writing this book is to help you gain some new insights and useful ideas for how to leverage Microsoft Lists in your daily work and your organization.

It would really help us (and other potential readers!) if you could leave a review on Amazon sharing your thoughts on Hands-On Microsoft Lists.

Your review will help us to understand what's worked well in this book, what you found useful, and what could be improved upon for future editions, so it really is appreciated.

Best Wishes,

João Ferreira

Rene Modery

Packt.com

Subscribe to our online digital library for full access to over 7,000 books and videos, as well as industry leading tools to help you plan your personal development and advance your career. For more information, please visit our website.

Why subscribe?

- Spend less time learning and more time coding with practical eBooks and Videos from over 4,000 industry professionals

- Improve your learning with Skill Plans built especially for you

- Get a free eBook or video every month

- Fully searchable for easy access to vital information

- Copy and paste, print, and bookmark content

Did you know that Packt offers eBook versions of every book published, with PDF and ePub files available? You can upgrade to the eBook version at packt.com and as a print book customer, you are entitled to a discount on the eBook copy. Get in touch with us at customercare@packtpub.com for more details.

At www.packt.com, you can also read a collection of free technical articles, sign up for a range of free newsletters, and receive exclusive discounts and offers on Packt books and eBooks.

Other Books You May Enjoy

If you enjoyed this book, you may be interested in these other books by Packt:

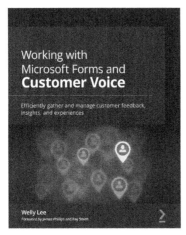

Working with Microsoft Forms and Customer Voice

Welly Lee

ISBN: 978-1-80107-017-1

- Get up and running with Microsoft Forms and Dynamics 365 Customer Voice services

- Explore common feedback scenarios and survey best practices

- Understand how to administer Microsoft Forms and Dynamics 365 Customer Voice

- Use Microsoft Forms or Dynamics 365 Customer Voice to monitor your survey results

- Set up the Microsoft Forms app for Teams for conducting live polls

- Automate feedback collection and follow-up actions

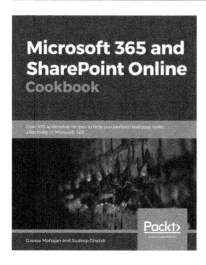

Microsoft 365 and SharePoint Online Cookbook

Gaurav Mahajan, Sudeep Ghatak

ISBN: 978-1-83864-667-7

- Get to grips with a wide range of apps and cloud services in Microsoft 365

- Discover ways to use SharePoint Online to create and manage content

- Store and share documents using SharePoint Online

- Improve your search experience with Microsoft Search

- Leverage the Power Platform to build business solutions with Power Automate, Power Apps, Power BI, and Power Virtual

- Enhance native capabilities in SharePoint and Teams using the SPFx framework

- Use Microsoft Teams to meet, chat, and collaborate with colleagues or external users

Packt is searching for authors like you

If you're interested in becoming an author for Packt, please visit `authors.packtpub.com` and apply today. We have worked with thousands of developers and tech professionals, just like you, to help them share their insight with the global tech community. You can make a general application, apply for a specific hot topic that we are recruiting an author for, or submit your own idea.

Leave a review - let other readers know what you think

Please share your thoughts on this book with others by leaving a review on the site that you bought it from. If you purchased the book from Amazon, please leave us an honest review on this book's Amazon page. This is vital so that other potential readers can see and use your unbiased opinion to make purchasing decisions, we can understand what our customers think about our products, and our authors can see your feedback on the title that they have worked with Packt to create. It will only take a few minutes of your time, but is valuable to other potential customers, our authors, and Packt. Thank you!

Index

Printed in Great Britain
by Amazon